Understanding

Student Affairs

at **Catholic**

Colleges *and*

Universities

Understanding
Student Affairs
at Catholic
Colleges *and*
Universities

A Comprehensive Resource

Sandra M. Estanek
Editor

SHEED & WARD

Franklin, Wisconsin
Chicago

As an apostolate of the Priests of the Sacred Heart, a Catholic religious congregation, the mission of Sheed & Ward is to publish books of contemporary impact and enduring merit in Catholic Christian thought and action. The books published, however, reflect the opinions of their authors and are not meant to represent the official position of the Priests of the Sacred Heart.

2002

Sheed & Ward
7373 South Lovers Lane Road
Franklin, Wisconsin 53132
1-800-266-5564

Scripture quotations are from the Revised Standard Version of the Bible, copyright © 1989, 1995, and 1999 by the Division of Christian Education of the National Council of the Churches of Christ in the USA. Used by permission. All rights reserved.

Printed in the United States of America

Cover and interior design by GrafixStudio, Inc.
Author photo by Studio 518 Photography;
48 East Mountain Ave,; Robesonia, PA 19551

Library of Congress Cataloging-in-Publication Data

Understanding student affairs at Catholic colleges and universities: a comprehensive resource / Sandra M. Estanek, editor.
    p.cm.
  ISBN 1-58051-116-3
  1. Catholic universities and colleges—United States. 2. Student affairs services—United States. I. Estanek, Sandra M.

LC501.U48 2002
378'.0712—dc21
                             2002019651

1 2 3 4 5   05 04 03 02

Contents

Introduction

In August 1990, Pope John Paul II issued an apostolic constitution, *Ex Corde Ecclesiae*, on the subject of Catholic higher education. The Vatican has several different formats for a communication about any given topic, but in this instance it chose an "apostolic constitution," which is the most authoritative statement on a particular subject. In this way the importance of the subject was clearly communicated. The document contained both the outline of the Vatican's understanding of the mission and identity of Catholic higher education and general norms for the governance of Catholic colleges and universities. Because the document was addressed to Catholic higher education throughout the world, it was left to local conferences of bishops to develop the normative application of *Ex Corde Ecclesiae* to their particular context. The development of the application to the United States has been hotly debated for the past decade and much has been written and said on this topic.

Ex Corde Ecclesiae did not arise in a vacuum. As Alice Gallin, O.S.U., demonstrated in her book, *American Catholic Higher Education: Essential Documents, 1967-1990*, the document was the result of almost twenty-five years of dialogue between the Vatican and Catholic educators and officials, particularly Americans.[1] Gallin's history of that period, *Negotiating Identity*, also demonstrated, however, that the dialogue stayed within the leadership circles of American Catholic higher education and did not permeate campus life.[2] The publication of *Ex Corde Ecclesiae*, then, pushed the dialogue into all corners of institutions of Catholic higher education.

The publication of this document and the resulting applications renewed and intensified discussions throughout American Catholic higher education about what it meant to be both "Catholic" and a "university." Most of the discussion has focused on the issues of university governance and academic freedom. Much attention also has been focused on the role of the faculty at Catholic institutions. Little has been said or written about the role of student affairs. However, it was logical that, in the spirit of the discussions that were occurring on campuses, in print, and at professional meetings, the question of what it means to do the work of student affairs on Catholic campuses would be raised.

This question is an important one because there is a significant body of student development research created over the past thirty years that indicates that students are influenced as much, if not more, by their experiences outside of the classroom as by what occurs in class.[3] This literature would indicate that students experience the "Catholic identity" of the university not only in their theology classes but also in residence hall policies and in student organizations, in opportunities for worship and for service, and in their interactions with others on campus. In other words, their experience of the Catholic identity of the university is "seamless." To understand this is to recognize that student affairs plays an important role in the mission of the Catholic college and university.

This body of literature also indicates that the college years are a time of significant personal development. Students experience a new level of freedom. Arthur W. Chickering and others have demonstrated that not only are students learning new academic skills, they are developing personal and interpersonal competencies.[4] They are creating their own adult identity. William G. Perry and others have demonstrated that establishing this adult identity entails examining and perhaps challenging the values one has inherited.[5] The college years can be a time of questioning and experimenting as one develops one's own sense of being in the world. Students often "push the envelope" in their behavior as they exercise their new freedom and crystallize their adult identities.

Thus it is not surprising that some of the most difficult issues related to Catholic identity are experienced in areas commonly supervised by student affairs professionals. Some examples of these issues are, Should birth control information be available in the health center? Should student groups be permitted to invite to campus speakers who disagree with church teaching? What are appropriate residence hall policies relating to students' sexual behavior and how should they be enforced? Should a gay, lesbian, bisexual, and transsexual student organization be recognized on campus? Student affairs professionals who work at Catholic institutions need to be grounded in both student development and Catholic identity to be able to wrestle with the issues that these questions raise.

One of the most important efforts to include student affairs professionals in the discussions of Catholic identity precipitated by the publication of *Ex Corde Ecclesiae* was the Institute for Student Affairs at Catholic Colleges. ISACC was a five-day summer institute that was sponsored by the Association of Catholic Colleges and Universities and funded in part by the Lilly Endowment as part of its Religion and Higher Education Initiative. The goals of the institute for those who attended were 1) to learn about the Catholic intellectual tradition, 2) to network with colleagues at Catholic institutions across the nation and internationally, 3) to discuss how to ground student affairs practice in Catholic identity, and 4) to apply this understanding to practical concerns on campus.[6]

ISACC was held on the campus of John Carroll University in Cleveland, Ohio, from 1996-1999. During that time, over 220 student affairs professionals from 59 Catholic colleges and universities throughout the United States, Canada, and Lebanon attended the institute. In 1999, rather than continue the institute itself, it was decided to create the Association for Student Affairs at Catholic Colleges and Universities (ASACCU) as a permanent organization that would hold an annual conference. In this way the conversation would continue.

This book also emerged from the ISACC experience. With the creation of the institute and the subsequent formation of ASACCU, there was the opportunity for student affairs professionals who work at Catholic colleges and universities to come together to discuss the meaning of their work for the "Catholic identity" of their institutions and to address issues and concerns that were common to their experience. But still there did not exist written, scholarly reflections on the practice of student affairs at Catholic institutions of higher education. This work fills that void. It is not intended to be the "last word" on that topic, but the "first word." It is the fervent hope of the authors that this work will initiate the development of a body of literature on the topic of student affairs at Catholic colleges and universities so that the conversation that has been initiated may be both widened and deepened.

This book is divided into two parts. The first section is a series of essays in which the authors reflect on topics that engage the relationship of student affairs as a profession and a body of knowledge to the context of the Catholic intellectual tradition. In chapter 1, Richard P. Salmi, S.J., compares the thought of *Ex Corde Ecclesiae* to two professional documents—*The Student Learning Imperative* and *Principles of Good Practice*—that define "good practice" in student affairs. In chapter 2, Sandra M. Estanek compares the epistemology that frames student development theory with the epistemology of the Catholic intellectual tradition as it relates to education. Where Salmi shows the similarities between *Ex Corde Ecclesiae* and student affairs literature, Estanek focuses on the differences. In chapter 3, Edward Jeremy Miller outlines six features that characterize the Catholic intellectual tradition. The next two chapters focus on sexuality. Because students in the college years are establishing adult relationships in an environment of freedom, the question of sexuality is one that is particularly difficult and important. In chapter 4, Robert M. Friday focuses on Catholic moral theology as it relates to sexuality, and he applies that context to our work with students. In chapter 5, Dolores L. Christie discusses student affairs in terms of conscience formation. Finally, in chapter 6, Martin F. Larrey proposes a model integrating student affairs and academic affairs.

Six case studies form the second section of the book. In chapter 7, Andrew J. Hill shares how the ISACC team from St. Mary's University, Texas, subsequently exercised campus-wide leadership in the discussions of Catholic identity. In chapter 8, Patrick Rombalski discusses how implementing an assessment process furthered the Catholic mission of a student affairs division at John Carroll University in Ohio. In chapter 9, Gregory Roberts describes the creation of university guidelines regarding controversial issues at the University of St. Thomas, Minnesota, and shares case studies of how the guidelines helped the university. In chapter 10, Deborah L. Ford discusses how Spalding University in Louisville, Kentucky, tries to meet the spiritual needs of a diverse student body while fostering the university's Catholic identity. Nancy B. Mathias and Julie Donovan Massey write in chapter 11 about how they united programs of leadership development and service learning to create a more integrated experience grounded in Catholic social teaching at St. Norbert College in De Pere, Wisconsin. Finally, in chapter 12 Robert S. Meyer and Laura A. Wankel discuss how their Catholic identity helped them to respond to the Seton Hall community in South Orange, New Jersey, in the aftermath of their tragic residence hall fire.

About the Authors

Dolores L. Christie is executive secretary of the Catholic Theological Society of America.

Sandra M. Estanek is Assistant Professor and Director of the College Student Personnel Administration Program at Canisius College in Buffalo, New York.

Deborah L. Ford is Vice President for Student Affairs at Spalding University in Louisville, Kentucky.

Rev. Robert M. Friday is Vice President for Student Life at the Catholic University of America in Washington, D.C.

Andrew J. Hill is Associate Director of Service Learning at St. Mary's University in San Antonio, Texas.

Martin F. Larrey is Vice President for Academic Affairs at the College of Saint Mary in Omaha, Nebraska.

Julie Donovan Massey is Campus Minister at St. Norbert College in De Pere, Wisconsin.

Nancy B. Mathias is Associate Director of Leadership and Service at St. Norbert College, De Pere, Wisconsin.

Rev. Robert S. Meyer is Associate Vice President for Student Affairs at Seton Hall University in South Orange, New Jersey.

Edward Jeremy Miller is Professor of Religious Studies at Gwynedd-Mercy College in Gwynedd, Pennsylvania.

Gregory Roberts is Vice President for Student Affairs at the University of St. Thomas in St. Paul, Minnesota.

Patrick Rombalski is Dean of Students at John Carroll University in Cleveland, Ohio.

Rev. Richard P. Salmi, S.J., is Vice President for Student Affairs at John Carroll University.

Laura A. Wankel is Vice President for Student Affairs at Seton Hall University.

Acknowledgments

This book is not about the Institute for Student Affairs at Catholic Colleges, but it is clearly a book that has emerged from the ISACC experience. Since 1994, many people from around the country have worked with me to create the institute, the organization that emerged from it, and this resulting book. Their dedication to these efforts has demonstrated the commitment of student affairs professionals who work at Catholic colleges and universities to the mission of Catholic higher education and to wrestling with the difficult and sensitive issues they face on their campuses.

Student affairs professionals supervise many areas of the college that affect students outside of the classroom. These areas include residence halls and student activities, health services and counseling, athletics, and, in many instances, campus ministry. The purpose that underlies each of these areas, and all the others under the umbrella of student affairs, is to provide students with a co-curricular environment that promotes their personal development and enhances their learning. This co-curricular environment also must be consistent with the mission of the college or university.

In the research I did in 1994, which led to the creation of ISACC, I found that student affairs professionals across the country understood that they needed to ground their work with students in the Catholic identity of the institution, but they indicated that they felt they did not know enough about how the Catholic intellectual tradition related to the work they did to do this effectively. ISACC was an effort to relate the Catholic heritage to student affairs. This book continues that effort.

The creation of ISACC was my dissertation project. The members of my doctoral committee at The Union Institute were creative enough to recognize that both analyzing *and addressing* a problem were legitimate academic work. Without their support I would have done a more traditional project, and ISACC would not have been born. I will always be grateful to Marjorie Bell Chambers, Sr. Alice Gallin, Patrick Love, Lyn Zanville, Walter Zielinski, and Edward Wingard. The support of Sr. Alice, in particular, opened the doors of the Association of Catholic Colleges and Universities and the Lilly Endowment. Special thanks are also due to Monika Hellwig, Rev. James Heft, Paul Gallagher, Frances Freeman, Dennis Golden, and Sr. Jeanne Knoerle.

While ISACC was my idea initially, it was given form and life by the faculty who worked together to create the structure and content of the institute. Several of the chapters in this book are revisions of the presentations that were the backbone of the learning experience at ISACC. My gratitude and affection will always go to Dee Christie, Fr. Bob Friday, Martin Larrey, Fr. Mark Latcovich, Ed Miller, and Fr. Richie Salmi. The work of the faculty was supported by the discussion leaders. These were ISACC participants who returned to facilitate the discussions that followed each presentation. The evaluations each year told us how important their contribution was to the learning process. Thank you to Kathleen Gausman, Deanne Hurley, Steve Mueller, Bob Pastoor, Greg Roberts, Wayne Romo, Linda Timm, and Lauren Zeefe. Finally, a special thanks is due to the more than 220 student affairs professionals from 59 Catholic colleges and universities who attended ISACC from 1996 to 1999.

I also wish to acknowledge several people to whom I am indebted for their support of this book. The book was written while I served as Vice President for Student Development at Alvernia College in Reading, Pennsylvania. The president of Alvernia College, Laurence W. Mazzeno, was steadfast in his support of my work with ISACC, ASACCU, and this project. He provided me with both time and good advice. Larry is a scholar and author in his own right, and his support and advice have been invaluable. Mary Haubrich, my administrative assistant at Alvernia, took the attachments, discs, and hard copies that came in several different formats and programs and turned them into one manuscript. Her expertise and good humor were essential to finishing this project. A final thank you is due to our editor at Sheed & Ward, Jeremy Langford, for his faith in this project and for his support throughout the process.

Sandra M. Estanek

1

Ex Corde Ecclesiae and Student Affairs Pedagogy

Richard P. Salmi, S.J.

On August 15, 1990, Pope John Paul II issued *Ex Corde Ecclesiae*.[1] This apostolic constitution describes the relationship between Catholic universities and the Church, and has received much attention, particularly in the United States, over the past decade. In that time, the renewed interest in maintaining and promoting the Catholic identity of our universities has been focused largely on the faculty. Much of what has been written and discussed has come from Catholic theologians and academics as well as from the U.S. bishops.[2] As a result, student affairs professionals at Catholic universities have generally not participated in the discussion of *Ex Corde Ecclesiae*. The importance of the document and the critical issues it raises for Catholic higher education, however, have not gone unnoticed by student affairs professionals. Yet, as collaborators in the mission of Catholic higher education, I believe that student affairs professionals have much to offer our colleagues in the conversations and discussions surrounding *Ex Corde Ecclesiae*.

The National Conference of Catholic Bishops (NCCB), in their final draft of the "Application to the United States of *Ex Corde Ecclesiae*,"[3] reminds universities that they "are called to continuous renewal, both as universities and as Catholic."[4] It states that this relationship between university and Catholic "is clarified and maintained through dialogue that includes faculty of all disciplines, students, staff, academic and other administrative officers, trustees, and sponsoring religious communities of the educational institutions, all of whom share responsibility for the character of Catholic higher education."[5] Student affairs professionals need to be a part of the ongoing dialogue on the

Catholic character of our universities. The following material highlights part I of *Ex Corde Ecclesiae*, "Identity and Mission," and shows the direct correlation of this part of the document to two documents from organizations devoted to student affairs, and demonstrates how student affairs professionals at Catholic universities can be instrumental in fostering the ideals of Ex Corde Ecclesiae through good student affairs practice.

In 1994 the American College Personnel Association (ACPA) published the *Student Learning Imperative* (SLI).[6] The SLI focused on "how student affairs professionals can intentionally create the conditions that enhance student learning and personal development."[7] In 1997, ACPA and the National Association of Student Personnel Administrators (NASPA) published *Principles of Good Practice in Student Affairs* (PGP).[8] These two documents have provided student affairs professionals with a basic guide to student affairs practice. Clearly, *Ex Corde Ecclesiae* (ECE)[9] and these student affairs documents demonstrate that student affairs personnel at Catholic colleges and universities are partners in both the educational mission and in the promotion of the Catholic identity of our institutions.

Social Responsibility

> **ECE:** "… the objective of a Catholic University is to assure in an institutional manner a Christian presence in the university world confronting the great problems of society and culture."[10]
>
> **SLI:** "…preparing students to lead productive lives after college including the ability to deal effectively with such major societal challenges as poverty, illiteracy, crime and environmental exploitation."[11]
>
> **PGP:** "Good student affairs practice provides opportunities for students, faculty, staff, and student affairs educators to demonstrate the values that define a learning community. Effective learning communities are committed to justice, honesty, equality, civility, freedom, dignity and responsible citizenship."[12]

In *Ex Corde Ecclesiae* the Church makes explicit that graduates of Catholic colleges and universities need to know that it is their responsibility to use their education not simply for their own welfare but for the world community. In *Gaudium et Spes*[13] the Church states, "The joy and hope, the grief and anguish of the women and men of our time, especially those who are poor or afflicted in any way, are the joy and hope, the grief and anguish of the followers of Christ as well. Nothing that is genuinely human fails to find an echo in their hearts."[14] Margaret O'Brien Steinfels, editor of *Commonweal*, in her published address on "The Catholic Intellectual Tradition"[15] writes, "That opening paragraph from *Gaudium et Spes* speaks of our responsibility for all that is genuinely human, for what draws the minds and hearts of women and men. The Catholic intellectual tradition is universal in its breadth and its interests; that is a notion set forth, defended, repeated, and encouraged throughout the 'Pastoral Constitution on the Church in the Modern World.'"[16]

The concern of student affairs personnel for the development of students who are capable of furthering the betterment of the world community is consistent with the Church's desire to form students who will work to address the "problems of society and culture." There will inevitably be some debate on what exactly these problems are and how student affairs can be involved in identifying them. However, higher education has generally held that the development of students' moral and ethical values is key to an educated person. Implicit in that belief is the hope that our graduates will use their education for the good of society and the benefit of humankind.

In Jesuit education we talk of forming "men and women for others."[17] This other-centered approach is not new nor is it limited to Jesuit universities. However, it needs to be reinforced by our mission statements and the methodology we employ in student affairs. We need to be certain this does not become an empty slogan but rather a true hallmark for our students and our graduates. David O'Brien, Loyola Professor of Roman Catholic Studies at the College of the Holy Cross, writes: "Jesuit schools continue to use the phrases 'faith and justice,' 'option for the poor,' and 'men and women for others,' and most Catholic schools join them in insisting that care for the poor and a general concern for justice are a part of their educational mission. But developing programs to implement these ideals remains unfinished business."[18]

Community

> **ECE:** "A Catholic university pursues its objectives through its formation of an authentic human community animated by the spirit of Christ... It assists each of its members to achieve wholeness as human persons."[19]

> **SLI:** "...learning and personal development occur through transactions between students and their environments broadly defined to include other people, physical spaces and cultural milieus."[20]
>
> **PGP:** "Student learning occurs best in communities that value diversity, promote social responsibility, encourage discussion and debate, recognize accomplishments and foster a sense of belonging among their members."[21]

The notion and importance of community both in the Church and within student affairs is certainly not new. The formation of community on any campus can be a difficult challenge for student affairs professionals. The creation of communities that reflect diversity often faces scrutiny from alumni, parents, and other concerned parties. Student affairs professionals at Catholic colleges need to be able to demonstrate that we are implementing the directive of the Church, especially as stated in *Ex Corde Ecclesiae* to create "authentic Christian communities."[22] The challenge is to be clear that the communities we are striving to create are "authentic" in terms of gospel values and the promotion of justice.

As we attempt to create communities that are diverse and welcoming to people of color, women, gays and lesbians, those with disabilities, and people of differing religious traditions, it is important to know that we are implementing the Church's desire to form "authentic human" communities. In this area, student affairs professionals at Catholic colleges will be well served by having at least a minimal understanding of the Church's teachings on social issues. It is important to go beyond our student affairs training and experiences to include the teachings of the Church in our efforts to demonstrate the importance of diverse campus communities.

For example, it is extremely beneficial to have some knowledge of the National Conference of Catholic Bishops' document *Always Our Children*[23] in defending programs and initiatives taken to promote acceptance of gays and lesbians into our university community. Gay and lesbian issues still draw a considerable amount of attention and are the source for anxiety among student affairs professionals not fortunate enough to have supportive administrations or open campus environments. However, armed with student development research and information on church teaching, student affairs professionals can offer support for gays and lesbians with the conviction that they are indeed doing the work of the Church in forming communities that are "authentically human."

Role Models

> **ECE:** "Christians among the teachers are called to be witnesses and educators of authentic Christian life, which evidences attained integration between faith and life, and between professional competence and Christian wisdom."[24]
> **SLI:** "…staff themselves model such behaviors as collaboration and reflection that are likely to promote learning."[25]
> **PGP:** "…student affairs educators should demonstrate the values that define a learning community."[26]

The value of personal example and modeling behavior has been a constant at all levels of education. *Ex Corde Ecclesiae* calls on "teachers" to live lives that provide an example of Christian living.[27] Richard McCormick, S.J., writes of those people in our campus communities who are "*animae naturaliter catholicae*,"[28] people who according to McCormick have "assimilated Catholic culture so personally and deeply that their attitudes, habits, and values are thoroughly stamped by it. This stamping reveals itself in their spontaneous reactions, judgments and actions."[29] Many of us at Catholic colleges can name one or more persons on our campuses who fit McCormick's description—the priest, sister, brother, or dedicated layperson whom everyone seems to know and who walks the campus spreading "good news" and is often sought out for advice. McCormick admits that it would be unrealistic to expect to find many of these people at any one university. However, for the rest of us, the message is clear: giving concrete example of what we believe by the way we live our lives is essential to our task as Christian role models and educators.

Student affairs professionals work with universities to establish codes of conduct for students and to set forth in some detail the standards for ethical behavior in the university community. In regards to these standards, student affairs professionals as role models must be willing to "walk the talk" and have the courage of our convictions. This is not to suggest adopting a self-righteous attitude or a "holier than thou" approach to our personal and professional lives. In fact, it will be through our honest witnessing to values that we will be most effective. This is not earthshaking news. In our mentoring, advising, coaching, counseling, disciplining, and countless other interactions with students, we have the opportunity to be role models. Student affairs professionals at Catholic universities need to encourage behavior that is consistent not only with university policies but also with gospel values.

Student affairs professionals need also to examine those activities within the university community that we choose to participate in. For example, when members of an athletic department staff attend a theatrical performance, or residence life staff members attend a scholarly lecture, they provide concrete examples of what we hope for our students. This is also a wonderful statement of support for our academic partners in the university. Similarly, the attendance of student affairs professionals at religious or liturgical events on campus gives witness to the importance of personal faith and public worship in the life of the campus community.

Educating the Whole Person

> **ECE:** "Students are challenged to pursue an education that combines excellence in humanistic and cultural development with specialized professional training. They should realize the responsibility of their professional life, the enthusiasm of being trained 'leaders' of tomorrow, of being witnesses to Christ in whatever place they may exercise their profession."[30]
>
> **SLI:** "Hallmarks of a college-educated person include: a) complex cognitive skills such as reflection and critical thinking; b) an ability to apply knowledge to practical problems encountered in one's vocation, family, or other areas of life; c) an understanding and appreciation of human differences; d) practical competence skills (e.g., decision making, conflict resolution); and e) a coherent integrated sense of identity, self-esteem, confidence, integrity, aesthetic sensibilities and civic responsibility."[31]
>
> **PGP:** "Effective learning communities are committed to justice, honesty, equality, civility, freedom, dignity and responsible citizenship. Such communities challenge students to develop meaningful values for a life of learning."[32]

Leadership and civic responsibility are commonly held traits of an educated person. Brian Daley, S.J., professor of theology at Notre Dame, writes: "The work of a Catholic university...must always be in large part a concern for the human implications of the knowledge acquired, for the relevance of teaching and study and research to the building of a more just and more unified human society."[33] Catholic universities, according to Daley, must go beyond academic excellence to the promotion of a more just world. Catholic universities must be attentive to the needs of the poor and encourage our students and our university community to service on their behalf.

Jesuits often speak of educating the whole person. The superior of the Society of Jesus, Peter-Hans Kolvenbach, S.J., in a talk given at Santa Clara University, stated that: "Tomorrow's 'whole person' cannot be whole without an educated awareness of society and culture with which to contribute socially, generously, in the real world. Tomorrow's whole person must have, in brief, a well-educated solidarity."[34] I believe that this concept of solidarity is applicable to the graduates of every Catholic university. Our graduates should be men and women who are not merely well educated but who understand that what they do with their education is connected to the injustices others experience. Student affairs professionals contribute to this education by providing experiences for our students to encounter injustice as it exists in our cities, our country, and around the world, and to witness the lives of those who are impacted by injustice. Programs that provide an opportunity for students to experience the Third World or the impoverished areas of the inner city are certainly not limited to Catholic universities. However, according to Daley, Catholic universities "have no choice but to involve themselves openly and energetically in these things, letting the pursuit of wisdom change the world. Social and human concern, for them, is not a luxury but a matter of basic mission."[35]

Integration of Knowledge

> **ECE:** "In promoting integration of knowledge, a specific part of a Catholic university's task is to promote dialogue between faith and reason."[36]
>
> **SLI:** "The concepts of 'learning,' 'personal development,' and 'student development' are inextricably intertwined and inseparable."[37]
>
> **PGP:** "Expectations should address the wide range of student behaviors associated with academic achievement, intellectual and psychosocial development, and individual and community responsibility."[38]

It is for the integration of knowledge that a Catholic university promotes dialogue between faith and reason. The programs we develop and the speakers we bring to campus should enhance student learning. It is important that we help students learn *how* to think and not *what* to think. Margaret Steinfels writes: "Reason and faith are not antagonistic or unconnected. In the Catholic tradition we do not accept what we believe blindly or slavishly; we are urged to think about and to understand what we believe."[39]

Michael Buckley, S.J., director of the Ignatian Institute at Boston College, has stated: "The Catholic university exists to further the development of both serious faith and all the forms of knowledge."[40] Student affairs professionals should be concerned that our programs include a wide range of views and thoughts. It is important to remember that we are in the business of education, not indoctrination. It is difficult to have a "dialogue" with only one point of view. Student affairs professionals should not shy away from presenting programs that involve controversial topics or speakers. But neither should we fall prey to the notion that education, especially at a Catholic university, is value free or neutral. It is especially important that the Catholic viewpoint be presented in a manner that is appropriate when presenting speakers or programs on topics that may be controversial. These offer opportunities to invite the participation and collaboration of the faculty with our own professional staff.

Partnerships with Faculty

> **ECE:** "...everyone in the community helps in promoting unity, and each one, according to his or her role and capacity, contributes towards decisions which affect the community, and also towards maintaining and strengthening the distinctive Catholic character of the Institution."[41]
>
> **SLI:** "...optimal benefits are more likely to be realized under certain conditions, such as active engagement and collaboration with others (faculty, peers, co-workers, and so on) on learning tasks."[42]
>
> **PGP:** "Good students affairs practice initiates educational partnerships and develops structures that support collaboration. Partners for learning include students, faculty, academic administrators, staff, and others inside and outside the institution."[43]

Creating partnerships within the academic community, especially between student affairs personnel and the faculty, have been advocated for many years. Alfred North Whitehead advocated this collaboration to provide a "seamless coat of learning" as early as 1929.[44] More recently the *Student Learning Imperative* indicated that "student affairs professionals attempt to make seamless what are often perceived by students to be disjointed, unconnected experiences by bridging organizational boundaries and forging collaborative partnerships with faculty and others to enhance student learning."[45] The importance of creating authentic Christian communities has already been touched upon in this chapter; however, if the communities we form are to be authentic we need to examine more closely the concept of partnership within the university community.

The American Association for Higher Education along with ACPA and NASPA indicated in their joint report, *Powerful Partnerships: A Shared Responsibility for Learning*[46] that "learning is done by *individuals* who are intrinsically *tied to others as social beings*, interacting as competitors or collaborators, constraining or supporting the learning process, and able to enhance learning through cooperation and sharing."[47] The report highlights the concept of relating students to one another as social beings and developing a campus marked by caring and helping one another. Student affairs professionals at Catholic universities who work to create this type of community, especially with students and faculty, are implementing *Ex Corde Ecclesiae*'s directive of involving everyone in the community. The cooperation and sharing we encourage among our students not only enhances educational opportunities but also works to promote gospel values that should typify our campus communities.

Catholic universities also have a responsibility to create partnerships with their local communities. Student affairs professionals are often involved with local civic officials regarding university policies and student conduct. We should explore ways to include local residents and civil authorities on committees whenever appropriate. An invitation to local judges or other elected officials, for example, will facilitate communication and hopefully conversation about issues concerning both the university and the community. The university's participation in city council or other regularly scheduled meetings in the community indicate our interest in the welfare of the community and not simply the university. In our willingness to be open and welcoming of those in our surrounding communities, we can create partnerships that will benefit our students and our universities. These partnerships may also provide opportunities to demonstrate our care for and commitment to the community.

Value Formation

ECE: "A specific priority is the need to examine and evaluate the predominant values and norms of modern society and culture in a Christian perspective and the responsibility to try to communicate to society those ethical and religious principles which give full meaning to human life."[48]

SLI: "Learning and personal development occur through transactions between students and their environments broadly defined to include other people, physical spaces, and cultural milieus."[49]

PGP: "Good students affairs practice provides opportunities for students, faculty, staff, and student affairs educators to demonstrate the values that define a learning community."[50]

As student affairs professionals, we are privileged to work with the young men and women who come to our campuses each year. They come to us with different backgrounds and experiences and often with a very different set of values and expectations. They are generally representative of their generation. Michael Lavelle, S.J., was president of John Carroll University in 1994 when he wrote: "Our young people come to us with the problems that face every teenager in the United States. To deny this is to deny reality. Questions about unwanted pregnancy, AIDS, drug addiction and a disregard for authority are endemic to our American culture at present. The students who come to Catholic colleges have drunk deeply from the wells of this culture."[51] Student affairs professionals must be willing to confront honestly the issues facing our students. The challenge for student affairs professionals is to be cognizant of the ethos of the student culture and to assist students in both their personal development and in the formation of their values within the context of a Catholic university.

Brian Daley suggests that a Catholic university ought to encourage "a level of serious Christian conversation and reflection and prayer that will make the community as a whole a place where faith in Christ can seriously flourish and will challenge each individual, whatever his or her religious position, at least to refine constantly the choices and motives that govern his or her life."[52] Student affairs professionals should be mindful of the environments we create on campus that provide for this level of conversation and reflection. This can be done informally in residence halls and student centers, or more formally through programming in collaboration with faculty, religious, and invited speakers.

The efforts of student affairs professionals to create spaces on campus for purposeful learning are important in conveying what we value. Residence halls that promote study and community formation, offer gathering spaces that are welcoming and conducive to conversation and communication, and provide offices that are open to students with questions and concerns indicate to students that how they study, live, and socialize on campus are valued.

At Catholic universities, student affairs professionals should also be attentive to the ways we convey the importance of our Catholic identity and faith. Do residence halls have a chapel or at least a room for quiet reflection or prayer? Is the university chapel used by student affairs for gatherings or for appropriate programming? Are materials (books, pamphlets, videos, and so on) on issues of faith or of importance to the Church readily available for students? Do student affairs meetings regularly include prayer? These are but a few of the questions we need to ask in assessing our effectiveness as witnesses to our Catholic faith. It is through our assessment and honest reflection that we can strengthen the ways we promote and foster the Catholic identity of our universities.

Support Staff

> **ECE:** "...the dedication and witness of the *non-academic staff* are vital for the identity and life of the University"[53]
> **SLI:** "Staff themselves model such behaviors as collaboration and reflection that are likely to promote learning."[54]
> **PGP:** "Partners for learning include students, faculty, academic administrators, staff, and others inside and outside the institution. Collaboration involves all aspects of the community in the development and implementation of institutional goals and reminds participants of their common commitment to students and their learning."[55]

Our notion of partnership with those others mentioned in the *Student Learning Imperative* is vastly important. We have expended much time and energy, and rightfully so, on partnerships with the faculty. Similarly, we need to examine how we create partnerships with those "others" in the university to promote community and enhance student learning. These others include secretaries and office staff, housekeeping and maintenance personnel, and food service employees, to name but a few. It is important for student affairs professionals to see these people as partners in the mission of the university. It is equally important for us to empower these people to know that they are "partners" with us. The food service employees, for example, even if they work at the university for an outside contractor, are critical to the smooth running of the university. A well-fed army travels on its stomach, or so the saying goes. How true this is for a university with a large residential population! I am constantly amazed at the number of relationships that exist between our students and food service employees. This year several food service employees received invitations to the senior class dinner. These invitations were limited in number and, in the past, were almost exclusively reserved for faculty or student affairs personnel.

The importance of staff members in the lives of our students and others often goes unnoticed. When a student, parent, or visitor comes onto campus and into our offices, the first person they meet is most often a staff member. It is important that the staff feel that they are partners in the mission of the university. I was pleasantly reminded of the importance of the staff recently when I walked into my own office and saw a student talking with my secretary. I assumed that the student had come to see me, but was quickly humbled when he informed me that he had come to talk with my secretary! Student affairs professionals need to provide opportunities for staff development in ways that are appropriate to particular institutions. The methods we provide for recognition of staff achievements and the reward structures for members of the staff should reflect our understanding that they are "vital for the identity and life of the university."[56]

Community Service

> **ECE:** "The Christian spirit of service to others for the promotion of social justice is of particular importance…to be shared by its teachers and developed in its students."[57]
>
> **SLI:** "Off-campus agencies (e.g., community service) and settings (e.g., work, church, museums) also offer rich opportunities for learning, and students should be systematically encouraged to think about how their studies apply in those settings and vice versa."[58]
>
> **PGP:** "Good student affairs practice provides students with opportunities for experimentation through programs focused on engaging students in various learning experiences. These opportunities include . . . field-based learning such as internships, peer instruction, and structured group experiences, such as community service."[59]

Community service opportunities abound at most universities. Student affairs professionals at Catholic universities have an obligation to provide service opportunities that integrate faith and civic responsibility. Ours is an attempt to assist students to see the connection between faith and the commitment to justice that is usually lived out in some form of service to the poor. David O'Brien maintains that faith is the heart of service work. He writes: "The world-transforming goodness of a Gandhi, a John XXIII, or an Oscar Romero arises from faith, from powerful convictions about meaning."[60] We must work to develop service opportunities that allow students to reflect on their own convictions of faith.

The connection of service and faith is not always easy and takes some time and effort. It requires preparation prior to any service opportunity and serious reflection following. This point was made perfectly clear to me not very long ago when I invited several students from a residence hall to join me in volunteering at an inner-city meal program. I was pleased that they were eager to go and that they worked hard once we were at the center. Alas, upon our return to campus, as we were walking back into the residence hall, someone inquired about where we were. "Out feeding the bums," came the reply from one of the students! Needless to say, the lack of preparation and reflection made the trip something less than a faith experience.

Students, and I suspect others in the university community, need to be assisted in making the faith connection and in understanding the gospel imperative to love our neighbor. Working with faculty, campus ministry, and others, student affairs professionals enhance these service opportunities not only by demonstrating the faith connection but also by connecting this service of faith with justice. According to Peter-Hans Kolvenbach, S.J., "The way to faith and the way to justice are inseparable ways. Faith and justice are undivided in the Gospel which teaches that faith makes its power felt through love."[61]

Reflection and Faith

> **ECE:** "Pastoral ministry . . . offers the members of the university community an opportunity to integrate religious and moral principles with their academic study and nonacademic activities, thus integrating faith with life."[62]
>
> **SLI:** "The learning-oriented student affairs division recognizes that students benefit from many and varied experiences during college and that learning and personal development are cumulative, mutually shaping processes that occur over an extended period of time in many different settings."[63]
>
> **PGP:** "Active learning invites students to bring their life experiences into the learning process, reflect on their own and others' perspectives as they expand their viewpoints, and apply new understanding to their own lives."[64]

Student affairs professionals strive to involve students in a variety of educational endeavors throughout their undergraduate years. Both the *Student Learning Imperative* and the *Principles of Good Practice* have demonstrated that involving students in meaningful activities outside the classroom is instrumental in their personal development and in furthering the educational mission of the university. For student affairs professionals at Catholic universities, this concept is enhanced through pastoral ministry.

Pastoral ministry achieves the integration of faith with life in many ways. Most Catholic universities have opportunities for students to participate in retreats. Often these retreats are planned and executed by students with direction from campus ministry staff. Retreats give students time for reflection on their personal and faith lives. This time away allows students the necessary space for putting their lives in perspective and evaluating their successes and failures in relationship to Jesus Christ.

Often retreats provide a place of quiet in the otherwise very noisy and active world of an undergraduate. At my university, we have recently begun discussions about the importance of introducing students to the concept of contemplation. We have begun examining ways to provide opportunities for students to experience silence and contemplation in their lives. The notion of contemplation is not new to religious and others who have been introduced to it through spiritual direction or other disciplines. Students, however, find silence and the idea of contemplation odd at best. Through retreats and similar activities, students may come to value contemplation as a method for prayerful reflection.

Liturgical and public worship activities provide Catholic universities with the opportunity to involve students in pastoral ministry. For example, reconciliation services allow students to reflect on their shortcomings and provide a ritual for personal and communal healing and forgiveness. Students should be encouraged to participate in planning and implementing liturgies and other forms of public worship. This planning and participation allows students to incorporate those issues important in their lives into the prayer of the campus community and furthers both their personal and faith development.

Pastoral ministry is also extremely valuable in times of crisis on campus. The sudden and unexpected death of a student or other member of the campus community is difficult for all. Student affairs professionals at Catholic universities have the advantage of calling on those involved in ministry to assist students to look on this and similar incidents through a faith perspective. The development of a mature faith in the lives of our students is an important aspect of pastoral ministry.

Assessment

> **ECE:** "Catholic universities will seek to discern and evaluate both the aspirations and the contradictions of modern culture in order to make it more suited to the total development of individuals and peoples."[65]
>
> **SLI:** "Student affairs professionals should adapt to their institutional setting promising practices from those fields that contribute to the body of knowledge about student learning and personal development."[66]
>
> **PGP:** "Good practice in student affairs occurs when student affairs educators ask, 'What are students learning from our programs and services, and how can their learning be enhanced?' Knowledge of and ability to analyze research about students and their learning are critical components of good practice."[67]

In religious life we often speak of "discernment." We discern how the Holy Spirit is working in our lives and what is being asked of us in response. In student affairs, we might call this discernment, *assessment.* Student affairs professionals at Catholic universities need to do assessment on several fronts. We should be assessing the needs of our students developmentally, but also spiritually and morally.

Student affairs professionals also need to assess the needs of the staff. In this assessment, we do well to examine what resources are available for staff development. While many universities provide funding for attendance at an annual national conference such as those sponsored by NASPA or ACPA, many do not. In addition to these student affairs events, we should be attentive to those national organizations and meetings primarily for people working at Catholic universities. It is through active participation in these national meetings that professional staff members have the opportunity to learn from their colleagues at Catholic universities. University administrators need to assure that there is sufficient funding for these national meetings.

Staff development opportunities are not limited to national meetings, however. Cities or regions with more than one Catholic university should examine the possibility of cooperating in staff development. This can be particularly helpful when introducing new staff to Catholic identity and traditions. I have found it advantageous to be able to collaborate with other universities in helping staff to understand the various perspectives and traditions on Catholic identity rather than just that of our own university.

Conclusion

It has been my intention in this chapter to show the relationships that exist between *Ex Corde Ecclesiae*, the *Student Learning Imperative*, and *Principles of Good Practice*. In examining these relationships, I have attempted to provide a starting point for conversation regarding the Catholic identity of our universities and how student affairs professionals, through our commitment to student learning and the principles of good practice, promote and strengthen that identity.

Pope John Paul II, in the introduction to *Ex Corde Ecclesiae*, wrote: "I turn to the whole Church, convinced that Catholic universities are essential to her growth and to the development of Christian culture and human progress."[68] Through good practice and dedication, student affairs professionals at Catholic universities foster the development of our students and of Christian culture. We should not be afraid of a bit of self-promotion in this regard. Our presidents, bishops, boards of trustees, and alumni, to name a few, need to know what we are doing to promote and implement *Ex Corde Ecclesiae*. The work we do in student affairs is the work of the Church. We are partners in the mission of our universities and in the mission of the Church to prepare men and women to live lives that proclaim the love of God and love of neighbor.

2

Student Development and the Catholic University: Philosophical Reflections

Sandra M. Estanek

Introduction

Scenario 1: A recognized student organization plans a film series devoted to the work of Martin Scorsese, offering discussions after each film. They plan to include *The Last Temptation of Christ*, expecting a lively discussion of the merits of the film. Another recognized group on campus objects to the film, saying that it is against the mission of the university.

Scenario 2: A group of gay and lesbian students approach the student activities office with a request for official recognition of their new organization, insisting they have followed all of the college's procedures for recognition and using as their model the African-American student organization, which is officially recognized.

Scenario 3: A college health center debates whether it can add women's health services to those services they already provide. They discuss how to handle situations in which a prescription for birth control pills would be medically appropriate. They also discuss how they will handle requests for birth control prescriptions from students.

Scenario 4: It is during visitation hours in the residence hall. A female student returns to her room to find her roommate in bed with a male student. She complains to the hall director. Her roommate responds that it was during visitation hours, and she violated no policy.

❖ ❖ ❖

Each of these scenarios happened at a Catholic college or university in the United States. In the first scenario the debate over *The Last Temptation of Christ* became public, and the administration canceled the film. Not surprisingly, the debate continued. Some thought this action was consistent with the mission of the university. Others thought it was an inappropriate act of censorship.

Many institutions have wrestled with the second scenario. Some institutions have granted official recognition to Gay, Lesbian, Bisexual, and Transsexual (GLBT) groups. Others have found other frameworks, such as "ally" groups or support groups. Still others have denied recognition altogether. Clearly, following the institution's rules for recognition is not sufficient.

In the third scenario, the institution decided to provide women's health services on campus, but the medical staff would provide birth control prescriptions only when warranted by a medical condition. They agreed they would not do exams solely for the purpose of providing birth control. Some thought this was consistent with the values of the institution. Others thought it was an intrusion into the doctor/patient relationship.

In the fourth scenario, the institution subsequently clarified in their next student handbook that fornication was against college policy. However, they wondered how far they should go in enforcing this policy.

These scenarios illustrate some of the difficult issues faced by student affairs professionals who work at Catholic colleges and universities. Some of the most controversial issues related to the Catholic identity of the institution emerge not in the classroom but in the areas traditionally supervised by student affairs professionals. Many of these issues involve a clash of values. For example, in the first scenario many believed that the presentation of *The Last Temptation of Christ* was consistent with the spirit of academic inquiry, especially because there would be a discussion of the film afterward. Others believed that the ideas presented in the film were offensive to Christianity, and that the university had no academic obligation to show such a film on campus because it was contrary to the institution's Catholic identity. The other scenarios revolve around the clash between the public and communal values of the Catholic Church with the private and individual values of some persons who make up the institution. Sometimes those persons are students and sometimes they are members of the faculty and staff. Sometimes the clash is between the values of the Catholic tradition and the values and perspectives of one of the professions represented on campus. It is this latter tension that this chapter will address.

Context

In recent years attention has been given to the role of student affairs in working with issues related to the Catholic mission of the institution, such as those described in the opening scenarios above. In 1990, the Association of Catholic Colleges and Universities (ACCU) published a special edition of *Current Issues in Catholic Higher Education* devoted to student life issues. The edition was published following the 1989 annual meeting of the association, the theme of which was "Student Life: Focusing on Our Catholic Identity." This meeting marked the first time that issues of student life appeared on the national agenda of Catholic higher education.

The theme of the meeting emerged from a discussion of the ACCU board of directors. As stated by Mary L. Funke, chair of the ACCU task force on student life, "At its June 1988, meeting, the ACCU board of directors discussed the cultural and social context within which Catholic colleges and universities in the United States attempt to carry out their missions. The board concluded that one area in which the impact of our American culture is clearly felt is student life."[1]

At that meeting the board established a student life task force and commissioned a survey of ACCU member presidents regarding the three most immediate student life concerns. The results of this survey and the discussion at the 1989 annual meeting were used by the task force to develop a questionnaire on student life that then was sent to presidents, chief academic officers, chief student affairs officers, and selected traditional-age undergraduate students at ACCU member institutions. The results of the survey were published in the winter 1990 edition of *Current Issues in Catholic Higher Education.*[2]

The findings of this study outlined student life concerns that have remained constant. Most of the issues cited were related to sexuality. As Dorothy M. Riley reported, "When asked 'What are your three most immediate student life concerns?' forty-three percent of the respondents list such issues as suicide, date rape, abortion, birth control, dating, sexually transmitted diseases, and eating disorders. Thirty-seven percent answer alcohol awareness, while twenty-seven percent name interpersonal relationships."[3]

Respondents were asked whether their colleges and universities were making an effort to address these issues and cultivate values. Seventy-four percent of all respondents indicated that their institutions were making considerable efforts in this regard. Sixty-eight percent cited the Catholic tradition as being extremely important in guiding these efforts.[4] When asked to rate the effectiveness of programs that address value issues, the respondents rated leadership development, value development, and spiritual development the highest, while they deemed programs addressing issues of sexuality not as effective.[5]

Two other findings were important to the emerging national discussion of student life at Catholic colleges. Riley noted that when asked to identify the greatest strength of the student life program, fourteen percent responded personnel. When asked to identify the greatest weakness, ten percent also claimed personnel. Eighty percent indicated that graduate training for student affairs personnel was important or extremely important.[6]

Based upon the findings of this questionnaire and subsequent discussions, the task force made four recommendations to the presidents of Catholic institutions: 1) to take a leadership role on campus in articulating Catholic values, 2) to get to know the diverse and changing population of the student body, 3) to involve the entire college community in student development efforts, and 4) to "encourage and actively support the formation of a national association which will provide a forum where student life issues will continue to be identified and through which programs, services, and models to address those issues can be developed."[7]

While presidents may have made efforts on their individual campuses to implement these recommendations, the national association was not created at that time and the discussion of the role of student affairs did not take root on the national level. It reemerged, however, in 1995. In preparation for the August 1995 national conference, "Catholic Higher Education: Practice and Promise," ACCU commissioned another study of student affairs practice. This study was subsequently published in a special edition of *Current Issues in Catholic Higher Education* devoted to the conference.[8]

The report was not technically a follow-up to the 1989 study because the researcher was unaware of the earlier study. However, some of the issues and concerns that emerged in 1989 resurfaced in 1995. The 1995 study consisted of a survey sent to chief student affairs officers at Catholic colleges and universities, plus a qualitative phase in which the researcher visited three institutions and asked follow-up questions based upon the issues raised in the survey. Like the 1989 study, the 1995 report discovered that issues of human sexuality were the most controversial issues faced by student affairs professionals at Catholic institutions. To the open-ended question, "In your experience, what have been the most important issues related to Catholic identity faced by student affairs?" the answers in rank order were 1) sexual behavior, 2) gay/lesbian issues, 3) the increasing diversity of the student body, 4) policies and social justice issues, 5) the lack of knowledge about church doctrine and practice and the role of women in the Church, 6) alcohol and drugs, and 7) racism, recognition of controversial groups, and the increasing diversity of staff.[9]

As the earlier survey indicated, these issues were being addressed in both programs and policies. However, the qualitative phase of the research uncovered discomfort among student affairs professionals in dealing with issues related to the Catholic identity and values of the institution. Most of them had been trained in traditional fields such as education, student personnel, and counseling, and they did not feel confident that they knew enough about the Catholic tradition.[10] Like the earlier survey, participants indicated that more conversation and training would be helpful. Again, a national organization was proposed.[11]

This time the idea for a national organization did take root. With the sponsorship of ACCU and funding by the Lilly Endowment, the Institute for Student Affairs at Catholic Colleges (ISACC) was created. The institute provided student affairs professionals with the opportunity to learn more about the Catholic context of their work. Sessions specifically addressed Catholic teaching on sexuality and the human person. Opportunities were provided for discussion and networking. During its five-year existence from 1995 to 1999, over two hundred student affairs professionals attended a five-day summer program. In 1999, participants in ISACC formed a permanent organization, the Association for Student Affairs at Catholic Colleges and Universities (ASACCU), which meets annually for a three-day conference.

These were not the only opportunities available for student affairs professionals working at Catholic institutions to gather together to reflect on their practice. The Jesuit Association of Student Personnel Administrators (JASPA), which was founded in 1954, continued to provide a forum for community and reflection for those working at the twenty-eight Jesuit institutions in the United States. Alternatively, the Cardinal Newman Society for the Preservation of Catholic Higher Education was created in 1993.

Reflection

The past decade has witnessed a growing recognition at national levels that student affairs professionals play an important role in the mission of the Catholic college or university. What has changed since the creation of the Task Force on Student Life in 1989 is that now there are regular opportunities for student affairs professionals who work at Catholic institutions to gather together to discuss issues and responses.

What has not changed is the nature of the issues that they face on campus. As a profession, student affairs continues to wrestle with the same difficult issues of student development that were articulated in the 1989 ACCU survey. However, several themes have emerged from the many formal and informal discussions over the past ten years that have begun to shape our responses to these ongoing developmental issues.

In dealing with controversial issues such as the ones already discussed, student affairs professionals have said in many venues that they experience a disconnect between the values and assumptions of their profession and the values and assumptions of the Catholic institutions at which they work. Several possible reasons for this have been articulated. Based upon these reasons, various solutions have been proposed.[12]

One of the reasons given is that the majority of student affairs professionals have received their graduate training at secular institutions. The 1995 study indicated so—the assumption being that the values they were taught are not the same as the values of the Catholic institution at which they work. Based upon this understanding of the problem, the solution has been proposed that Catholic universities begin their own graduate programs. The presumption is that because the programs are housed at Catholic institutions, graduates of these programs will receive a professional training that will better prepare them to work at Catholic institutions. Such graduate programs exist at Boston College, Canisius College, Seattle University, and the University of St. Thomas in Minnesota.

Another reason is that professionals took the jobs at Catholic colleges without having an adequate understanding of the mission and values of the institutions at which they worked. Several possible solutions have arisen from this understanding. One is the movement to "hire for mission," that is, to make sure that the Catholic identity and mission of the institution are discussed fully with each candidate in the hiring process. A candidate's potential contribution to the Catholic mission of the college would be a significant factor in deciding who should be hired. This solution does not require that the candidate be Catholic; however, a related proposal recommends the preferential hiring of Catholics.

These solutions address the issue of new hires. Another group of solutions address the ongoing in-service training of staff, which are consistent with the recommendations to the presidents of the Task Force on Student Life in 1989. Examples are participation in formation programs such as the Institute for Student Affairs at Catholic Colleges and in organizations such as ASACCU, JASPA, and the Cardinal Newman Society. Similarly, a call for greater ongoing communication on campus regarding the Catholic identity and mission of the institution has been stressed. At many institutions a "mission office" has been established for this purpose.

However, these solutions, while important, do not address the fundamental problem; therefore, even if all of these ideas are implemented, the tension experienced by student affairs professionals will not go away. There are no administrative solutions because at its heart the problem is one of epistemology; that is, what we know and believe and how we come to know and believe it, or "the nature of knowledge and justification."[13]

Student affairs professionals stand at the uncomfortable practical interface of two epistemological systems, the one stemming from the Catholic intellectual tradition and the other from the professional field of student development. These systems hold different understandings of the nature of the human person and the nature of society and, therefore, while each tradition may on the surface hold dear the same values, such as community and freedom, each means something completely different. This conflict, especially when it is not understood, complicates our efforts to ground our practical decisions in both the values of the institution and an understanding of good professional practice.

This is not to deny the connections that were drawn in the previous chapter. It is important to recognize that *Ex Corde Ecclesiae* places the work done by student affairs professionals at the heart of a Catholic higher education. *Ex Corde Ecclesiae* takes seriously the idea of the "holistic education of the student" and argues that the Catholic identity should be experienced in all aspects of the life of the campus. Such a holistic approach to student learning is also at the heart of the *Student Learning Imperative* and *Principles of Good Practice*.

I challenge student affairs professionals to reflect more deeply upon this connection. By understanding the epistemological framework, we will be able to develop a more nuanced approach to the issues we face on campus.

A full discussion of this epistemological debate is a book in itself. My purpose in this chapter is to briefly outline the epistemological framework of student development and illustrate the dissonance with the Catholic tradition. By doing so I hope to begin to raise the awareness of this philosophical issue so that a full discussion can be initiated in future work.

The Epistemology of Student Development

On the surface it would seem that the student affairs tradition would allow for multiple responses to questions of values. Support for the mission and values of the institution at which we do our work have been part of the tradition of student affairs as a profession. This was stated as much in the 1937 document, *The Student Personnel Point of View*, and was reaffirmed in *A Perspective on Student Affairs*, which was published fifty years later. It states, "Student affairs in a college or university is influenced by the distinctive character of the institution, including its history, academic mission, traditions, and location. The composition of the student body and faculty, the priorities of the chief executive officer and governing board, and the beliefs and knowledge of the student affairs staff also shape the responsibilities and the manner in which programs and services are delivered. Since the character of an institution largely determines the nature of student affairs programs, organizational structures and services may vary widely from one campus to another."[14] A similar statement is found in the 1997 *Principles of Good Practice in Student Affairs*: "Institutional contexts influence how principles for good practice are applied. Such contexts within higher education include institutional missions, expectations, and student demographics. In realizing institutional goals, each student affairs division is responsible for managing resources effectively in support of its institution's mission. This document provides a framework to aid student affairs in meeting these challenges without sacrificing the individuality of their institutions."[15]

According to this tradition, it would be perfectly acceptable for different resolutions to the above scenarios to exist depending upon the institution at which they arose. In terms of the four examples, while Institution A could decide to show *The Last Temptation of Christ* as an expression of the value of freedom of speech, Institution B legitimately could decide not to show the film and argue that this decision was consistent with the value of community. Different institutions could make different decisions as to the appropriateness of a GLBT organization on campus. An institution could determine that the health center would not distribute or prescribe any form of birth control, and college policy could state that any student who engaged in fornication on campus could be subject to disciplinary action. This variation would seem to be consistent with the professional premises of student affairs, which would seem to be silent on the relative merits of these positions.

Such an assessment is too simplistic, however. In the intervening years between the publication of *The Student Personnel Point of View* and the present, a professional body of knowledge has been created. Like any body of knowledge, over time an understanding has emerged as to what is known and how one goes about creating and confirming knowledge. This is the functional definition of an epistemology.

The underlying epistemology of the body of knowledge known as "student development" can be discerned through a reading of the "great books" of student affairs.[16] In 1992, Florence Hamrick and John Schuh conducted a research project to identify the works that have been the most influential in the field of student affairs since the publication of *The Student Personnel Point of View* in 1937. Their list of twenty-two books was compiled by conducting a survey of selected student affairs program faculty members and recognized writers in the field. Their purpose in compiling the list was threefold: first, to determine if a common knowledge base existed for student affairs; second, if such a knowledge base did exist, to provide an explicit description so that it might be more effectively integrated into the curriculum of professional preparation programs; and third, to provide a "permanence and opportunity for reflection" to a profession that is more often focused on the immediate and the practical.[17]

Since the publication of this list, its value has been debated, while the goal of the project that it be used to inform graduate education in student affairs has not been met. However, the compilation of this list of seminal works has been essential to our task of articulating the underlying epistemology of student development. If one reads the "great books" in the order in which they were published, one is able to discern the development of a dominant epistemology in the field of student affairs. The epistemology that emerges from this reading may be characterized as "belief-empiricism." According to the *Cambridge Dictionary of Philosophy*, "...for one's beliefs to possess one or another truth-relevant merit, they must be related in one or another way to someone's experience."[18] In other words, knowledge is inductive, or derived from experience, rather than deductive, or derived from principles. Nevitt Sanford first applied this epistemological framework to student affairs in the 1962 "great book," *The American College*.

Because it is an applied field and its writing always has served the purpose of informing practice, student affairs has never seen itself as value-free, as have other fields grounded in an empiricist epistemology. Students affairs as a profession always has had a dimension of "values-transmission," as has been stated by Robert B. Young in *No Neutral Ground*, a work to which we will return later. What it means for student affairs to be grounded in belief-empiricism, however, is that the values to be transmitted are derived from the structured observation of experience rather than from principles, a perspective that was first articulated by Sanford.

Sanford argued that American colleges and universities were doing a poor job of socializing students because their practices were not grounded in empirical research. He did not challenge the idea that the teaching of values was an appropriate goal of higher education, but he did argue that colleges and universities were failing in this task because their work was not empirically based. Sanford argued further that education should have specific goals, methods for reaching those goals, and appropriate strategies for assessing success or failure. For this to occur, the methods of the social sciences should be applied to the study of student behavior. Sanford wrote, "The major purpose of the present volume is to put the resources of the newer social sciences into the service of liberal education."[19] He continued, "It may be hoped that the work will not only further the development of a scientific approach to higher education but stand as a contribution to social science in general."[20]

That the methods of the social sciences have been applied to the study of student behavior is evidenced in the body of literature that has emerged since Sanford's clarion call in 1962. Chickering, Perry, and Astin have written within this framework also. One of the seven "principles of good practice" is using "systematic inquiry to improve student and institutional performance." What we know about students, what values we hold as a profession, and what we believe we should be doing in our practice are grounded in our study of student experience. This way of thinking is clearly consistent with the epistemology known as "belief-empiricism."

Values and Student Affairs

In her 1998 keynote address to the Association of Catholic Colleges and Universities, "A Critique of Values in the Social Sciences," political theorist Jean Elshtain argued that the social sciences that emerged in the 1960s aspired to become value-free. Because of their devotion to the scientific method, they saw values solely as "subjective preferences,"[21] and thus have become increasingly unable to make a case for the holding of one value over another. Values were empirically demonstrable, but could claim no moral authority. Consequently, as bodies of knowledge, she argued, they have become devoid of values, not free of them. They are not value-free because "value neutrality" itself is a value.

Despite its acceptance of these social science methods, student affairs never aspired to become value-free. The teaching of values has been an essential aspect of the profession throughout its history. For example, the teaching of values as a role of student affairs is cited throughout *The Student Personnel Point of View*. This role is also cited in the earliest of the "great books," *Student Personnel as Deeper Teaching* (1954) and *Student Personnel Work in Higher Education* (1961). Values remain a part of the literature of the "great books" despite the epistemological revolution that occurred in the field in the 1960s. They also remain a part of the understanding of good practice today. One of the "principles of good practice" states: "Good practice in student affairs helps students develop coherent values and ethical standards."[22] The values listed are justice, honesty, equality, civility, freedom, dignity, and responsible citizenship. Thus, not only is student affairs as a profession not value-free, it holds certain values as a profession.

One writer who has explored the values held by student affairs is Robert B. Young. The values professed by the university in general, and student affairs in particular, is the topic of his 1997 book, *No Neutral Ground*.[23] In that work, Young argues that certain values have been central to higher education. These values are freedom, equality, individuation, justice, and community. In *No Neutral Ground* he defines and discusses each of these core values and how student affairs as a profession implements these in its practice. It is clear from Young's work that these values work together to provide a context of understanding for the student affairs professional.

Young's analysis may be summarized as follows. The first value of the academy is freedom. The key attribute of freedom is choice.[24] Higher education improves a person's ability to choose from among the many goods and opportunities society provides. The ability to choose is tied to the opportunity to do so. Thus, the next value of the academy is equality. By this, Young does not mean equality of outcome, but equality of opportunity. Everyone should have a fair opportunity to succeed. Even with a fair chance for success, however, individual differences will emerge. The outcome of education is not to make people equal; it is to create individuals who can better exercise their freedom to choose. Thus, individuation is the third value of the academy. This is what we mean when we speak of the "education of the whole person" and "educating for character."[25] The freedom of the individual is never totally unrestrained because each is an individual among other individuals. Thus, the fourth value of the academy is the value of community, that is, of "mutual empowerment."[26] Young defines the academic community as "an assembly of colleagues."[27] Balancing the needs of the community and the prerogatives of the individual is the purpose of justice, which is the fifth value of the community. These core values and how they are defined inform what we understand to be good student affairs practice.

Contrasting the Catholic Point of View

By taking an overview of the literature of student development that has emerged in the past fifty years, one is able to see that, in fact, a dominant "student personnel point of view" does exist. This point of view includes both content (values) and method (belief-empiricism).What is understood as "good practice" is grounded in this point of view. Good practice includes both specific values and a specific methodology. Despite the stated commitment to ground our practice in the multiple missions of different kinds of institutions, what has emerged is a dominant understanding of good practice, which has its own set of fundamental assumptions about the way the world works.

By reflecting philosophically on this body of literature, one can discern three such fundamental assumptions: 1) knowledge is inductive, not deductive, that is, it is derived from the structured observation of experience; 2) the individual is primary and the community is a voluntary association of individuals; and 3) individual choice is the fundamental social value. From their professional training, student affairs practitioners bring these perspectives to the issues they face on campus.

The problem for the student affairs professional who is trained in this worldview, and who works at a Catholic institution, is that the Catholic intellectual tradition does not hold the same assumptions about the nature of the real. The "Catholic point of view" is based upon assumptions that are different and definitions that also are different, even though the words sometimes may be the same. If a student affairs professional who works at a Catholic college is unfamiliar with this perspective, and also is ignorant of the assumptions of his or her professional training, he or she will be unable to understand the different contexts in which the problems and issues he or she faces, such as the scenarios with which we began this chapter, are grounded.

In contrast to the three fundamental assumptions stated above, one may discern from reflection on the Catholic intellectual tradition three alternative assumptions. From the Catholic point of view: 1) truth is deductive, not inductive, that is, it is derived from fundamental principles that interact with and interpret experience; 2) human beings are fundamentally social beings and not isolated individuals; and 3) the common good, not individual choice, is the fundamental social value.

In his introduction to the apostolic constitution, *Ex Corde Ecclesiae*, Pope John Paul II challenged the Catholic university "to consecrate itself without reserve to the cause of truth."[28] He continued, "Without in any way neglecting the acquisition of useful knowledge, a

Catholic University is distinguished by its free search for the whole truth about nature, man and God. The present age is in urgent need of this kind of disinterested service, namely of proclaiming the meaning of truth, that fundamental value without which freedom, justice and human dignity are extinguished."[29] This challenge by the pope is grounded in the Catholic understanding of "...all aspects of truth in their essential connection with the supreme Truth, who is God."[30]

When the pope writes of this pursuit of truth, he does not understand the endeavor within the framework of belief-empiricism. Put very simply, the pope is presuming the following: the primal fact is the existence of God. God made all of creation. God made creation knowable and understandable to human beings through their reason. God also revealed God's plan for the human person in the person of Jesus Christ. Through their reason human beings are able to discern God's plan for them and for creation. What is true is what is consistent with God's plan. However, human beings are finite and bound by time and space, so the continuing discernment of God's plan is a task that falls to each generation. But the nature of God's plan and, thus, what is true, does not change. Through this process over time, principles are developed. These principles guide each subsequent generation's process of discernment. To this process human beings bring their reason, their faith, and their experience. This is what is meant when one says that truth is deductive rather than inductive. In *Catholicism*, Richard P. McBrien notes: "Principles do not appear full-blown apart from experience. They are attempts at coming to terms with the multiplicity and ambiguity of experience. Principles are formulations which try to bring a measure of consistency and coherence to human experience, to find common threads which hold that experience together."[31]

In contrast to the second assumption, that the individual is primary and the community is a voluntary association of individuals, the Catholic tradition posits that human beings are fundamentally social beings, not isolated individuals. Again, this alternative assumption stems from the Church's understanding of the nature of God and from the picture of communal responsibility that emerges from the Gospels. Again, very simply, at the heart of Christian belief is the mystery that God is a triune God, that is, a unity composed of three distinct persons: Father, Son, and Holy Spirit. In other words, the very nature of God is communal. Because human beings are made "in God's image" we, too, are communal as well as being individually unique. This understanding is described in the entry on "individualism" in the *HarperCollins Encyclopedia of Catholicism*:

> The rise of modern individualism owes something to the his-
> torical Christian emphasis on the sanctity and dignity of the
> person, though the often exaggerated distinction drawn by
> modern individualism between the individual and the com-
> munity—particularly in the moral, social, and economic
> spheres—is inconsistent with the traditional Christian belief
> in the inherently social nature of the person, the unity of
> humankind, and the ultimate dependence of the human
> being upon God.[32]

The third assumption stems from the second. If one believes that
the individual is primary, then choice is the fundamental social value.
However, if one believes that human beings are fundamentally social,
then the common good is the fundamental value. The common good
was defined in the Vatican II document, *Gaudium et Spes* (*The Church
in the Modern World*) as "...the sum of those conditions of social life
by which individuals, families, and groups can achieve their own fulfillment in a relatively thorough and ready way."[33] This understanding
was defined further in the *HarperCollins Encyclopedia of Catholicism*
as follows:

> The concept underscores the basic claim in Catholic teach-
> ing that the person is fundamentally social. This is opposed
> to certain modern understandings of the person as funda-
> mentally autonomous and separate from society, entering
> into society by contract only because it is to the individual's
> advantage. The concept of the common good, in contrast,
> forms the basis for both societal claims on the individual and
> individual claims on society.[34]

The purpose of these comments is not to defend or analyze the
Catholic point of view. The purpose is to illustrate through this admittedly simplistic overview of an ancient and complex tradition that the
assumptions upon which human behavior is understood are different
from the assumptions that form the basis for student development
theory. Without understanding these fundamental philosophical differences, one will not be able to understand the full complexity of the
tension that arises when one tries "to use theory" to ground one's
practice.

This may be illustrated by returning to the five values articulated
by Young as being fundamental to the university in general and student affairs in particular: freedom, equality, individuation, justice, and

community. We can now understand that these values are also held by the Catholic tradition; however, they are understood in a different context and, thus, may mean something different and may call for a different response from the practitioner. In contrast to Young's analysis, summarized earlier in this chapter, we can posit this alternative: God created each individual human being with the capacity for reason and freedom. This means that each person has the innate capability to know God and to do God's will. The purpose of education, including higher education, is to develop both reason and the ability of the person to exercise his or her freedom. This is what we mean when we speak of the "education of the whole person" and "educating for character." Because all persons are created by God, all persons are fundamentally equal regardless of any differences between individuals. Because all persons are equally children of God, all persons are connected to each other in community. The university, as well as all social institutions, is called upon to manifest this community. As members of this human community, all persons owe each other fundamental respect as children of God, which is the foundation of justice.

This also may be illustrated by returning to the scenarios with which we opened the chapter. Each of these scenarios present the student affairs administrator with a problem to be solved. Should a film that some believe is blasphemous be shown on a Catholic campus? Should a GLBT organization be officially supported? Should medical services that are legal be limited because they violate a religious principle? How far should the university go in regulating student behavior that is contrary to traditional Catholic teaching? If the administrator approaches the problem from within the dominant epistemology of student affairs, he or she will ask certain questions to come to an understanding of what to do. What is college policy related to scheduling of events and establishing organizations? Did the groups involved follow established college policies and procedures? What does the literature say about this? What have colleagues at other institutions done? What is student opinion? From the Catholic perspective, one would ask different questions. What is the teaching of the Church in this matter? If I don't know, how can I find out? How is that teaching applicable in this instance? What principle is at stake? How can we engage students to understand this?

Both sets of questions need to be asked for the administrator to come to a decision that respects the full complexity of the situation. It is still possible to come to different conclusions, as occurred in the scenarios presented. It is possible, even likely, that the decision reached will remain controversial, but it will be the quality and openness of the discernment process that will determine if the administrator will ultimately be successful in crafting a response.

Conclusion

The successful student affairs administrator at a Catholic institution will be professionally "transcultural," that is, he or she will know the professional literature of student affairs, and will develop a sophisticated understanding of the assumptions of this body of literature. At the same time he or she will understand and respect the Catholic tradition. Both will inform practice. This transcultural approach will not make the tensions and controversies go away, but it will allow the administrator to work with them successfully over time.

It is this transcultural approach that is called for in *The Student Personnel Point of View*, *A Perspective on Student Affairs*, the *Student Learning Imperative*, and *Principles of Good Practice*. Student affairs is, in fact, practiced within the mission of the institution. Hopefully, this chapter has demonstrated that the "principle of good practice" remains true and valid once we realize the depth and complexity of the challenge that is presented to us by that statement.

This transcultural approach also is called for by *Ex Corde Ecclesiae* when it asks for a dialogue between "faith and culture." By its very nature, the document states, the university "…develops culture through its research, helps transmit the local culture to each succeeding generation through its teaching, and assists cultural activities through its educational services."[35] Such a process certainly goes on in the classroom, and in the decade since the publication of *Ex Corde Ecclesiae* there has been much written about the "dialogue between faith and reason" from the perspective of the faculty. However, as this chapter also has demonstrated, that dialogue should go on in student affairs. Student affairs administrators are not simply disinterested problem solvers. Our work is grounded in a body of knowledge that has its own epistemology. How we understand our work is colored by that epistemology. In other words, like our faculty colleagues, we have a "field." In this way, too, we are like our faculty colleagues at Catholic colleges and universities who are challenged by *Ex Corde Ecclesiae* to reflect on "the methods proper to each academic discipline," in other words, on their field, and to "determine the relative place and meaning of each of the various disciplines within the context of the human person and the world that is enlightened by the Gospel, and therefore by a faith in Christ, the *Logos*, as the center of creation and human history."[36]

Student affairs has called for a holistic approach to education. We have called for greater collaboration with our faculty colleagues to provide a "seamless" experience of student learning. In its call for dialogue between faith and culture, *Ex Corde Ecclesiae* provides those of us who work at Catholic colleges and universities with support for those collaborative efforts and with a place to start.

3

Characteristics of the Catholic Intellectual Tradition

Edward Jeremy Miller

The work of student affairs professionals on a Catholic campus happens within the environment of the Catholic heritage of the institution. Sound and effective student affairs work operates within many parameters and warrants, such as state and federal laws. No less important a parameter is the mission statement of a Catholic college or university, because the *mission* defines the milieu and the vision within which the student body and student affairs personnel interact. As varied as are the several hundred Catholic colleges and universities spread across the nation, their mission statements appear to have a common element. These colleges and universities assert that the heritage of Catholicism, particularly its faith tradition, stamps their missions and influences the work of their campuses. It is then incumbent for all those in the Catholic campus environment to understand the Catholic heritage and utilize it to their advantage.

The Catholic heritage is a complex reality having many aspects. A most important aspect of the heritage is the manner in which Catholics have pondered religious matters over the centuries, that is to say, how the Catholic tradition has thought about the nature of God, what God wills for human beings, and so forth. The Roman Catholic tradition has evolved into exhibiting a characteristic way of engaging these important religious questions that distinguishes it from other belief traditions such as Protestantism or Islam. This essay will delineate six characteristics of the Catholic intellectual tradition that, taken together, define and describe how it has begotten a recognizable heritage.

The present chapter has a more theoretical relationship to understanding student affairs at Catholic colleges than do other chapters in the book. This chapter portrays an environment of thought, a set of religious principles, within which student affairs is practiced. Most of the time the insights and strategies of student affairs practitioners are far more concrete than is the cluster of intellectual features I wish to describe. Nevertheless, a theoretical grasp of the Catholic intellectual tradition is necessary for student affairs work if obstacles are to be avoided.

A few obstacles should be noted, and hopefully they will suggest the applicability of this chapter to more effective student affairs practice. Many students, especially non-Catholic students who might fear being proselytized, come to Catholic campuses convinced that Catholic heritage is equivalent to church authorities pontificating on this or that topic. To them, Catholicism is simply doctrinaire. So pervasive is this sentiment even in the wider American culture that many Catholic laity themselves have not much more grasp of Catholic heritage than something reducible to the notion of authoritative indoctrination.[1] People beginning college life with this stereotype of the Catholic tradition are generally closed to the richness a Catholic campus can offer them. It is important that student affairs personnel realize why the stereotype is false.

Another problem arises from the "indoctrination" stereotype. Very conservative students, and the conservative parents of some traditional-age students, would wish a Catholic college to continue the doctrinal catechizing that had been begun in the lower grades of parochial schooling. For them the Catholic heritage means a collection of doctrines, and these ought to be propounded authoritatively. They believe that a Catholic college no longer in the business of doing this has lost its way; its light has died. Two falsehoods are being perpetuated with this kind of thinking. First, the Catholic intellectual heritage is reduced to indoctrination, as in the above case. Second, a college should operate much the same as a parochial high school in terms of religious teaching. Closely connected to this expectation is another. Such parents also expect the student affairs division to run residence halls as these parents ran their households, because the college ought to be acting *in locus parentis*.

From a quite liberal vantage point arises another kind of obstacle to student affairs practitioners. Many students come to campus or live in residence halls imbued with the relativistic thinking that characterizes much of American culture today. Some of its shibboleths are "If it doesn't hurt anyone, what's wrong with it?" "I have my opinion. I respect your opinion. And everything is a matter of opinion after all, isn't it?" It is important for student affairs personnel to appreciate that the Catholic intellectual tradition is not relativistic, that it claims truths can be reached, and that the path to truthful insights is a quite nuanced process. Other illustrations could be drawn, but hopefully these three situations point sufficiently to the applicability of this chapter's more theoretical contribution to understanding the work of student affairs.

I begin by defining what is meant by the *Catholic intellectual tradition*. Over the centuries the Catholic Church has developed ways of thinking about sacred realities that are distinctive of Catholicism and differentiate it from other religious traditions.[2] I refer to realities such as God's will for the individual, for the Church, and for the world; the role of prayer; the ways of discerning divine providence; the effects of sin and subsequent reconciliation, and so forth.[3] The Roman Catholic Church has come to reflect on such matters in a characteristic manner, and when this intellectual tradition is viewed on a large and centuries-long scale, different characteristics of the tradition come into focus. I am not proposing a listing of doctrines from the Catholic tradition, no *Enchiridion*[4] or catechism of religions truths, as it were. I propose, rather, that the Catholic intellectual tradition has six characteristics: It is developmental, incarnational, integrating, self-criticizing, authoritative, and social/dialogical. Of these six traits, I wish to make three prefacing remarks before proceeding to a description of each trait.

1) These ways of thinking tended to emerge over time; they are not present in clarity and in operation right from the beginning. I will present them in a chronological way, but the order of treatment should not be interpreted too strictly. For example, I shall present in sixth and last place the dialogical/social way of thinking evident at Vatican II, but a social way of thinking characteristic of the intellectual tradition began long before the 1960s. In fact, the early Christian church thought far more socially than did Catholicism of two centuries ago. Vatican II was a retrieval of an earlier heritage that had become clouded over due to the individualism of the Era of Enlightenment in Western culture.

2) These ways of thinking are characteristic of the Catholic intellectual tradition only when all six of them are viewed together. For example, an incarnational way of thinking describes the Roman Catholic tradition, but the case can be made that incarnational thinking describes more strongly, some may even say more fittingly, the Eastern Orthodox tradition. Think only of the Greek Orthodox understanding of icons. The same caveat applies to the other descriptors and even to smaller groupings of them. (To be unique and different from other religious traditions would not be a blessing of Roman Catholicism but rather a dark suspicion hovering over it. It would be an ironic prayerful

wish to want God to shepherd Roman Catholicism so uniquely that God's provident actions in other religions are perceived to be stingy or withheld.)

3) Rather than arguing a heavily footnoted thesis, I will use illustrative stories and depictions of Catholic "phenomena" to make my "case" that these six aspects are properties of the Catholic intellectual tradition that, taken together, define it. My examples should elicit other examples from a reader's memory that might serve to corroborate my contentions or at least make them plausible.

1. The Catholic intellectual tradition is developmental or, "What do you do when you can't quote Jesus?"

The developmental characteristic is placed first because it is most fundamental. Development refers to the notion that religious teachings undergo a kind of expansion or growth in understanding without ceasing to be grounded in the same original teaching. The development of a teaching enables the teaching to retain what is old and achieve what is new. If Christianity were not developmental, then Christianity is simply the unvarying implementation of a blueprint Jesus left behind. Admittedly, Christianity implements many things Jesus commanded, such as the "Do this in remembrance of me" eucharistic prayer, a first-century tradition Paul had received in the late 30s in Antioch or Damascus and in turn passed on to the Corinthians in the mid-50s (1 Cor. 11:23-24). There are, however, many more situations that Christianity had to face after Jesus' final resurrection for which it had no blueprint or direct teaching from the Lord. One such situation, with two dogmatic issues at stake (to use a later heavier language) asked: How Jewish must you be to follow Jesus? And, can you even be non-Jewish and be saved?

There is an important story in Acts[5] that unfolds during Christianity's first fifteen years, if one reads carefully between the lines. After the Pentecost experience, when Jesus had appeared to a group of disciples a mere fifty days after the Crucifixion and narrated by Luke in terms of its charismatic effects on them, the disciples settled down into a commune. The choice for commune—rather than going out to evangelize the world, which Luke knows is the ultimate result of resurrection appearances, though the disciples do not quite know this yet—made initial sense. Experiencing the resurrected Jesus was so powerful and transforming that the disciples were convinced Jesus would return very soon to consummate history as they knew it.[6] They shared all things in common, they prayed in the Temple by day, and they broke bread (their early word for the Lord's Supper) in their homes at night. They were doing what I would call "Jewish things" (Temple practice) and "Christian things" (Eucharist). I am being anachronistic in imposing on the first months of church existence the much later Jewish/Christian distinction, but I wish only to indicate that the first disciples thought of themselves as fully Jewish, yet they are also my own eucharistic ancestors.

The first disciples evangelized locally as well. Acts records Peter's Jerusalem sermons.[7] This preaching introduces the story's next element. Diaspora Jews were always visiting Jerusalem, since there were three pilgrimage feasts held each year. Pilgrimage Jews from the Diaspora more than likely were bilingual, Greek and Aramaic, and some of them were converted by the preaching of Jesus' earliest disciples. Thus they joined the growing commune. Luke terms *Hellenists* the Greek-speaking Jews who believed in Jesus; he calls the Aramaic-speaking Jewish believers (for example, James, Simon Peter, Levi, Mary the mother of Jesus, the other Miriams, and so on) *Hebrews*.

Eventually tensions developed between the two groups, which openly erupted over "money," as it were, that is, over a power play about the common holdings. The Hebrews withheld food from the Hellenists' widows. If this were all there was to it, it might seem petty; instead, the "food fight" was a kind of leverage strategy over a doctrinal dispute between Hebrews and Hellenists, but I jump too fast. Luke simply offers the peace-at-all-cost solution. The Twelve were not going to become the food distributors to keep the peace. Instead, they split the commune in two. The Hellenists were given their own leadership, a seven-man group that included Stephen.[8] Although not mentioned here, the Hebrews also get their own leadership, because a few chapters later we are reading about James, the brother of the Lord, as the elders supervise matters in their own commune community. It is not at all strange that pastoral leadership in both groups was modeled on the synagogue, a ruling committee of elders, because these Jesus-believers were all Jews; the synagogue was a familiar religious organizational structure.

Luke has us follow Stephen's ministry. He preaches about Jesus to arriving Diaspora Jews. Eventually he is accused of preaching against "this holy place and the law," the same charges brought a year or two earlier against Jesus. Like Jesus he is brought before the Sanhedrin, the Jewish assembly of leaders that treated religious violations of Jewish law. Unlike Jesus, he mounts a spirited defense. I have no doubt Luke transposes some later Christian preaching onto Stephen's lips, but the uprising that Stephen's speech causes is historically authentic. Why did the Sanhedrin explode and kill him? After describing the history of their own people and Solomon's construction of a temple to house the sacred

Ark of the Covenant, on top of which Yahweh was felt to dwell, Stephen informs the Sanhedrin that "God does not dwell in buildings." Now we see for the first time in Acts how the Hellenists understand their Judaism in relation to a belief in Jesus, since Luke has painted Stephen as spokesperson for Hellenist theology. The Hellenists do not believe in Temple practice nor do they observe the Torah in full (for example, charge of preaching "against Moses"). I suspect the Hellenists have dropped the food laws, the sexual purification laws, the festival laws, and so on. The Hebrews have been observing all of these torahs (commandments) religiously. Now we grasp why there was a fight over food. The Hebrews in the original commune were disturbed by this Hellenist "liberalism," and they tried to force compliance by using as leverage the common food supply.

How observantly Jewish must you be to be a Jewish Christian, for example, a Jew like Stephen (a Hellenist) or like Simon Peter (a Hebrew) who both believe in Jesus. It is not certain. Jesus left no clear instructions. This much so far is known: it is more important to believe in Jesus and accept diversity in Torah practice than to force uniformity or fight over it.

The story continues with enigmatic verse 8:1, that a persecution of the Jerusalem church broke out the very day of Stephen's martyrdom, and "all were scattered . . . except the apostles." Luke uses *apostles* here to mean the *Twelve*. Ironically, Luke's entire Book of Acts turns on this verse, for if a forced dispersal had not happened, Christianity would never have become a world-evangelizing religion. Who was attacked and scattered by the Temple authorities? The Hebrew commune, with the familiar Synoptic names we know? No. They were left untouched because they continued Temple practice and Torah observance. The Hellenists? Yes, indeed! Like Stephen, they were a threat to Jewish Sanhedrin leadership, and they had to be silenced by whatever means.

Young Saul, who carried the double name Paul—many Diaspora Jews had two names—was no Diaspora Hellenist. He was an ultra-orthodox Sanhedrin supporter, and his work was to round up these anti-Temple Jewish misfits. On one such sortie he received a resurrection appearance from Jesus so transforming that Paul became one of them, one of the Hellenist enemy. Our story is almost over. Paul joined the Hellenist community in Antioch, Syria, which had already begun preaching to the so-called unclean Gentiles. On one evangelizing trip from the Antioch church in the mid-40s, Paul and Barnabus converted a slew of Gentiles—the two of them can be said to have created the "Gentile problem." Sense the tension among the Hebrews in the Jerusalem commune: the Hellenists, their brothers and sisters in Jesus, pushed them on the Temple issue, pushed them on Torah observance, pushed them when some Hellenists evangelized a few Gentiles, but at least (we think) circumcised them, and now learned that large numbers of Gentiles were being baptized but not being made Jews at all (through circumcision). Envoys rush from Jerusalem to Antioch, telling the new Gentile converts they must become Jews to get saved by Jesus. Paul and Barnabus explode. A delegation from Antioch is sent to Jerusalem to resolve this issue of belief in Jesus and Jewish identity.

A conference ensues. Sides are debated. What is at stake? The doctrine of salvation and who can be saved! Is there a blueprint from Jesus? Clear instructions are lacking, for otherwise there would have been no debating assembly we now call the Council of Jerusalem. After the debates and testimonies and prayers for discernment ended, James, the leader of the Jerusalem church, renders the decision that the baptized Gentiles need not be made Jews but they must observe four strictures (the so-called laws of Noah, which Jewish enclaves in the Diaspora had always imposed on pagans living in their midst).

Unfortunately, Luke does not report the arguments of the parties. The far right likely argued: Jesus never reached out to the Gentiles, nor should we. The far left might have argued: if you really live in the spirit of Jesus, all the traditions are abrogated. I think a middle position won out. Against the far left it argued that the past counts; after all, Jesus lived among them and they keep him in their memory. Against the far right it argued that Jesus did not reach out to Gentiles but he did reach out to men and women outside the law, that is to say, to Jewish men and women who were public sinners, who were lepers, or who worked with Romans, such as tax collectors. We have now Gentile believers who are so far outside the Torah law that they were never inside it. In this new situation, the middle position likely argued, we discern the "mind of Jesus" to conclude we should embrace Gentiles as family of God, as *qahal Yahweh*.

My first story thus ends but its point must clearly be drawn. Within its first fifteen years, the Jesus movement faced two crucial issues on which Jesus left no instructions: how Torah and Temple relate to Jesus, and how Jewishness relates to salvation. There needed to be an understanding of what Jesus' gift of salvation meant. There was no blueprint carrying Jesus' lines of thought. The mind of Jesus had to be discerned to unfold the sheer richness of the gift of salvation. I could have taken later church stories of development, such as the Council of Ephesus's *theotokos* teaching about Mary, but such post-biblical examples would not give pause to a biblical literalist mentality that thinks in the necessity for blueprints drawn from Scripture. It is better to show development

within the biblical period itself. The New Testament portrays developments of understanding, and I am justified in making development a
cornerstone of any Christian self-understanding, and incontestably it is
for the Catholic intellectual tradition. Catholicism allies itself with
Eastern Orthodoxy and Anglicanism, and opposes biblical fundamen-
talist groups, in thinking developmentally.[9]

*2. The Catholic intellectual tradition is incarnational or, "Hertz versus
Avis: Are you second class if you didn't know Jesus of Palestine?"*

Although the old Avis versus Hertz rental car advertisement may
date me, I am not being cute or comical about a serious matter and way
of thinking. When one says, "Moses gave us the Torah" or "Mohammed
gave us the Qu'ran," the fact that readers live generations later matters
not at all. The written revelations matter. But when one says, "Jesus is
God's Word," then personal access matters. Therefore, are later generations of Christians, who never experienced what Jesus looked like or
sounded like, disadvantaged? This question matters a lot.

From its characteristic way of thinking, the Catholic answer is that
the same Jesus who brought God's gifts of enlightenment and healing
to Palestinian contemporaries will meet later believers with the same
gifts, and the meeting will be just as personal and direct. This way of
thinking is rooted in the Bible itself, especially in the Gospel of John.
My illustrating story is, in fact, Johannine Christianity's own story
about a healing miracle Jesus performed in his lifetime. To appreciate
the story, one must recollect that Jesus performed it about the year
30 A.D. and that the Fourth Gospel was composed in the mid-90s, a gap
of over sixty years and during which interval Johannine Christianity
had come to a deeper insight into the miracle's import for them.[10]

The story comes from John 9, where Jesus restores sight to a blind
man. The disciples see the man and ask Jesus if the blindness is due to
his own sin or the sin of his parents. Jesus responds by saying the blindness serves to reveal the work of God in the man. Jesus then says that
he is the light of the world. With that, Jesus takes dirt and his spittle,
smears the man's eyes with the paste, and tells him to clean himself off
in the pool of Siloam. The man, blind from birth, does as he is told and
receives the gift of sight.

In the synoptic Gospels of Matthew, Mark, and Luke, this is where
the story would end, with Jesus exercising power over evil (Satan) in
this world. In John, though, the story is just the beginning. Many conversations follow about what really happened and what it all means.
Notice all the speakers in the story: Jesus, his disciples, the blind man,
his parents, the Pharisees, and the onlookers themselves. The Fourth

Evangelist crafts these conversations to teach the deeper meanings of Jesus' miracle, the Christological meaning that Jesus is the light of the world and enlightens people, and the sacramental meaning that God's gift of real light is not physical sight but faith-insight that comes in and through baptism. Let me focus on the baptismal level of the story.

John 9, between the lines, as it were, is filled with baptismal allusions. The motif of the story is enlightenment, which we know was a very early church term for baptism.[11] Jesus daubed (*epechrisen*) his eyes—and the same Greek verb was employed in early baptismal ceremonials to describe the anointing in the rite of initiation. Then there is the very name of the pool where Jesus directs the man to go, Siloam, which the Evangelist tells the reader means "sent." (Probably many original readers of this Gospel in the mid-90s did not know Aramaic.) Significantly, Jesus is the one who is "sent" from the Father throughout the Fourth Gospel, and so the man washes off the grime in a pool of water bearing Jesus' heavenly name. How more baptismal can one get?

But the baptismal allusions do not end there. As the man is questioned in the story about who restored his sight, his depiction of Jesus becomes ever more insightful. First, he is a "man named Jesus," then he is someone "come from God," then Jesus is a "prophet," and at the story's conclusion, the man confesses to Jesus himself that Jesus is the "Son of Man" whom the very same man worships (that is, does to Jesus what alone is allowed God). The man received physical sight in the beginning of the story, but his spiritual sight (that is, faith) grows incrementally, not unlike what happened to early church baptismal candidates. To the man's responses there may also be a hint of the question-and-answer motif of the baptismal ceremony, but we do not know how early this format came into the rite of initiation.

Notice also the Pharisees are depicted as Jesus' enemies. They become ever more blind as the story progresses, as if they and the man are traveling in opposite directions. They "end up in sin" whereas the man at the start is alleged to have been "born in sin." The Pharisees end up in unbelief (about Jesus and his divine role).They have physical sight all along, but they cannot really see.

This story is no mere metaphor for baptism in the manner one might retell a saint's story, as Hrotsvit of Gandersheim does of St. Pelagius.[12] John 9 is about Jesus' healing ministry, and the baptismal catechesis asserts that the Jesus who conferred miraculous sight in the early 30s is the same Jesus conferring the miracle (power) of enlightenment at the end of the century for the first readers of this Gospel, and consequently for every later Christian generation. The same Jesus is acting on a baptismal candidate to be given sight, real sight. To not have lived back in the Palestinian days of Jesus is no disadvantage for a later disciple. One meets the same Jesus, personally, beneficially, and without diminution, in a sacrament, and it is Jesus who acts in sacramental baptism when one is washed in the water bearing his name.

Sacramental thinking is really incarnational thinking for Catholics, given the sense of sacramental realism Catholics profess. Amazingly, *stuff*—and I include human gestures and words—express the risen Jesus' presence in the sacramental ritual: poured water, oil, bread, wine, a hand imposed on a head, "this is my body," "you are forgiven," "receive the gift of the Spirit." These words make Jesus present and encounterable.[13] This way of thinking is blasphemy to anyone with so transcendent a notion of God (for example, Muslims) that God and matter are distinct and untouchable. Not so with Christian faith in Jesus. Jesus is the human expression of divine being, not just its cover. We are accustomed to name this doctrine *incarnation*, whose boldest translation (in + *caro/carnis*) is simply the *enfleshment* of God.

Incarnational thinking focuses on a *communing* between the visible world and the invisible world, to use Cardinal Newman's favored terms. It accepts distinction between created and uncreated realities, but it shuns their dichotomy and the tendency to attribute sullied status to created matter. As a characteristic of the Catholic intellectual tradition, incarnational thinking looks, with poet Gerard Manley Hopkins, for the grandeur of God in matter, reaches for spiritual growth through engagement with the world, expresses love of God in love of neighbor and in cherishing the earth, builds churches whose materials nurture imagination and memory, listens for God's voice in our consciences and in features of the Church and in everyday events, and tastes God's sweetness in consecrated wine and in conjugal embrace. Because incarnational, the Catholic intellectual tradition does not desire escape from matter as do the Buddhists, and does not exalt spirit over matter as did the Puritans and many Protestants today (and older Catholics of a Jansenist persuasion).

3. The Catholic intellectual tradition is integrative or, "Secular knowledge counts."

The Christian movement could have dug a moat around itself and cut off the temptations of a sinful unbelieving world. It could have practiced sacred sacramental rituals in isolated enclaves and waited until its eschatological meal (the Eucharist) met its complement, the end-of-the-world eschaton. It would have been a sect and likely would have withered as a sect, not unlike religious sects today and religious sects then, such as the John the Baptist disciples who only lasted into the early second century before dying off. But the Christianity that Catholicism sees as its earlier expression[14] went a different direction and did so by choice (by "discerning the Holy Spirit" is the theological way of putting it).

The mid-second to the early third century evidences a clear rejection of the sectarian temptation to remain isolated.[15] A group of Christian writers, the so-called Apologists, made a public defense (*apologia*) of Christianity to prove that this no-longer-Jewish-protected religion was not a threat to the state and, in fact, was morally superior to pagan sects such as Mithraism, the Persian-imported cult promising immortality. The defense was likely to appeal to the second-century Stoic emperor, Marcus Aurelius, a kind of philosopher-king who wanted to encourage virtuous living in the empire. (Curiously, Aurelius's demented son, Commodus, made Mithraism an imperial cult when he came to the throne.) Apologists like St. Justin Martyr writing in Greek, and Tertullian in Latin, used the common coinage of secular culture and philosophy to dispel popular prejudices against Christians and to show the compatibility of Christianity with the best attainments of Greek and Latin thought by expressing Christian teachings in secular language.

The engagement of secular thought for Christian purposes perhaps becomes clearest in the adoption of Neoplatonism by Christian writers and preachers during the next two centuries. In the Latin West one has only to mention St. Ambrose and St. Augustine. Let me cite a clear example by St. Augustine of a cardinal Neoplatonic teaching that claims all being emanates from one eternal and immaterial source and is meant to return to this source if able to escape the chains of materiality.

In the following passage from his *Confessions* about the "ascent of the soul" to God, St. Augustine describes withdrawing deeper and deeper within himself, and in an experience of unchangeableness and timelessness—how unlike the world of matter—he experiences God.

> In the course of this inquiry why I made such value judgments [about beautiful bodies] as I was making, I found the unchangeable and authentic eternity of truth to transcend my mutable mind. And so step by step I ascended from bodies to the soul which perceives through the body, and from there to its inward force to which bodily senses report external sensations, this being as high as the beasts go. From there again I ascended to the power of reasoning. . . . It withdrew itself from the contradictory swarms of imaginative fantasies, so as to discover the light by which it was flooded. . . . So in the flash of a trembling glance it attained to that which is [*id quod est*]. At that moment I saw your "invisible nature

understood through the things which are made" [Rom.1:20].
But I did not possess the strength to keep my vision fixed.
My weakness reasserted itself, and I returned to my custom-
ary condition.[16]

Who can remain unmoved by this fleeting experience of sheer
divinity? In telling his story, Augustine speaks to us of our own quest
and hunger for God. Here the categories of Neoplatonism are put to
evocative use, in enabling Augustine to give expression to his own
experiences and in fortifying us to undertake the same pursuit. If the
secular knowledge of Neoplatonism would never have counted, then
we would never have heard those other intoxicating words from him,
"Late have I loved you, O Beauty so old and so new, I loved you late.
And all along you were within me, and I outside, and I sought you out
there. I rushed crassly toward those beautiful things you had created.
You were with me and I was not with you. Things held me distant from
you."[17]

Thinking is impossible without a linguistic and philosophical world
within which it happens. This is a lofty way of asserting what should be
obvious to common sense. You can no more deny to St. Augustine's
mind his Neoplatonism than you can deny to a man's lungs his air. We
do not judge, think, feel, sense, and recollect in a vacuum. In an appeal
to a biblical-age purity and uncorrupted innocence, some religious
groups today anathematize secular knowing and worldly philosophy,
substituting shibboleths that are neither true to the Bible nor helpful in
the long run to anyone. This is not the way Christianity evolved, and it
is not the way Catholics think.

Some precision is needed, however. Secular knowing counts but it
does not count without caveat.[18] All secular ways of knowing carry their
own limitations. Philosophical views have myopia. Therefore the integrative feature of the Catholic intellectual tradition presents a constant
call to vigilance and circumspection. Where do we go too far? When is
there a sellout? It is more likely that a particular limitation of a secular
way of knowing will be perceived later, not as it is being utilized. It is
likely to be perceived when another secular way of knowing has come
to the fore and has illuminated the limitations of the earlier way.

St. Augustine provides a good example of philosophical myopia in
regard to sex. If the Neoplatonist in him saw the beauty of the exterior
world as a distraction from an introvertive path to God, then the lure of
the female body, by which I really mean a person and femininity in all
her attractiveness for a heterosexual man, must have battered him all
the time. Remember that he was sexually active many years and

fathered a child before he had his conversion and accepted baptism from St. Ambrose. St. Augustine, it would appear to me, comes down against sex simply too hard. It is being too hard to say, as he does, that every act of intercourse between husband and wife is at least a venial sin.[19] It is more than just too hard; it is not Christian self-understanding. This was a myopia of his Neoplatonism.

4. The Catholic theological tradition is self-critical or, "Can you be a loyal Catholic and a maverick too?"

What does the Catholic intellectual tradition do with myopia? It corrects it. At times, when the error is destroying Christian faith, there is solemn anathematizing, as the ecumenical Council of Nicea did against Arius.[20] Usually, however, the corrections come about imperceptibly and without fanfare, and the errors are of a more minor nature. I want to tell the story of critiquing a great figure, St. Augustine, by another great figure, St. Thomas Aquinas. My purpose is to write about being Catholic and being critical, because it is wrong to equate being Catholic with being docile. It is a common misapprehension of the Catholic intellectual tradition, especially by people who do not know it, that loyalty to one's Catholicism means abdicating one's use of reason, especially its self-critical function, and foregoing dissent. I realize there are many examples of criticism by some Catholics of the church tradition that are "over the edge," and I am not going to identify and justify them. My aim is simple: there is a place for being critical. Being critical does not impugn one's loyalty. Indeed, some great luminaries, later honored by popes and the people, have critiqued the intellectual tradition they have received.

I can site many examples, but I am choosing someone who is thought to be as safe and solid and stalwart in Catholic matters as is imaginable. I refer to St. Thomas Aquinas, the *doctor communis* of the Roman Catholic Church and the patron of all Catholic schools. And I am positioning him *vis-à-vis* St. Augustine, whom Aquinas venerated. You will not find anywhere Aquinas writing, "Beatus Augustinus is wrong here." Rather, you see what Aquinas does with the Augustinian legacy, which in most cases he adopted straightaway. I am taking one small portion of the Augustinian legacy about sex, where Aquinas corrects Augustine ever so respectively but corrects him nevertheless.

Calling Aquinas a maverick is not being excessive. I also want to reclaim this word for Catholics. For too many Catholics, loyalty and faithfulness have become identified with total compliance and "not making waves." Regarding Aquinas, I could begin with his condemnation by the archbishop of Paris in 1277, but the story needs to focus on him earlier, at the moment he is correcting Augustine on the matter of sex and intercourse apropos original sin.[21] For Aquinas to go against so long and entrenched a position as Augustine's on intercourse as deviant or suspect requires a touch of the maverick. We see indications of this independent streak in his personality early on. At age twenty he resisted family pressures to become a Benedictine and instead entered one of the new mendicant (begging) fraternities, the Dominicans, whose novelty upset those who preferred the tried-and-true brand of monasticism. Shortly thereafter, he immersed himself in the "new" philosophy of Aristotle, a philosopher who unsettled popes. Aquinas was no domesticated Italian!

For Augustine, the sinful rebellion of Adam and Eve, with all its consequences (original sin), was visited upon posterity through the sexual intercourse which conceives life. Coitus is not just the occasion for transmitting original sin; it is its implementing vehicle. "The whole race was corrupted in Adam [and Eve], . . . being the offspring of carnal lust on which the same punishment of disobedience was visited."[22] If one looked within oneself for the struggle between obedience to God and self-willed rebellion, one need not look beyond libido, and it is here where Augustine placed his emphasis. It is true for him that spiritual sins, such as pride, are in themselves worse, but it is also true that one's ungodliness, on balance, is sexual libido, inevitably uncontrolled libido. Is it not understandable? Do we not see political careers undone by dalliances and marriages unraveled by trysts? If for the Letter of James the uncontrolled organ of sin is the tongue, Augustine locates it lower on the anatomy.

Aquinas also sees Adam's sin as rebellion, and its effects on us all as a disorder we cannot control or harness. But he is too much the Aristotelian to make the bodily features of human life inherently sinful. Desire is a healthy dimension of being human. Aquinas calls it *passio* (passion), better understood as emotion. In Aquinas's psychology, the human person is filled with powers meant to be exercised, such as the power to will, to know, to desire, to emote. If original sin had never existed, these human powers would coexist coherently and be integrated among themselves within a unified personality.

Aquinas works from a positive first principle. God created human beings; their every dimension was good. A better gift of God yet was the coherence and personal integration of the personality. Aquinas called it *original justice*, the fundamental gift of personhood. Adam's sin destroyed the coherence, and, in domino fashion, loss of control at every level set in. The human will becomes wayward (from God), the intellect becomes muddied, the emotions lose their grounding in the human spirit (mind and will) and become unruly. Furthermore, the internal chaos of the personality feeds off itself and worsens. It is this "unglued" nature, to use the trendy modern term, that each generation of sexual partners begets. Like begets like. Original sin is not about the act of intercourse itself. It is about us as people. When, in point blank fashion, Aquinas asks if Augustine is correct in identifying original sin's transmission with sexual intercourse, he replies, in his respectful maverick fashion, both yes and no. Concretely speaking (*materialiter*), yes, because libido's disorder expresses original sin. Fundamentally speaking (*formaliter*), no, because original sin is the loss of the integration the Creator intended for humanity, and without their freely willed alienation from God, this personal integration would today be their crowning gift.[23] In Thomas's description of sin, sex is not a dirty word in and of itself.

Permit me to draw from Aquinas another example about sex that can be quite useful in the student affairs work of counseling, assuming students might bring forward for discussion such matters of conscience. For Aquinas there is a world of difference between sexual temptation and sinful sexual thought. A sexual thought is a conscious act of will because *willfulness* is necessary for any sin to happen. Sin cannot sneak up on you unwittingly or unwillingly. A sexual temptation involves an *imagined* situation (for example, an act of adultery) that "possesses" us before we might come to will it, that is, will its performance or will its lingering for the sheer titillation of it. How long can it linger in the imagination in a pre-willed state? Hard to say. How long do people unwittingly daydream? Here is a more important question. Is a sexual temptation pleasurable? Of course it is. Every temptation is, or it would not be a temptation. Aquinas's moral theology distinguishes temptations from willed acts of thought or deed, and his realistic Aristotelian psychology reminds us, as if we needed reminding, that matters sexual are pleasing and appealing, both the licit kind and the illicit kind. But are the illicit kind consciously willed? That's the question for the matter of sin. Augustine, on the other hand, would see the merest sexual imagining of something as sin having its pervasive grip on us.

5. The Catholic intellectual tradition is authoritative or, "Can the Church subsist on Scripture alone or reason alone?"

In maintaining a consistent subtitle format, I found it difficult to choose a single adjective to express the role of teaching authority (*magisterium*) in the Catholic Church. *Magisterial* would suffice for Latin lovers, but it is off the mark in modern English. By *authoritative* I mean the rightful role of teaching authority in Catholic self-understanding of the faith. There is no Catholic intellectual tradition without place given to the teachings of past councils and synods, the ongoing teaching of popes and bishops, and the teaching of liturgical books and catechisms. Magisterium is a very broad topic and I have no intention of delineating it.[24] Instead, I want to make four suggestions about teaching authority in Roman Catholicism; there are two groups envisioned in the back of my mind in my choice of suggestions. On the one hand there are many people, Catholics included, who collapse the Catholic tradition to the teaching authorities and their dicta. What I have discussed up to this point should have unmasked the narrowness of such a mindset, but a few matters remain. There is another group of people who shun all church authority, either in the name of enlightened reason (*sola ratio*) that sees church authority as the darkness from which western culture has finally emerged, or in the name of "the Bible alone" (*sola scriptura*) that sees church authority as the wicked Babylon foretold in the Book of Revelation into whose clutches early Christianity slipped.

First, the exercise of teaching authority and pastoral administration has existed in the Church from the beginning. As well as in the post-apostolic age, which no one seems to deny, it is important to note the exercise of church authority in the New Testament period. Its presence from the beginning, and especially from the second century onward, indicate how constitutive of the Church is teaching authority. Even in this essay, we saw that James, the blood relative of Jesus who led the Aramaic-speaking Jerusalem church (the mother church, if you will), delivered the decision that Gentile believers in Jesus need not become Jews. How awful it would have been if the Jesus movement experienced immediate schism between Hebrews and Hellenists due to an inability to decide the matter authoritatively. St. Paul was most desirous of "not having run in vain" (Gal. 2:2), that is, of having a non-circumcising ministry to the Gentiles that would have been rejected by the Jerusalem mother church. He continued to make financial collections in his Asia Minor churches for the impoverished commune community in Jerusalem to show solidarity (or communion) with it. Schism was avoided by James's pronouncement to recognize both non-Torah observing Christianity on the same footing with Jerusalem's Torah-observing Christianity.[25]

Second, a very muscular form of teaching authority existed in the Catholic Church after and due to the sixteenth-century Protestant Reformation. The Protestants rejected church authority and taught that the Bible alone was the authority for Christians. Their battle cry was *sola scriptura*. In reaction, the Catholic Church asserted the legitimacy of church teaching authority and exercised it vigorously in order to contain the revolt. (What is reform for one side is revolt for the other side.) An aggressive exercise of teaching authority continued in what is called post-Tridentine Catholicism[26] up until our own times.

Two commonsensical observations must be made. Other periods of Catholic church life have existed without such a strongly exercised ministry of authority. Therefore, the style of exercising authority is somewhat conditioned by historical circumstances. Second, if this style is all that some Catholics today have seen or read about, it is small wonder they conclude that strong, centralized teaching authority is alone what constitutes the Catholic intellectual tradition. The more firmly rooted is this image of Catholicism, the more difficult it is to convince them of a larger picture and greater nuance.

Third, the misuse of teaching authority is inevitable. I make this statement, not to whip church magisterium but actually to shore it up in the popular mind and maintain its legitimacy. In this sinful world in which people desire to act conscientiously, if I may use a recurring idea from Cardinal Newman, the exercise of power and authority will inevitably be misused, even if the one exercising authority continues to maintain "good intentions." This is simply the nature of the beast, as the phrase goes. Who can think of any power enclave, anywhere, and at any historical period, that did not know abuses? Like Newman, I prefer to "take things as they are" and to judge legitimacy and authenticity on its own merit, not on the principle that "it is, has been, and ought to be, abuseless." When someone points out an abuse of Roman Catholic teaching authority, it could be that the situation "can be explained," and that the charge lacks merit. But not everything falls into place in this way. There have been abuses and they should be acknowledged.[27] What is more important for the Catholic intellectual tradition are the self-corrective features of the Catholic Church that come into play as the tradition unfolds in a creative fashion.

This matter is too broad to receive treatment here. I would, however, direct interested readers to what is now a classical depiction from Cardinal Newman on the issue. I list simply its main points: The presence of the risen Jesus in the Church as its Prophet, Priest, and King is given concrete sacramental expression (for example, by people) in the prophetical or theological office, the priestly or devotional office, and the kingly or authoritative office of the Church. Left to itself, theologizing can drift to rationalism, devotion to pietistic superstition, and pastoral authority to tyranny. (The descriptors are Newman's.) The living out of the life of two offices acts as a check and balance on any tendency of the third office to cause abuses. Newman's depiction runs ninety pages, and so there are nuances to be appreciated.[28] My third suggestion is only to emphasize that abuses of authority can be expected and ought not lead one to reject its legitimate role.

Fourth, without teaching and pastoral authority, Christian community would self-destruct. The Church is a community, and if its unity is fractured irreparably, this is the self-destruction to which I refer. The experiment of "the Bible alone" as a centering and congealing force has been tried. In my opinion, it does not work. Protestantism offers a history of fractures and breakups. When there is a contentious and divisive issue, and some persons can interpret the Bible one way on the matter and others interpret it oppositely, there is nothing to fall back upon for adjudication other than "let's agree to disagree." But if the matter is really divisive, this tolerance principle will not work and only one solution is left: the group splits and the parties go their separate ways. To show how ill-equipped the Bible is for adjudicating contentious issues between well-meaning believers, consider this observation made long ago by John Henry Newman: If Unitarians sit down and read the Bible, they get up Unitarians. If Trinitarians sit down and read the Bible, they get up Trinitarians. Newman's advice is to take things as they are, then theorize about them.

What alone has worked in the history of Christianity to maintain the community in unity is an exercise of teaching authority that defines issues, either in an enduring claim on reflection (Mary as *theotokos* or Mother of God) or if only for a particular period (dating of Easter), that proposes limits, that ensures the voice of tradition is being heard on the matter, and that brings a conserving and slowing-down force to the fore as a counterbalance to a progressive and opening-up force (say, of theological work, or of new devotional practices taking off). Most importantly, style is at times as important as substance. You may have all the correct ingredients for exercising authority to the larger community, but if you can only compel allegiance by fiat and dicta and not win the hearts and affections of the community, you will win the battle but lose the war. Anyone vested top to bottom with God-given parental authority and who has parented successfully will attest to the truth of this observation.

6. The Catholic intellectual tradition is social/dialogical or, "From talking to listening, and from I count to we count."

So much has been written about the Second Vatican Council that I hesitate to assert what it represented. Generally speaking, it did represent a change in focus from prevailing Catholic viewpoints. It reclaimed the Catholic intellectual tradition which had slipped out of focus; a more social and communal way of thinking was retrieved.

Take this question: Is the individual or the community to be emphasized more? It is fair to respond that the biblical period, the early church period, and the medieval period of Catholicism emphasized community more than the individual. Social-centered thinking is quite rooted in the Old Testament. Israel is a community chosen and called together by Yahweh (the *qahal Yahweh*). The New Testament word for church, *ekklesia*, means literally "called together;" *convocation* would be a better English word for it. The patristic writings are about the Christian life of the baptized *people*. Further, it is a rare and refreshing experience for the imagination when medieval writings (or architecture) bring you face to face with individuals, as the letters exchanged between Heloise and Abelard do, since the individual medieval personality hides behind the social visage of the Christian enterprise. This all changes with the Renaissance when the focus on the individual bursts out. It is also fair to say that Roman Catholic life from the later medieval period until the present emphasized the individual in a manner hitherto unknown.

Let me illustrate the point with two rather high-profile Catholic practices: sacramental confession and Mass. Catholics lined up for individual private confessions to a priest in a confession box. The Catholic penitent was preoccupied with "my sins," with "my act of contrition," and with "my firm purpose of amendment." Truly pious penitents in a confessional line kept "custody of the eyes" and never made eye contact with fellow penitents. This experience of isolated individuality was replicated at Mass. One went to "Father Smith's Mass." Not that the expression meant he was simply the celebrant, but people thought of themselves as onlookers at "his Mass." Some did not even look on. Mrs. Jones read her prayer book and was lost in it, or immersed in her rosary, except when the Sanctus bells caused her to look up momentarily for the truly important portion of Mass, the words of consecration. When did Mrs. Jones consciously connect with her down-the-street neighbor, Mr. Brown, who was also at Mass? Not during Mass (because both were lost in private prayers) but outside on the church steps after Mass! And all during 7:30 Mass, what was happening on the St. Joseph side altar? The visiting priest, Fr. Ward, was saying his private Mass. (If you in the pew were really distracted, you might be wondering who will reach the consecration first, Fr. Smith or Fr. Ward.) No doubt subject matter for next Saturday's confession: "I let myself get distracted during Mass two times." I do not ridicule this piety—in fact I have warm nostalgia and deep respect for it. But these two sacraments were conducted—celebrated would not seem the right word—in such a privatized and individualized atmosphere.

This way of experiencing sacraments changed with Vatican II. Consider the sacrament of penance, now called the sacrament of reconciliation to underline that it is not simply "my penance" (contrition) but also my reconciliation to God, to the Church (and to this parish), and to myself. Except for those rare situations when church law justifies communal absolution, the actual confession of sins remains private as do the words of absolution, but everything else is meant to heighten the sense of community. Many Catholics now "go to confession" at an Advent or Lenten penance service. Hundreds of people convene, joined by a dozen or so priest-confessors. Congregational singing, Scripture readings, a sermon, and a public examination of conscience prepare for the actual confessing of sins. When it is time to line up to confess at fifteen or so "confession stations," one might see a priest confessing to another priest and everyone else assuming a posture of "seeking reconciliation." We, clergy and laity, are all sinners. An actual confessing and absolving of sins is expedited—this is not the occasion for the twenty-minute "confessional box" situations of years ago—and people returning from a confessional station may remain in the church for the last portion of the ceremony, a joyful hymn of having experienced God's forgiving love. A strong sense of community (communal Christianity) has been returned to the sacrament of penance.[29]

Mass after Vatican II is more obviously social and dialogical. The congregation prays with the priest, in its own mother tongue, engaged together in various ways (the hymn singing, the gifts carried forward, the sending forth of eucharistic ministers with Holy Communion for sick or immobilized parishioners). When priests are visiting the parish, they concelebrate at the same liturgy with the people. Rarely seen anymore are mass congregants immersed in their private prayer books, and more rarely seen are priests celebrating private Masses. In fact, the phrase *private Mass* is contradictory for eucharistic faith, which is the prayer of the whole Church, when you consider it in a strictly literal fashion; a more suitable phrase is needed.

If I would sum up the change in focus from "I count" to "we count," I would recall a prayer from today's Mass that captures for me, in most moving fashion, the communal dimension of eucharistic faith and the communal experience of sins being forgiven. As the congregation readies itself to go to communion, the priest prays aloud after the Our Father prayer but in the name of all gathered, ". . .[Lord], look not on our sins but on the faith of your church. . . ." Lord, look upon me as a member of this larger Church, and not just the Church of this calendar date but the Church from the beginning, the Church of all the martyrs and confessors and of all the holy men and women who ever lived or will live, all of them present to your eternal gaze. By their faithfulness and witness, judge me because my identity before you involves them and their faithfulness. An older privatized Catholic might fret: Is my act of contrition perfect or is it only imperfect? Have all my sins been forgiven? When you pray the above prayer and take the words to heart, you do not carry the burden that everything depends only upon you in your isolation, and you approach the reception of Communion not as if it is nourishment for the perfect and sinless but as heavenly manna for sinners and pilgrims in the desert. A sense of "we count" is truly a cause of inner peace and joy.

The Catholic intellectual tradition is not only social but dialogical. The former implies the latter and is its rationale. Like the social dimension of being Christian, the dialogical way of being a Catholic Christian was a focus of Vatican II, especially in its pivotal document, *Gaudium et Spes*[30] If personhood is a "being for" others and a "being from" others, and not just "my unique being," then to be social in this sense, is also to be dialogical and to be a partner in conversation. Communication is a weaker personal term than conversation. Teaching is a form of communication, and even one-way teaching (when someone is doing all the teaching and another is doing all the receiving) is a form of communication. But conversation is never as thin as one-way communication any more than radio listening is reckoned conversation. Not all communication is conversation, but all conversation is communication and customarily its most effective and persuasive form. Plato's Socratic dialogues are a classic illustration of persuasive teaching in the form of conversation.

Conversation entails listening. We listen to learn from one another. We listen to sense the other so that our response is apropos. And we listen to impress upon the other that he or she is worth being heard. In this sense, listening affirms. *Pastoral* is a religious term that implies all of the above, and more. Under a rallying cry to read the signs of the times from Pope John XXIII, who convened it, the Second Vatican Council intentionally chose to be pastoral in its teaching mission to its own Catholic faithful and to the rest of the world. It committed itself to listening as a consequence.

In the long period prior to Vatican II, the Catholic Church exercised a teaching ministry to its own members and to the world, but the style seemed one-way. Catholics and others were to be taught. Errors were to be exposed. Items were to be insisted upon. In and of itself, this is not a false style, as evidenced by the New Testament letters to Timothy that urge it on him as a presbyter-bishop. Situations dictate style, and certain situations call for this kind of teaching style. But the bishops of

Vatican II chose to be pastoral *vis-à-vis* Catholic laity and the wider human family. They wished to enter into conversation with the world.

They crafted the very first sentence of *Gaudium et Spes*, a document labeled a pastoral constitution of the Council, by defining the Church (and consequently themselves as teachers in the Church) as listeners, and this was a crucial choice. "The joys and the hopes, the griefs and the anxieties, of the men and women of this age, especially those who are poor or in any way afflicted, are the joys and hopes, the griefs and anxieties of Christ's followers." For what do you hope? What are your anxieties? Speak, we listen, for these become the goals we set before us, the matters we must ponder, before we speak to you or speak out about you on your behalf.

Again, risking oversimplification, let me identify three "listening" rooms: 1) The Church chose to listen to its own members. Laity and lower clergy (priests) began to be consulted. Parish councils and associations of priests were formed. 2) The Catholic Church chose to listen to non-Catholic Christians, to the members of other churches and ecclesial communities. At the Council itself, Orthodox and Protestant observers were invited to attend, and while they were not members of the working committees, they were asked their opinions of proposed texts. The choice to listen brought the Catholic Church more fully into the ecumenical movement, and discussions with other churches began. 3) The Council chose to listen to the non-Christian world, and conversations began between Catholics and Muslims, and between Catholics and Buddhists. All of this characterizes the period after the council, not before it, and it would not have begun unless there was a change of focus from "I teach" to "I listen."

Postscript on the Catholic Intellectual Tradition

The Catholic tradition does not own any one of these six defining adjectives as if any one of them was a unique bequest from above for Catholicism alone. For example, liberal Protestantism of the early part of the twentieth century was very much involved in a social and dialogical engagement with American industrial society. Again, the European Protestant intellectual tradition has been always self-critical, and yet loyalty to the fundamental principles of the Reformation did not seem at stake. In addition, as mentioned earlier, the Eastern Orthodox way of thinking is as much incarnational and epiphanic as Roman Catholicism is, if not more. It is the ensemble of these six characteristics that form a portrait or mosaic of the Catholic intellectual tradition.

Yet the portrait or mosaic simile also obscures the reality. A mosaic is static; each element retains its individual properties. A red tile square in a mosaic remains as red as when it stood alone. What is missing from the simile are the organic implications of the individual elements in an ensemble. It is not enough to say that the Catholic intellectual tradition is incarnational and it is developmental. Rather, it is developmental in an incarnational way. But it is also integrative in a self-critical and developmental way. The very presence of one of the six elements (characteristics) influences all the other elements of the Catholic intellectual tradition. Thus, the Catholic intellectual tradition is integrative in a developmental, incarnational, self-criticizing, authoritative, and social/dialogical way. It is authoritative in a social/dialogical, developmental, incarnational, integrative, and self-critical way. Admittedly, it is elusive to describe an ensemble composed of elements, but the ensemble is not like a tossed salad; rather, it is itself an organic reality: living, breathing, moving forward, sometimes one or two steps backward, momentarily slipping now and then and not having the best of days, but always strong and lively enough so as to engender confidence in itself. This is the Catholic intellectual tradition.

4

Student Affairs and the Catholic Moral Tradition

Robert M. Friday

The 1990 document *Ex Corde Ecclesiae* has generated significant controversy and often passionate on-line discussion in theological circles because of its requirement that Catholic theologians request a *mandatum*[1] from the local bishop in an effort, presumably, to ensure orthodoxy in the classroom and a more discernable Catholic identity for the college or university. In one of these on-line exchanges, a theologian observed that what goes on in the student life office is often far more telling about the institution's "Catholic identity" than what the theologian says in class. Those of us actively engaged in student affairs on Catholic campuses would heartily agree with this assessment.

The presence of crucifixes in the classroom, the prominence of a well-appointed chapel, and a visible campus ministry team are expected symbols on a Catholic campus, each contributing to its Catholic identity. But so, too, are the mission statements, policies, and "standards of student conduct" that reflect the values and teachings of the Roman Catholic Church. To be an effective contributor to the life of the learning community, student affairs professionals need to understand and be supportive of the doctrinal and value presuppositions imbedded in the mission of a religiously affiliated college or university, even when not personally espousing those beliefs and values. What follows will be an abbreviated exposition of Catholic moral theology to assist the student affairs professional in better understanding and appreciating the underpinnings of the policies and rules ordering life on campus, perhaps, especially in the residence halls. The purpose in doing this exercise is not to evangelize but to assist understanding.

The majority of student affairs professionals receive their training in degree programs at secular or state institutions. These programs, while providing excellent preparation for working with students in general, cannot be expected to prepare student affairs personnel for the potential challenges and the expectations of them to be encountered on a Catholic campus. For example, abortion counseling for an unplanned pregnancy or condom distribution to prevent pregnancy and sexually transmitted diseases will not be permitted on a Catholic campus, even though sexual activity may not be less common among college students on a Catholic campus than it is on a secular one.[2] Certain controversial speakers or programs may be rejected as unacceptable by the administration because of a presenter's identification with or advocacy for positions judged to be inimical to the mission and values of the institution.[3] It is imperative, therefore, that the student affairs professional working on a Catholic campus understand not just *what* the Catholic tradition teaches in these matters but, more importantly, *why*. This chapter will provide a framework for understanding Catholic moral teaching by addressing such fundamentals as the nature of Christian morality; the role and authority of the teaching Church; scriptural and rational sources for this moral teaching; some necessary distinctions between "evil" and "sin"; and the role of personal conscience.[4] Anyone working in student affairs knows that sexual issues are often some of the more troubling and time-consuming areas of concern when interacting with young persons. These concerns are compounded on a Catholic campus because of the Church's widely known conservative position on sexual ethics when measured against the more liberal attitudes encountered in a sexually open society such as ours. In what follows, issues from sexual ethics will be utilized to illustrate theological points with a special care to present the "why" behind the "what" of Catholic teaching. In most instances real-life examples from campus experience will be used to concretize the more theoretical theological methodology.[5]

The Nature of Christian Morality

It is not uncommon to hear a remark such as: "The measure of a 'good Christian' or of a 'faithful Catholic' is whether or not he/she obeys the commandments of God and the precepts of the Church." Implied in this statement is the centrality of "rule keeping" in an ethical system. In reality, contemporary Catholic moral theology is more person-centered than rule- or law-centered.

Theology is the study of God, literally, "the word about God" (Greek *theo* + *logy* (meaning "word"), similar to biology being the word about "bios," or life. In biology one learns about life by a hands-on empirical study of living things, or things that were once living. The difficulty in theology is that we cannot bring God into a laboratory for observation or dissection, as we can a frog or a leaf. Our knowledge about God must rely on a different set of sources, namely, what God has revealed about him/herself in the sacred writings we call the Bible and what we can discern about God through a rational study of all that God has created. In these resources we find that God has revealed not only something about God but also about humankind in relationship to God.[6] In Catholic theology the primary theological sciences are biblical study and systematic theology. The former seeks to discern and understand God and God's will for humankind in the sacred Scriptures. Systematic theology uses both Scriptures and the living tradition of a believing people to develop teachings about who is Jesus Christ, what is the Church, what are the sacraments of the Church, and so on. Moral theology is a "conclusionary science" that focuses on the kind of relationship existing between God and humankind, asking the question, What counts as an appropriate response in and to that relationship? Judaism and Christianity believe that the relationship found in Scriptures and the tradition of believing peoples is a love relationship, that is, a relationship in which God desires and seeks only what is good for the human creature and, in return, asks the human to love God, self, the neighbor, and the rest of creation. The task for the human is to determine what counts as love, or what does love look like? Moral teachings are an attempt to articulate what does and what does not look like or count as "love."

Rules, even the Ten Commandments, are human formulations of guidelines for loving response. For example, "thou shalt not kill" expresses the belief that killing the neighbor whom I am to love is an inappropriate way to say, "I love you." "Thou shalt not steal" recognizes the inappropriateness of taking the property of, or failing to compensate fairly, someone whom we are to love. A residence hall policy prohibiting smoking expresses the medically sound position that smoking is contrary to both self-love and neighbor-love. The rejection of premarital sex is rooted in the belief that the physical act of sexual intercourse, while legitimately pleasurable, is also a human act to be vested with symbolic interpersonal meaning, namely, it is to be a physical expression of a mutual commitment to a faithful, permanent, exclusive, creative, and possessive relationship with an openness to procreation. The casual sex on the tube and the silver screen seldom has such meaning. In the traditional Christian understanding of this act, only intercourse within a heterosexual marriage has the potential to meet all of these criteria. Therefore, premarital (and extramarital sex and even homosexual genital acts) are judged to be inappropriate, or unloving in that theological (not Hollywoodian) understanding of love.

To the question, What does love look like? the Christian has one answer. Love looks like Jesus Christ, because Christ is love. Jesus gave us one uncompromising commandment: "Love one another as I love you" (John 15:12). Christ gave neither a new set of rules nor a list of "do's" and "don'ts." Christ offered himself and his example of love for us as the measure and model for what love looks like. The Christian is called to imitate Christ's example of loving response in his or her relationships with God, self, neighbor, and creation. Therefore, the nature of Christian morality is not keeping the rules but responding appropriately in and to the love relationships we are called to have with God, self, neighbor, and the cosmos. Does this mean that we are each free to determine for ourselves what a loving response is in any situation or decision confronting us? Yes and no. Loving response is not arbitrary or relative in the sense that I might decide X and you decide Y and we are both ethically correct. The institutional Church, using its sources, attempts to provide guidance in making ethically and morally correct decisions.

The Role of the Teaching Church

In the minds of many, including many Roman Catholics, the official Church intends that its moral teachings be accepted as "infallible," incapable of being erroneous. In fact, the teaching Church, called the *magisterium*,[7] makes a careful distinction between what it calls "extraordinary magisterial teachings" and "ordinary magisterial teachings." The former are solemn pronouncements about articles of "faith or morals" that, the Church believes, are so fundamental to the gospel message of Christ that in presenting them the teacher (for example, the pope)—even though humanly capable of error as human—will be so protected by God in the exercise and expression of this authority that a specific teaching will be infallible. This very formal exercise of teaching authority has been used rarely, and never in regard to a moral teaching. Are moral teachings, then, simply "up for grabs" or a matter of personal choice? Certainly not. They are presented with varying degrees of authority and are to be taken seriously by Catholics as they form their consciences and make their decisions. But the Church recognizes that these teachings are still subject to ongoing study, research, greater nuance, clearer expression, and even possible change. What sources does the teaching Church use for the formulation of its teaching?

Sources for Moral Teachings

The Bible

Some Christian traditions use Scriptures in a literal manner: if you find it stated in the Bible, that's the law. Catholic theology and most mainline Protestant Christian churches today approach the interpretation of sacred Scripture from a more scientific, historical-critical perspective asking such questions as, Who wrote the passage? When was it written? Where was it written? What were the social, economic, and religious factors of that era that might have influenced the human author? Questions about language (usually, Hebrew, Greek, and Aramaic) and its meaning are also quite relevant. After sorting through the human components of a passage, the scriptural exegete then seeks to discern what God has revealed or said through the human author.

The Bible is a collection of writings by diverse human authors, mostly unknown, who tell the story of God's interaction with humankind over hundreds, even thousands, of years. One thing it is not: it is not an ethics book. Although there are many rules and commandments addressing human behavior scattered throughout the Bible, these need to be read within the context of culture and historical circumstance. The familiar commandment, "Thou shalt not kill," is translated from the Hebrew language where it most likely meant "Thou shalt not unjustly kill a fellow Israelite." Killing itself was not proscribed, as is clear from even a cursory reading of the Old Testament where there is much killing, some of it ordered by the Lord. Interestingly, demonstrators for an end to the Vietnam War often carried banners quoting Isaiah 2:4: "They shall beat their swords into ploughshares, and their spears into pruning hooks; nation shall not lift up sword against nation, neither shall they learn war any more." For those using this quote, the will of God, clearly, was that killing and war must cease. On the other hand, those supporting the war might have countered with their own banner with a citation from a later prophet, Joel, who lived in a different time when God's Chosen People were being sorely oppressed. Here Joel has the Lord say: "Proclaim this among the nations: Prepare war, stir up the warriors. . . . Beat your ploughshares into swords, and your pruning-hooks into spears; let the weakling say, 'I am a warrior'" (Joel 4: 9–10). The literalist looking for direction from the Lord about war would find very opposite messages in these two passages!

Think of the Bible as a drama unfolding on the human stage. There are two actors: God and humankind. In the Old Testament,[8] God (Yahweh) interacts with Israel; in the New Testament God in the person of Jesus Christ interacts with "the church," that is, with all those whom

God has called into relationship with him and with one another. The two characters are the lover and the beloved. The Christian ethicist, or moral theologian, studies the interaction between the divine lover and the beloved human searching for moral themes that exemplify "what love looks like." In both the Old Testament and the New Testament, God always seeks to liberate the beloved from what is oppressive or enslaving: for example, Yahweh freeing Israel from bondage in Egypt and, in his time, Christ freeing the people from the onus of the Law.[9] Someone who loves another will seek to free the other from what oppresses him or her, from what keeps him or her from developing and exercising his or her fullest human potential and giftedness. Contemporary examples include racism, sexism, poverty, ignorance, hunger, addiction, domestic violence, and so on. This liberation could be on a global scale, as the need to liberate peoples in African countries from the scourge of HIV/AIDS, or it can be far more personal and local, such as liberating an inner-city child from ignorance and illiteracy by giving an hour a week to tutor her in reading skills, or simply visiting an elderly neighbor who is imprisoned by loneliness. There is no biblical passage that commands us to liberate, although there are a plethora of examples of God liberating his beloved human creatures. "Liberation" is an expression of love; an example of what love looks like.

Other examples would be compassion, forgiveness, mercy, and justice. On campus, love might mean confronting a hall mate who triggers a fire alarm at 3:00 a.m., thoughtlessly endangering the lives of peers who must vacate the residence hall in the dead of night. If the culprit dismisses or makes light of this rebuke, love might demand turning him in to the resident assistant on duty. Love can be painfully countercultural!

The central, all-encompassing commandment of Jesus Christ, as noted above, is found in John 15:12: "This is my commandment, love one another *as* I have loved you." Note the emphasis (mine) on *as*. Jesus did not offer a new code of laws. He offered only one commandment—that we love one another—and he offered himself as the model for what love looks like. In the face of this new commandment, the Christian is called to study the Scriptures for examples of what love looks like in the interaction between the divine lover and the beloved. The role of the institutional Church is to bring Christ to the consciousness of the faithful, there to "unpack," insofar as possible, the meaning of Christ and his teachings. When faced with a decision, the question for the Catholic is not, What would the pope or the bishop or the priest or the sister do? but What would Jesus do?

A Biblical Sexual Ethics

How do we derive teachings about sexual behavior from the Bible if not from direct statements condemning specific sexual acts, for example, fornication and homogenital acts?[10] How is it that the Catholic Church rejects contraceptive acts that are not specifically addressed in the Bible? Catholic theology discovers an operating principle relative to sexual behavior in the Genesis creation story or, more correctly, stories, for there are two of them. The human author of the first creation story tells us "God created humankind in his image, in the image of God he created them; male and female he created them. God blessed them, and God said to them, 'Be fruitful and multiply, and fill the earth and subdue it" (Genesis 1:27–28). From this the Church has discerned that in the plan of God, revealed in the nature of the human, sexuality is for procreation.

But that is not the whole story. A second account of creation (Genesis 2:18) is a bit folksier. God formed the man out of the clay of the earth and set him to the Garden of Eden. Then God said: "It is not good that the man should be alone; I will make him a helper as his partner." God then proceeded to make the animals and birds—"but for the man there was not found a helper as his partner. So the LORD God caused a deep sleep to fall upon the man, and he slept; then he took one of his ribs and closed up its place with flesh. And the rib that the LORD God had taken from the man he made into a woman and brought her to the man. Then man said, 'This at last is bone of my bones and flesh of my flesh; this one shall be called Woman" (Genesis 2:20–23). God had a dual purpose in gendering the human creature: procreation and companionship (love and unity).

These two stories have given rise to an ethical operating principle that has been applied, even if not explicitly articulated, especially in the Catholic tradition, to all areas involving sexuality: *When sexuality is expressed in its fullest sense, including genital expression, the physical act must remain open to its love-giving and its life-giving potential.* For example, acts of masturbation are seen as self-centered genital acts that exclude the possibility of procreation. Premarital sex (fornication) generally intentionally excludes biological life-giving and, relative to "love-giving" as understood in this context, such acts of intercourse lack the communication of self-giving marked by permanency of commitment and a pledge of exclusive fidelity to this one person. Contraceptive acts intentionally seek to exclude the procreative potential of the act of intercourse. Homosexual genital acts by their very nature cannot be procreative and will, in this calculation, always be judged "objectively disordered."[11] Sexual intercourse only within a heterosexual marital relationship would be justifiable according to this principle derived from sacred Scripture.

Once adopted, this principle and its application in traditional, official Roman Catholic sexual ethics are very consistent. Catholic theology has found support for its sexual ethics and much of its other ethical teaching in the philosophical natural law tradition.

Natural Law

Catholic moral teaching has not depended totally on the Scriptures as a source for its moral guidance and rules. Human reason, more specifically, a philosophical natural law theory, has played a major role in the development of Catholic moral teachings, especially those having to do with sexual behavior. The roots of the natural law tradition go back to the ancient philosophical ethics of Aristotle and the Stoics. Formally put, "natural law is human nature under the aspect of its inherent obligations."[12] More simply stated, "natural law dictates that things should act or be used according to their nature, that is, according to what they are and, therefore, what God intended them to be when God gave them their specific nature."[13] Knowing what the nature is will be key in determining what is or is not "natural" or appropriate behavior. This said, it is also important to recognize, as will be discussed later, that there is not unanimity of opinion about human nature among Catholic moral theologians. Perhaps applying the theory of natural law to the question "How should we use our sexuality?" will help to exemplify both the theory and its traditional application in official Roman Catholic sexual ethics.

Although it may not have been immediately self-evident to early humans, they eventually began to understand, probably by observing other creatures with a shorter gestational period, that there is a causal relationship between biological heterosexual intercourse and, approximately nine months later, a baby. They concluded that, in God's plan, the nature of human genitalia included these objectives: the possibility of procreation, a deeply human way of expressing unity and love, and, of course, an avenue to sensual pleasure. From an ethical perspective, the use of human genitalia that excluded one of these objectives was considered to be "unnatural," or (once the philosophical natural law was "baptized" and incorporated into Christian theology) contrary to the will of God reflected in the creature's nature. Understandably this natural law perspective found masturbation, contraception, and homosexual acts unnatural or disordered. Premarital sex acts, while physically natural, were judged to be immoral because of the injustice done to a potential child conceived apart from a nurturing, father/mother relationship as well as the injustice foisted upon the mother who would shoulder the burden of single parenting, to the likely detriment of the child and her own personal development.

At a Catholic college or university, premarital and homosexual sex acts by students are considered to be immoral and unacceptable behaviors, contrary to the values espoused by the institution. Most students and their parents understand and are supportive of the position taken by the university in these matters, even when they do not fully understand (or even agree with) the theological or philosophical bases for the church teaching. One recognizes, however, that students are products not only of their parents and their parents' value systems but also of a societal culture that may oppose sexual practices among the unmarried, but for reasons related more to unwanted pregnancies and sexually transmitted diseases than to violations of tenants of sacred Scripture and natural law. In the face of the more pragmatic cultural concerns, condoms and their availability in residence halls, Greek houses, and campus convenience stores will take priority over considerations of a moral nature on the majority of state and secular campuses. The student affairs professional working on a Catholic campus should understand the basis for the teachings embedded in the codes for student conduct, and be prepared to be supportive of those rules, even when he or she does not agree with them personally.

A student affairs professional considering a position in residence life at the Catholic University of America would be expected to uphold the following policy found in the residence hall handbook:

Behavior

Students are expected to exhibit appropriate behavior within the community of the residence hall. Individuals who participate in or display inappropriate behavior while in a residence hall will be subject to disciplinary action. Inappropriate behavior is defined as an activity that disrupts, endangers, or interferes with the environment of the residence hall community. This includes any sexual expression inconsistent with the teachings and moral values of the Catholic Church: "human sexuality . . . is to be genitally expressed only in a monogamous heterosexual relationship of lasting fidelity in marriage." Violators may be suspended from the university, evicted from the residence halls, relocated to another residence hall, placed on probation, and/or receive additional educational sanctions.

Stating an actual policy relative to expected sexual behavior provides the area coordinator (AC), resident director (RD), and the resident assistants (RA) with something specific to support interventions in situations where a student invites a "significant other" to "sleep over." The policy also presents an opportunity for a knowledgeable administrator, faculty member, or campus minister to address at a student residence hall program or at AC, RD, and RA orientation the Church's teachings about sexual morality and the expectations of the Catholic institution in this regard. It might also serve as a caution to prospective job applicants should they be unwilling to enforce this policy.

It was alluded to above that there is less than unanimity of thought within the Roman Catholic theological community in regard to the application of natural law to ethics, especially in areas concerned with sexual morality. Two schools of thought emerge, one identified with the traditional, official Church natural law position, sometimes referred to as a "classical worldview of man," and the other a more contemporary, even personalist perspective characterized as a "historically conscious worldview of man."[14]

The classical position maintains that what it means to be human is known principally through the physical/biological nature of the creature as, for example, determining that human genitalia are oriented toward procreation. Once the nature of the organs is known, the resulting conceptualization is static and unchanging, and serves as a normative model or standard against which sexual actions in any age or culture may be judged. This view, with its absolutist concept of the nature of human sexuality rooted in the physical, biological orientation of the organs then provides a base for articulating moral absolutes of a very specific nature. In the male, for instance, masturbation, understood as the manipulation of the generative organ, the penis, to ejaculation of semen, will always be "unnatural" and objectively immoral, that is, never to be permitted. No distinction is made between an act done for self-gratification and the same physical act done to procure semen for fertility testing in an effort to possibly affect a pregnancy. The physical make-up of the act determines its intrinsic morality. Personal intentionality is given no determinative moral significance.

The "historically conscious" natural law moral theologians, on the other hand, give greater weight to the nonbiological, more distinctive attributes of human nature, namely rationality and free will, which prompt human creatures to use their intellect and freedom in the pursuit of becoming fully, truly human. Biology, while not unimportant, is not determinative. Utilizing the example above, the historically conscious natural law moralist may consider the physical act of masturbation to possibly enhance chances to procreate as unnatural, even objectively evil, but justifiable and not immoral. The historically conscious natural law proponent will maintain that no judgment about the morality of an act can be made apart from the circumstances and human intentionality surrounding the act. If the objective good is greater than the objective evil, the act may be justified even though regrettable, as in killing in self-defense and procuring semen through masturbation for fertility testing.

The issue of the morality of homosexual acts further exemplifies the differences between the classical and historical approaches. Official Catholic teaching (classical) rejects every homosexual genital act as intrinsically disordered (unnatural) and objectively immoral.[15] Such acts will always lack procreative potential, thereby falling short of what natural law, biologically considered, requires, as well as failing the scriptural requirement of openness to procreation. Homosexual orientation is generally recognized in official church documents as a state not chosen by the person and, therefore, not culpable in itself.[16] The expression of this orientation in a genital act, however, is considered to be objectively immoral. Theologians and pastors following the historically conscious position may be more inclined to accept the fact that persons who are lesbian or gay need to develop close interpersonal relationships and that sexual acts that might occur within this context, while outside the natural orientation of human sexuality toward procreation, may be justified if they are genuine expressions of unity and love within a permanent, faithful, and exclusive relationship (similar to, but not synonymous with, marriage). Advocates for this position see sexuality as a means to the attainment of higher human ends, and not as an end in itself or one that should unduly occupy the psychic and spiritual energies of the person.[17] Obviously, Catholic moral theologians employing this historically conscious natural law system in moral analysis find themselves in conflict with the Church and its official teachings, especially in matters dealing with human sexuality.

How does all of this affect life and rules on a Catholic campus? The policies and rules on a Catholic campus must correspond to the official teachings of the Church and, therefore, they will reflect primarily the classical natural law perspective. Neither premarital nor homosexual acts will be acceptable behaviors. Condoms will not be distributed or sold through the institution. This does not mean that presentations and discussions of sexuality, as in residence hall programming or in the classroom, may not address methods encountered in our society for preventing pregnancy and sexually transmitted diseases from abstinence to contraception. In these presentations and discussions, the Church's position must be clearly and accurately presented and explained. That there are students on Catholic campuses who are gay, lesbian, bisexual, or transsexual will be recognized as a matter of fact and, on some Catholic campuses, these students will be allowed to organize for educational but not recreational or social purposes.[18] Residence hall programs might feature gay speakers to address the issue of being gay on a college campus, or simply presentations to help the "straight" better appreciate, so as to repudiate and oppose, the kinds of discrimination and harassment persons who are homosexual (or simply "different") face in our society.

A university is a place where ideas can and should be presented and debated, even when some ideas may run counter to the mission and values of the university. This can be an unsettling proposition for some students, parents, and church leaders. However, it is at a university that students have the opportunity to test and have tested their own value systems before being exposed to diverse currents in society where, perhaps, there are few or no safeguards or opportunities for rational discussion and argumentation.

Sin and Objective Evil: Necessary Distinctions

Mention was made above about the importance of distinguishing between calling something "objectively evil" and calling it "sin" (subjectively evil). In Catholic theology care is *generally* taken not to label actions themselves to be "sins" because sin includes a judgment that the "sinner" has separated himself or herself from God and the faith community—and that simply cannot be judged from knowing the action alone. The importance of this distinction is significant and eminently pastoral. There is no quicker way to end a reasonable discussion about the rightness or wrongness of an action than to call the action "a sin" with the presumption that the one contemplating or doing the action is rejecting God, or worse, has been rejected by God (which is never the case). To tell a female student, for example, that she sinned in having an abortion is both judgmental and potentially inaccurate. It is also contrary to Catholic theological teaching. In traditional Catholic theology an action such as a directly procured abortion is judged to be "objectively evil," but the determination as to whether or not the doer of the action has sinned will hinge on subjective elements of the decision, namely, what she knows *and believes* about abortion and why it is considered (at least by the Catholic Church) to be objectively evil, and how free and voluntary is her decision to abort.[19] Relative to other actions, the *Catechism of the Catholic Church*, stating the long-standing church tradition, designates masturbation "an intrinsically and gravely disordered action" (#2352); fornication (premarital sex) is judged "gravely contrary to the dignity of persons and of human sexuality which is naturally ordered to the good of spouses and the generation and education of children" (#2353); and, as noted above, homosexual acts are consistently labeled "intrinsically disordered" (#2358). "Sin language," with its judgmental overtones, is carefully avoided in official church documents but not infrequently it is encountered in homilies, media reports, and conversations among Catholics. "Sin" is a bigger stick than "it's wrong."

When an action is designated "objectively evil" or "intrinsically and gravely disordered" the sense of this is that, in the judgment of the Church, such actions go contrary to the good of persons and hinder the doer of the act in his or her pursuit of being fully and truly human. The actor may not immediately perceive this, especially when the act is pleasurable or results in a desired good end, for example, a student "liberates" (read: "steals") a comfortable chair from the residence hall lounge for his own personal use in his room. The "meaning" of the act of liberating the chair is not insignificant in terms of what it communicates about the student's personal value system, his self-centeredness, his lack of concern for the rest of the residence hall community, his disregard for property rights, and so on. The act of taking the chair is wrong (objectively evil). Depending on what he understands, taking the chair of his own free will affects the issue of "sin" (subjectively evil). When confronting him with the issue of his stealing the chair, one has a "teaching moment" opportunity to explain the distinctions made above. A similar "teaching moment" is occasioned when a student elicits approving laughter from his peers when he calls another student a "fag." The judgmental, hurtful comment may be an expression of a more deep-seated prejudice, which violates both justice and charity, providing an opportunity to talk about the meaning of this action and what it says about him, the kind of person he is and is becoming. Jumping in with "it's a sin" will kill the "teaching moment." Incidents such as "acquaintance rape," harassment of gay and minority students, "sleeping around," drugs, and the ever-present abuse of alcohol are all situations where objective evil needs to be addressed, even if formal sin is not present.

If the essence of "sin" is not law or commandment breaking, or even bad actions considered in themselves, what is it? Consistent with the description offered for the nature of Christian morality,[20] sin is a broken relationship—alienation from God, self, neighbor, and the cosmos. The *Catechism of the Catholic Church* (#1849) describes sin as a "failure in genuine love for God and neighbor caused by a perverse attachment to certain goods." In light of this understanding, it is not surprising that the Catholic tradition speaks of the "communal dimension" of sin, meaning that our personal sin, because it is self-centered and self-seeking, always affects the community by denying to it the best possible person we committed ourselves to be in our baptism. The sacramental ritual of baptism initiates us into a new and special relationship with God and the faith community that includes a commitment on our part to use our unique giftedness in the communal project of "kingdom building," that is, establishing a society characterized by love, justice, and, ultimately, peace. Sin is a rejection of this communal relationship in favor of self-interest. This estrangement is then concretely symbolized in actions that are signs of sin, not sins in themselves. Our actions, the "thoughts, desires, words, deeds, and omissions" of the old Baltimore Catechism must be unpacked to see what they mean about us as persons. However, regardless of whether the brokenness and alienation of sin is truly present, inappropriate and "bad" actions detract from both personal and communal well-being.

Conscience

In Catholic theology "conscience is the most secret core and sanctuary of the human person. There he is alone with God, whose voice echoes in his depths."[21] At that deep level of the person, which is not an organ of the body but a function of the intellect and the will, values are learned and stored, and decisions are made that concretely reflect our values and help to define our moral character. The development of our conscience is an ongoing process from the moment of birth (at least) to our last dying breath, as values are learned, prioritized, challenged, confirmed, changed, and activated in the choices we make. Parents and family get first crack at us as value communicators, either by specific directions ("Smoking is harmful") or more subtly by their own actions and choices (Dad smoking a pack a day!). There is a host of other value communicators in society that impact our conscience formation: the entertainment media, in all its forms; civil laws that, on the one hand, value and protect life through traffic regulations while cheapening life, on the other hand, by choosing "reproductive rights" over the lives of the unborn; and religious institutions that teach the Ten Commandments and virtues to their faithful.

The young persons encountered on our campuses possess consciences with already well-formed value data banks that are the products of their unique life experiences. Student life professionals, especially those working in the close, interactive confines of a residence hall, will soon begin to discern the values that fund the decisions of individual students in their charge. As they surface, positive values should be reinforced, negative disvalues should be challenged by offering counter values and other correctives. Religiously affiliated institutions, unlike more secular schools, are not neutral on values. Specific expectations relative to values are included in the mission statement and policies of Catholic colleges. While a Catholic institution will recognize and respect the right of every individual to follow his or her own rightly formed conscience,[22] the institution will require adherence to and support for the mission and values of that institution. An unmarried student, for example, who honestly believes in her or his conscience that sexual intercourse with a significant other is moral and right, is physically free to exercise that option—but not in the residence hall of the Catholic school. A group of students on a Catholic campus who are committed to a pro-choice agenda will be denied formal recognition and funding under the logo and banner of a Catholic school.

Conclusion

Few if any Catholic colleges or universities require that student life professionals be practicing Roman Catholics as a condition for hiring. All institutions of higher education, however, expect those serving the students and the university community to be knowledgeable about and supportive of the mission and values of the institution. It is difficult to imagine that a staff member would be comfortable or effective doing otherwise. The abbreviated summary of fundamental Catholic moral theology in this chapter is intended to assist the student life professional toward a better integration into the culture of a Catholic institution, recognizing that the 200+ plus Catholic schools in this country will each have its own distinctive identity along with the common base outlined above.

For wider and more in-depth reading, I suggest the following selected bibliography of contemporary writings on Catholic moral theology and moral issues.

Always Our Children: A Pastoral Message to Parents of Homosexual Children. Committee on Marriage and Family, NCCB, 1997.

Collins, Raymond F. *Sexual Ethics and the New Testament: Behavior and Belief.* New York: The Crossroad Publishing Co., 2000.

Curran, Charles E. *The Catholic Moral Tradition Today: A Synthesis*. Washington, D.C.: Georgetown University Press, 1999.

Fagen, Sean, S.M. *Does Morality Change?* Collegeville, MN: Liturgical Press, 1997.

Friday, Robert M. *Adults Making Responsible Moral Decisions*. Washington, D.C.: NCCD, 1992.

Gula, Richard M, S.S. *Reason Informed by Faith*. New York/Mahwah, NJ: Paulist Press, 1989.

_____. *Moral Discernment*. New York/Mahwah, NJ: Paulist Press, 1997.

_____. *The Good Life: Where Morality and Spirituality Converge*. New York/Mahwah, NJ: Paulist Press, 1999.

Keating, James, ed. *Spirituality and Moral Theology: Essays from a Pastoral Perspective*. New York/Mahwah, NJ: Paulist Press, 2000.

Keenan, James F., S.J. *Commandments of Compassion*. Franklin, WI: Sheed & Ward, 1999.

Liuzzi, Peter J., O.Carm. *With Listening Hearts: Understanding the Voices of Lesbian and Gay Catholics*. New York/Mahwah, NJ: Paulist Press, 2001.

McCormick, Richard A., S.J. *Corrective Vision: Explorations in Moral Theology*. Kansas City: MO: Sheed & Ward, 1994.

O'Connell, Timothy E. *Making Disciples: A Handbook of Christian Moral Formation*. New York: The Crossroad Publishing Company, 1998.

Sloyan, Gerard S. *Catholic Morality Revisited: Origins and Contemporary Challenges*. Mystic, CT: Twenty-Third Publications, 1990.

Williams, Elizabeth. *Understanding Catholic Morality*. New York: The Crossroad Publishing Company, 1997.

5

Student Affairs and Conscience Formation

Dolores L. Christie

Since colleges designated "Catholic" often market themselves as different or even unique in light of the faith tradition they espouse, those who work in them are perceived to have a different task from those who work at other kinds of institutions. Catholic colleges are viewed as offering a "value added," that is, the opportunity for students to learn about and practice the faith of their fathers and mothers. Those who do not profess Catholic belief may find in Catholic colleges an atmosphere of morality and order, a system of values that they want their children to have. Student affairs professionals at Catholic colleges are a part of this promise and the process needed to achieve it. Although it is certainly not their role, such personnel may be seen as the authority and court of judgment for "Catholic" issues. I suggest there are two functions that relate to conscience that fall under the domain of student affairs. First, flowing from their professional training, student affairs professionals must encourage the unique process of development into adulthood of each student. Generally this means holding a high degree of toleration for various value systems. Most people who work in these fields have both the training and the inclination to do just that. But there is a second task. Flowing from the articulated mission and identity of the institution for which they work, they may be expected to bear some responsibility to represent the tradition of the Church and to encourage the development of other human-worthy values it espouses. Whether those employed at Catholic institutions like it or not, students do not view them to be value-free, nor should they be. They will be seen, in some sense at least, to represent the identity and mission of the school.

If that representation is overly emphasized, students may rail against it; if it is underplayed by saying nothing in the attempt to be "inclusive," students may perceive it as agreement with a point of view different from what the institution holds.

Complicating the second task of representing the identity of the institution is the fact that in today's college world many who function in student affairs may have little or no background in the Catholic tradition, whether or not they themselves are Catholic—and many are not. Like the students with whom they work, many receive their Catholic theological training from sound bites on the evening news, whether covering the visit of the pope to America or condensing into a few sentences some titillating Catholic issue. With the difference in perspective and background of the various players and the perception of what "Catholic" teaching means, it is easy to see that there is a kind of functional oxymoron going on in the work of student affairs. On the one hand, how does one remain faithful to the professional task of acceptance and nurture? On the other hand, how can one represent a tradition about which one knows very little? Both these tasks must be held together in a single job. How to do that is the critical question.

This chapter addresses some aspects of these issues by considering the role of student affairs in the formation of conscience in college students as part of their total education—a complete "leading out," as the word implies. It also gives an overview of conscience, how it functions, what place it holds within a contemporary view of the Catholic moral tradition, and what laws and values define it. Finally, this chapter will offer some suggestions for the connection of the two.

What Is Conscience?

The meaning and function of conscience is one of the most enduring and ubiquitous topics in the Catholic moral tradition. Agreement about what conscience is and how it should function is less universal. Often the different aspects of conscience are isolated and presented in such a way as if to suggest they each tell the whole story. This is an incomplete approach to the topic and, ultimately, it is not helpful in the task of nourishing the growth of a healthy mature conscience.

In a first definition, *conscience* is taken to mean the knowledge of right and wrong inherent in the human person. This knowledge asserts that either human persons have by nature the capacity to discern right and wrong and to do the good[1] (basic Catholic anthropology) or that there is a specific content to the good. If the latter interpretation is emphasized, it is often assumed the breadth of that content is defined, guarded, and enforced by the teaching authority of the Church.

A second approach is found in the thinking of the first century, at the birth of Christianity. The early church thought less philosophically and more holistically about conscience. Conscience was more than a human power used to deal with moral questions. Paul, writing in the first century of Christianity's existence, draws from his own historical context to speak of the "heart" or "wisdom" of human beings. Conscience is perceived as an integral aspect of the self, not merely a tool of judgment.[2] It is the core of humanness rather than a body of content or tool of the human person. This insight may be an important one to recall in thinking about the place of conscience in the lives of college students.

A third approach views conscience as the concrete application of the person's knowledge of right and wrong to individual choices. In this view, the primary emphasis is not on the total quality of the person but on the evaluative function of conscience. It is "me coming to a decision" or "the specific judgment of the good"[3] that should be done here and now. This notion can be found in many twentieth-century texts on the subject.

For those whose theology finds its source in a world of Walt Disney, conscience is an external reminder of the good to be done, one's own personal Jiminy Cricket who appears just in time to avert bad moral choices by a foggy-brained Pinocchio. Modern psychology uses the term *superego* to speak of sanction from outside the person, finding the root of moral constraints in a kind of knee-jerk reaction set in one's formative past. Superego is not owned morality, that is to say, a moral perspective based on values freely and consciously chosen by the person. Rather, it is learned or inherited from authority figures from childhood. As such, it is open to the sometimes flawed judgment of others' conclusions or constructs. As Richard M. Gula notes, it is a *submission* of rather than a *commitment* of one's freedom.[4] The novel *Lord of the Flies* portrays a community of young men who have lost the external safety lock on their behavior. The consequence, as William Golding sees it, is a community that descends to an almost bestial state of existence. While the scenes from the Golding novel are not quite those on college campuses, and the subjects are somewhat older than the characters in the book, many who enter college can be located developmentally at the stage of moral development where the governor of rightness or wrongness comes largely from an external source. They often have not yet gained a maturity to own values as mature adults. Hopefully college is a time when moral maturation may occur.

A fourth definition, perhaps a variation on the above theme, sees conscience as primarily a conformity to the law.[5] In what might be considered a contemporary Catholic caricature, Catholic moral teaching is all about rules. This approach reduces the exercise of conscience to nothing more than following the rules, in particular, rules about sexual morality. An informal poll of what makes a Catholic "Catholic" may yield no comments about the importance of social justice or a centrality of a community of believers together in the Eucharistic celebration. Even sitcom television may portray those identified as Catholic as somewhat sweet but simple people who do not think for themselves but who are expected to conform their actions to church tenets. It is the rare show that considers serious struggles of conscience in the manner of, say, a Graham Greene, the twentieth-century Catholic novelist.

This phenomenon is likely explained by the fact that many Catholics were trained in the faith at a time when their place in the continuum of moral growth was at Lawrence Kohlberg's conventional stage. Kohlberg's research on moral reasoning postulated a cognitive-developmental role, which demonstrated that a significant number of adults make moral decisions based on living up to roles and rules and what is expected by others, particularly those close to them. While growth continues to occur in other facets of Catholic lives—Catholic physicians grow in their sophistication about medicine, believing accountants keep up on new tax laws, and so on—many adult persons of faith remain fixed morally at the stage of development where obeying the rules is what morality means. Often the Sunday liturgy and homily are all that nourish growth; and these can be, as one wag put it, a caffeine-free instruction, guaranteed not to keep one up at night.

From this last definition it is not difficult to see that freedom of conscience or personal discernment in moral matters is often thought to be located outside the Catholic sphere, the purview perhaps of Protestants and others who do not have the clear guidelines of the *magisterium*. No one who professes to be a Catholic need take moral freedom too seriously. While this is not the conclusion this chapter will draw, it is the tacit position of many.

Who Are the Players?

There are several groups of people who have a stake in the question of conscience and conscience formation. Often the parents of today's Catholic college students are a product of the thinking mentioned above: morality as it connects to the Church means conformity to rules. Parents who come from this model may send their children to a Catholic college with the idea that this is a "safe haven," a place that will teach and enforce the moral rules that they perceive as the bedrock of Catholic thought. Most parents hope that children will reach adulthood with the values that they themselves hold. Such a pattern affirms the rightness of such values and assures a connection across the generations.

Catholic colleges are expected to have clear prescriptions for behavior and values, as well as an environment that teaches and enforces them. This scenario most certainly defined the Catholic college of parental experience, and these middle-aged Catholics have little data to expect anything different for the next generation. Most have been much too busy to have kept up with any changes in the methodology of education since they attended college. The naiveté about the real aspects of college life that characterizes many parents' perceptions is bolstered by the fear that a different setting will challenge what the children have been taught. Parents may forget how they were at that age.

College students, in contrast to their parents' expectations, are at the stage of moral development where they are testing rules, trying to discover for themselves who they are, what values they will hold as adults, and what rules they will honor or which they will jettison as they grow out of childhood. Packed tightly in the expansive family vehicle among the computers, compact disks, and comfortable jeans are an assortment of values and beliefs. Only time will confirm which of these will be unpacked and used and which will remain neglected, kicked into the back of the residence hall closet, and ultimately left for the cleaning service to throw out after graduation. Some of the values students bring with them to college come from the family or the Church, but many are absorbed from the culture without much thought—much like the unseen particles that come into one's body with each breath of air. The influences of the culture, often seen to emphasize nonjudgmental pluralism and perhaps even a relativism,[6] are strong ones. As a professor teaching a class of predominantly Catholic students, it is clear to me that cultural values trump what could be called traditional Catholic values every time. Eighteen-year-olds do not yet discern distinctions among such things but take in elements of the culture without much critique. Consider how they eat, consuming with equal vigor bad pizza or Mom's pot roast (if any moms still make pot roast!). That is not to say that the culture does not contain both the human-enriching and the human-destroying, but little is offered to distinguish the two. Particularly in sexual behavior, students accept unnuanced and uncritiqued the message of the desirability of multiple partners, little commitment, and sex as a casual accompaniment to a good evening with beer—a message not likely to come from home or church community but quite clearly presented in prime time television and other media.

Students look forward to college as the occasion to explore new values and ideas without the watchful and dictating eye of parents. This expectation on the part of students is appropriate and necessary for growth. College is the normal time and place for young adults to consider using a metaphoric scissors to sever the ties with their inherited past and to embrace with confidence their own unique future. Perhaps they will eventually use the "apron" of their parents, but this time it will be worn by their choice. Without the tools and practice to sort what they inherit, however, the students are ill-equipped to perform the task.

Enter those who work at the colleges these students attend, Catholic colleges and universities, in specific student-centered jobs. In contrast to the expectation and experience of many parents, student affairs professionals have been trained to address students at the stage of growth and development described above. As partners in the educative process, these professionals provide opportunities for experiences that will allow students to make good choices. The professional mandate of student affairs is not one of judgment or sanction so much as it is one of acceptance and encouragement in a somewhat controlled environment. Although *in loco parentis* was the situation of those who worked with students a generation ago, those who interact with the college student today do not perceive themselves as surrogates for enforcement of parental beliefs. One psychologist at a small Catholic college, herself a Catholic, affirmed that it was not her job to articulate whether the abortion contemplated by one of the students who sought her help was right or wrong. Her job was to listen and not to judge. It is this kind of situation that gives rise to the difficult conundrum that faces many student professionals at Catholic institutions.

Vatican II: A Perspective on Conscience

It is important to consider the perception versus the reality of what the Church teaches, particularly about the human person, sexuality, and conscience. For the person who is working at a Catholic college or university, an understanding of the Catholic perspective on conscience is essential. The meaning and function of conscience as treated in Catholic tradition must be understood. Since the anthropological perspective is the foundation for an understanding of how conscience functions, we will look at the human person through the filter of *Gaudium et Spes* (*Pastoral Constitution on the Church in the Modern World*), the groundbreaking document of the Second Vatican Council, which convened in Rome from 1962 to 1965.

The council drew from the early church in its portrayal of conscience as a most fundamental aspect of a human being. Conscience is the heart or center of the person, that which defines him or her morally and existentially, and what ultimately determines meaning for the person. It is developmental and incarnational, informed by the experience and integration of value. Ongoing dialogue with community and with one's own set of values is essential to its robust function. It has content: the individual meaning system and values that each person holds. It moves the person toward action—the moral choices that support or deny the content. In a contemporary context, which sees knowledge as constructed rather than given, it may seem difficult to integrate the values and norms that the Church proposes—in some cases as absolute—and the development of a free and knowing human person.

Let us consider conscience from a personalist perspective.[7] *Gaudium et Spes* characterizes conscience as "the most secret core and sanctuary" of the human being, where God's voice "echoes in . . . the depths" of the person.[8] To enter into the core of the individual person is to stand with awe at the uniqueness and individuality of each one. It is the conscience, with its personal set of values and its movement toward concrete choices, that defines and shapes the individual as unique. Characterizing conscience in this way, Vatican II embraces a more biblical and expansive definition than any one of those considered above. The council also moves the understanding of conscience's function from a more rule-centered or legalistic approach to a person-centered holistic approach. This shift locates the mature conscience in the later stages of moral and personal development outlined by Erik Erickson and Lawrence Kohlberg.[9] It is in this developmental mode that student affairs will find its niche.

Vatican II emphasizes other characteristics of the human person that have bearing on the development of a mature and healthy conscience.[10] In this modern take on a Catholic perspective, human beings are seen to be the *imago dei*, the image of God. Such a designation attributes to humanity an intrinsic dignity and equality. "I am somebody" is not a phrase unique to black pride; it is foundational to Catholic thinking about all humanity. Human beings possess an inviolable freedom, which others are called to respect. While Martin Luther may be the one who popularized freedom of conscience, the idea can be found in pre-Reformation Christianity. A contemporary Catholic anthropology retrieves the idea and affirms that persons are naturally able to identify and do the good, because they are themselves good and have an affinity by nature toward what is like them. This viewpoint grounds a confidence that to allow freedom is not risky and frivolous but rather acutely foundational to how persons should be treated as they create themselves in the conduct of their lives. This attitude is not reserved merely for emancipated adults, but must be part of how one looks at the on-the-way adult who attends college. There is not some magic moment in which a child suddenly becomes a free and functioning adult. While at first this may be a frightening thought, it is part of the Catholic tradition. Confidence in a basic and value-oriented freedom is the seminal anthropology from which approach to conscience and conscience formation must spring.

In contrast to a previous perspective in Catholic moral theology, which placed significant emphasis on *what* a person did—the action itself and its moral character—Vatican II details the uniqueness of the person, seeing each as a developing individual. Many have seen the poster: "God isn't finished with me yet," which demonstrates this belief. This notion is most compatible with the job descriptions of student affairs professionals, who deal with students as not completely formed; but it is not the whole picture. The emphasis in Catholic thinking has turned from *WHAT is done* to the character of *WHO is doing the action*. Therefore, the contemporary concern must be with the formation of the whole person, rather than a tally of specific good or bad actions. What I do contributes to who I am, but it is not the complete story. Forming conscience is about growing mature and integrated people, who draw from an appreciation in the concrete of what is good and act upon that appreciation.

To emphasize persons rather than actions is not to jettison a belief in an objective moral order, however. Catholicism has generally and consistently taught that there are certain things that are of value to human beings and certain things that, in themselves, are not. It is objectively good, whether a person is Catholic or not, to have concern about the well-being of the neighbor. If the campus ministry department is collecting money and food for the poor in the inner city, it may be good for a student to participate in that activity. It will achieve a goal that is helpful for the poor as well as build generosity and concern in the character of the student who participates. If a classmate is drunk, it is not good for his roommate to help him find his keys so that he might drive home. Whatever the reason the roommate would do such a thing—he was asked, friendship, and so on—the real harm present in allowing a drunk person to drive outweighs any motivation to comply with the request. The former example shows something that is good for persons, not exclusively from a religious perspective; the latter demonstrates the process of weighing the good and bad in a possible action. Both examples embody an objective calculation of a potential choice for the good. Neither example embodies specifically "Catholic" values.

Vatican II laid the groundwork for a different way of thinking about objective good when it put the "human person and his [or her] actions" at the center of the moral project as the standard of what constitutes the good. Since the human person is no longer viewed as a static entity but as an evolving one, certain conclusions follow. If persons change, so do communities. As communities evolve, a new understanding of values—what is good for human persons—will be developed. It follows, then, that there must be a corresponding shift in thinking from a definitive and for-always understanding of right and wrong to an existential or historically conscious approach.[11]

Since persons exist in an imperfect and incomplete world of experiences, one could also say a personal world of incomplete experiences, two things follow. On the one hand, a person or a community can be held morally responsible only for what he or she knows: at two years of age a baby cannot be expected to discuss the intricacies of calculus or to consider giving a portion of her wealth to the poor, much less refrain from wandering into a street in front of a car. Adults, however, would be accountable for the moral implications of such actions. On the other hand, the current community in the form of parents, teachers, even student affairs professionals, bears at least some responsibility for passing on the wisdom of the total human experience to younger persons. It is the community that holds the discovered and embraced values of the past in trust for the future. The individual should not have to experience personally the consequences of every wrong action to see it as such, but should be able to draw upon the experience and wisdom of those who have gone before.[12] To some degree, those who are the "elders" in the college community are the caretakers and dispensers of the human tradition. For those in Catholic institutions, the tradition, which holds a place of primacy in that passing on, is the wisdom of the intellectual and moral tradition of the Church. For Catholic tradition, there is indeed an objective moral order that defines the good, even if this good is seen incompletely because we have not discovered it all yet. Not all values are appropriate for human beings to have—not all are fulfilling and advancing of persons.

Another point must be made regarding the meaning and place of freedom, an essential component of moral action. As focus shifts to the good of persons, it is easy to place human freedom as the dominant element in the moral calculus. Not every act is moral simply because it is a free act of a human being, however. Lizzie Borden was, in a sense, free to bludgeon her parents. She had the opportunity, the ax, and a strong pair of arms. That freedom did not make what she did morally right, however. Very few people would endorse the grizzly murder on the basis that it was done freely. Another example might be helpful. In the abortion debate, the woman's right to choose is often given as a justification for procuring a termination to a pregnancy: "It's her choice" is used as the trump for any other moral consideration. The Church teaches that freedom of choice is only one element of the moral equation. To fully assess morality, one must look also at the content of the action—what is done. Does the action embody something of value, something that is worthy and enhancing of persons? As Lizzie wields her ax, she must consider what she does and not base moral assessment solely on the freedom with which she does it—likewise for the woman contemplating an abortion. Although freedom is a prerequisite for any moral activity, what is done—in this case the removal of natal human life from the woman's body—must also be considered. Since life is a value, terminating any life, most especially human life, is not to be taken lightly. It is always a tragedy, no matter what the circumstances.

To summarize: the traditional calculation of moral rightness and wrongness that Catholic moral theology has embraced is that there are three elements that enter in: the act itself, what is done; the motivation or intention, or why the act is done; and the circumstances, or the how. The final element is crucial, in that it helps determine if the action is done with complete freedom and knowledge. How many Lizzie Bordens fear for their lives with abusive parents? How many women who seek abortions do so under extreme pressure from family, a sense of desperation, and often a lack of knowledge of what the alternatives might be? Such elements act to diminish freedom in moral action and therefore may diminish moral responsibility. All three elements must be considered to judge the moral reality of an action and ultimately in judging the moral reality embodied in a person.

The personalism that flows from Vatican II affirms that there is a clear objective standard for the "what" or content of moral decision-making, which means the person and what is good for the person. That standard includes moral values—those which tell us the character of someone, such as courage, honesty, truthfulness—but also material values, which itemize those things that are limited but good when chosen rightly (life, money, food). One could see persons who work with college students being interested in encouraging the planting of moral values to build good persons. Learning to care about others, to be honest, to have courage—all these are possible and desirable traits in mature adults. Opportunities to nourish them in college students should be a conscious consideration for student affairs. I suggest that the Catholic college or university should reflect consciously and purposely on how to help students learn to prioritize their choices with regard to material values as well. A college with a Catholic identity will teach its students to use the good things of the world in ways that reflect a personalist standard.

Such a standard does not refer simply to what is good for one particular person, but must be expanded to consider the good for all persons. Such a thought process enlarges the discussion to ask questions that get at that idea. With regard to the abortion example above, the woman should be helped to ask such things as What is good for the child to be, for the father, for the family, for the rest of humankind? Some see this shift in emphasis from clear objective moral norms as a collapse into "a do whatever is good for me" approach. On the contrary, the "person" as a standard for deciding rightness and wrongness is not subjective—what is good for this person here and now—but objective—what is good for all persons who exist in the contemporary now of today's culture and those to come in the future. This standard exists not in the whim of the individual but in the collective wisdom of the community. The documents of Vatican II call people to reflect on how specific values can be chosen with this idea in mind.

The personalist standard is objective, having value content, while at the same time it is evolutionary. As the human community grows and its experiences increase, its collective wisdom is expanded. It is this collective wisdom that is formulated in teachings that the Church offers as guides for moral action. For example, as humanity has come to a clearer understanding of the importance of preserving natural resources such as water and timberland in order to maintain them for future generations, the moral imperative to have conservation as part of the content for moral activity increases. Now and in the future, taking care of resources is and will be good for human persons. This insight was not a part of human understanding—at least in western European thinking—until very recently. Having entered human collective consciousness, however, this insight calls for a moral response by contemporary human communities unknown to past communities.

While the elements of a personalist standard for determining morality may change, they must be a part of the "content" from which decisions are to be made. The concrete decision of a person here and now can be informed by such a standard, even if what the person should do may not be so clear. One of the realities of decision making, particularly with regard to the material values, is that the concrete working out of what is to be done is often individual and unique. Sarah Student may decide, in thinking about conservation, to plant trees on campus to help clean the air. Sam Student may decide to become a vegetarian, to eat lower on the food chain and thereby help the earth. Sylvester Student may plan to monitor his parents' stock portfolio to ensure the companies whose stocks they buy are environmentally responsible. All three hold the value of preserving the earth for the future—the good of persons—but how they work that out in choices is unique. Those who interact with these students are required to help them learn the values to be incorporated in decision making. It is up to the free choice of the individual as to how those values come to fruition.

The task of promoting moral development in college students is complicated by the fact that each person's ability to receive and act on objective moral information is different. Although the capability to know good is universal, that capability is clouded, as Christian tradition affirms, by the existence of original sin[13] as well as by personal limitations. While there is a fundamental ability in the human person to know and do good (a kind of built-in moral Windows operating system for the human being), the appropriation of content of the good in each person will differ (programs on computers are not all the same); and sometimes the person may lack the totality of knowledge and freedom needed to be a moral agent (the poltergeist in the computer system).

Further, good decision making in the concrete may be compromised by factors that diminish or destroy the elements of knowledge and freedom that are essential for moral thinking and action. An individual may lack knowledge about the implications of the action anticipated. The first time a person drinks a number of beers with her buddies, she may not appreciate that the effects of alcohol can compromise her thinking and ability to function. Lack of such knowledge may diminish moral responsibility. If a person purposely does not find out what needs to be known for proper moral judgment, moral responsibility remains: "I didn't know there was a test today, so you can't hold me responsible." The test was listed on the syllabus.

Many factors can compromise freedom. Peer pressure, habitual patterns (smoking comes to mind as an example), emotional constraints such as anger, passion, and so on can all lessen the freedom with which a person acts. In the task of conscience formation, those who work with students should endeavor to eliminate for individuals those impediments that can be eliminated. Perhaps an example might help. A student speaks candidly to her adviser as she signs up for classes. "I guess I had better take that marketing class this semester. My mom and dad want me to major in business. I don't want to disappoint them, but I really want to be a Spanish major and teach high school. I hate business!" Note the lack of free choice here. The student is making a decision based on a fear of parents' disapproval (superego) not on freedom (true exercise of conscience). The adviser can encourage growth by affirming the student's choices for her own life, assuming they are thoughtfully considered. Helping the student obtain knowledge about the two possible professions may be useful. The student will then have the information necessary to make a better decision. In general, those working with students can enhance their moral growth by promoting the exercise of freedom and the development of knowledge.

Vatican II tells us that human beings are essentially related to their personal selves, to one another, to the earth they share, and to God.[14] The first, the relationship to the self, includes an understanding and an appreciation of human materiality as integral to humanity. For many centuries the human body has been considered by some to be suspect, to be in need of control, to be transcended by a more spiritual approach. While this perspective is not really from the tradition—Genesis tells us that the body is precisely the receptor of the breath of godly life, the "mortal coil" that God pronounces "good"—there persists a tendency to see it otherwise. Much of Catholic thinking and teaching, especially in the area of sexuality, reflects this negative and dualistic approach to the body. Materiality is seen as not only suspect, but in need of domination by the more rational aspect of the person. I surmise that much of the teaching about things sexual is tainted by this anthropology.

On the whole, Vatican II views the person as an awesome being made in the divine image, whose unique and equal status with regard to conscience and its freedom must be respected. The person is essentially related to other entities, which requires that a decision of conscience cannot be made without taking into account the well-being and rights of the other. Morality is objective, based on what is good for persons, but not a-historical and fixed for all time. Human communities, as they evolve, discover more deeply God's call and God's law. Human growth and human understanding of rightness and wrongness is a process for both the community and the individual. Human beings are embodied—the only life and experience they have is body, their biological selves—in a unique and incomplete way. It is the body that touches reality. It is the body that is open to experience. On the other hand, the human body, bound to materiality as it is, limits the person in his or her ability to take in the vast scope of reality. These limits are imposed by the boundaries of time and place, including the historical context[15]—one's place in history—as well as by the natural margins and capacities of each unique body.[16] This teaching is the basis for an understanding of human conscience and must underlie any other specific consideration of rightness and wrongness.

Calling the Question

We turn now to questions of morality that seems to be uppermost in campus concerns. The common understanding of church teaching is that important pronouncements are anything to do with sex. For many, preoccupation with what occurs between the knees and the navel defines a common compendium of what Catholic identity means. Sexual intercourse belongs only in marriage, which has two inseparable purposes: unitive and procreative. Therefore, any form of artificial conception is immoral, since it thwarts the procreative purpose of marriage while allowing the unitive. Abortion, sexual activity before marriage, and homosexual activity at any time are objectively immoral. It is not that these statements do not reflect the official position of the magisterial teaching. They do. The teaching is clear and enduring, even in the face of Catholic practice to the contrary. Nevertheless, it must be kept in mind that the focus on this one dimension of Catholic thought deemphasizes the importance of other aspects of teaching, the full picture of Catholic moral thought. It even clouds the broader teaching on marriage itself and on how persons should relate to one another with respect and love.

There may be a perception that the work of student affairs, as it relates to the Church, concerns itself primarily with issues of sex, that is to say, what *not* to do or be. While this may indeed be part of the job, it should be kept in mind that exposure to a broader scope of values and practices from the tradition is equally important. Uppermost in the minds of those who work with students should be the Church's positions on social justice and the common good, care of the earth, and the use of money and power in positions of authority. All of these issues embody values that reflect an adequate understanding of the human person as pictured in a Vatican II Church. As student affairs divisions of Catholic colleges plan their activities and educational projects, all of these elements must be addressed. They will help give content to the conscience base of students as they progress toward maturity. To accentuate certain prohibitions is to impoverish the potential for a rich content on marriage and personal relationship. The shift in approach to morality that occurred at Vatican II sought to deemphasize individual actions as morally wrong and to concentrate on the moral reality of the whole person. To continue to focus on the moral wrongness of individual actions is to return to a preconciliar view of morality. Those who work with students must see their task in the broader context of building persons of character and sound judgment rather than constricting certain behaviors.

The Process of Conscience Formation

Now we turn to the concrete task of student affairs professionals. Formation of conscience begins with the experience of being loved and continues with the building of the system of meaning that forms the basis for moral choice. The college or university meets the young person at some place along the continuum of this development. I suggest that student affairs professionals who work at Catholic institutions have three functions related to conscience. First, they must encourage without judgment the unique process of development into adulthood for each student, contributing to the ground of conscience: a good self-image. This requires active listening. Second, they have a responsibility to represent as definitive the tradition of the Church and to articulate other human-worthy values that will help develop the content component of conscience. They must challenge and guide students. Finally, they must encourage the development of a true freedom, which is able to move toward good and person-affirming choices. How can these things be accomplished?

First, the person must have a healthy self-image as well as a sense of trust born of early relationships with family and friends. Louis Janssens, in his reflection on conscience, notes the importance of early loving parental context to the development of a mature conscience.[17] Walter Conn, in his classic book on conscience, notes the importance of early trust, self esteem, and a sense of control or freedom.[18] As children come into college, their experiences in this regard are not always completely good ones. They have collectively been damaged by divorce, abuse, betrayal of friendship, derision by friends, failure to get into the first college of their choice, to name only a few. They have been told they are ugly, cannot do math, or will never make it on the ball field. The litany that details the perpetuation of evil on human development is long. Perhaps the college years can be the occasion to mitigate the results of this exposure to evil that is part of everyone's life. The affirmation and acceptance of students as they are by those who work with them at the college level may be helpful in recovering the self-image damaged by bad experiences. The conception of each student as made in the image of God, not in some pious sense but as a truth, will go a long way toward making this real.

It is part of the job of student affairs to provide experiences for students. Programs are a part of student life. These experiences, thoughtfully constructed, have the potential to shore up self-image as well as embody the values promoted by the institution. Experiences, which reinforce values while allowing freedom of choice, also encourage self-development. Student affairs professionals must reflect on what kinds of personal interaction with students and what sort of experiences will contribute to the development of a good self-image. Certainly this task begins with a real love of students and an appreciation of the good that is concretely in each of them. One does not stay in this work for very long if that perspective is absent. Different from parents, who may seek to "fix" what they see as not quite right in their children or project their own insecurities on their offspring (original sin, alive and well), the resident assistant or the chaplain or the judicial affairs officer has no personal stake in who or how this student is. Such a dispassionate stance allows a certain objectivity about the good and bad in a student, which can be translated into a kind of acceptance of each one. In a certain sense, the people who interact with students professionally have the potential to fill in the gaps that even the best of parenting leave out. Individuals are more likely to engage in person-destructive behavior when they do not feel good about themselves. Helping to counteract that position will ground movement toward good and person-affirming actions.

The second element where student affairs can be helpful is to provide content for the basic goodwill and focused freedom that we claim students have. By way of example, let us look again at the sexual teaching of the Church. In his controversial 1968 encyclical letter, *Humanae Vitae*, Pope Paul VI outlined the purpose and context of sex. Sex is best expressed in the committed relationship of two people that we call marriage. It is a celebration of that relationship. Two persons reach out to each other in an ongoing intimacy of permanence and trust. In the sexual act they celebrate who they are, what they mean to each other, and where their relationship will go in the future. The act is both conjugal and generative. Other relationships have some of the same elements. This is good stuff. It reminds human beings of their need to be loved and to love. It forms the basis for reaching out with confidence to do justice and, as Rosemary Haughton notes, to "'make love' for all kinds of people."[19] This rich message is easily obscured in the formal and structured language of the papal letter, however. Nor does it likely correspond to either student experience or to what the culture tells us are student needs.

If we were to reflect fairly on the Catholic perspective, certainly we would expose students to the Church's teaching. But this is not the 1950s with its Mary-like dresses[20] and high school proms in decorated gyms.

A twenty-first century version of the quaint pamphlet, "Modern Youth and Chastity," is not enough. What is needed today is serious reflection on what is valuable about the idealized picture the Church presents, and how this value might be articulated to today's college students. Simply to articulate prohibitions—"Don't have sex before marriage, and if you do and get pregnant, don't get an abortion"—will not sell in a modern context. Besides, most students already know what the rules are; but they are not always convinced that those rules apply to them.

One approach might be to ask, What experiences help a growth in understanding of the ideal and what experiences will help the student to move toward that ideal? What experiences hinder the growth? Why? How can we take the person where he or she is and at the same time offer experiences that will help build a solid appreciation of the ideal? Looking at the long term, it is more important that a student become practiced in such things as how to make relationships work and how to be related to significant others without using them or betraying them, than it is to avoid a particular type of sexual expression. Certainly individual actions contribute to who the person is, but alone they cannot exhaust the core or totality of the person.

An appreciation of other aspects of Catholic identity, especially in the area of social justice and the common good, are largely absent from the Catholic experience or even American experience; where love of God and neighbor often pale in juxtaposition to egoism. It is easier to repeat church teaching that homosexual activity is forbidden than it is to understand what it means to be gay and to promote just treatment of gay people on campus. These elements, too, are part of Catholic tradition. Catholic parents, the culture in general, and consequently the average college student may be content to live the life of individual goals, seeking the individual good life with little regard for the situation and needs of other persons. This can be demonstrated in such simple examples as playing loud music in a residence hall with little consideration for sleeping roommates, or the cruel isolation of a student whose heritage, financial situation, or appearance is different. Student affairs programming and philosophy can help develop content for decision making by introducing students to a broader perspective of diversity and the connectedness of all human beings, as the council documents affirm.

Some practical questions arise. Where and in what format should experiences that promote the incorporation of values occur? Is it best to offer seminars or student in-service or merely to create an environment where the ideals are promoted—and what might that look like? The time to talk about the Church's teaching on sex within marriage is not at the moment a young woman is crying in the office because her boyfriend, with whom she has been having sex, has just dumped her for another woman. I leave it to the expertise of those who do this work to find adequate answers to these questions.

The third element of conscience formation is the promotion of freedom. This may be the most difficult area. Certainly a good self-image goes a long way toward grounding a healthy and responsible freedom. So does creating opportunities to exercise freedom among different goods and allowing students to make mistakes. Those who work with students must know when to look the other way and when to crack down. All these strategies can be used to encourage growth in freedom. Pope John XXIII, who convened Vatican II, was noted for a saying that is pertinent here: "Conformity in essentials, freedom in non-essentials, charity in all things." This is a good working rule. Where better than in the somewhat sheltered environment of college life to try out the choice making that wasn't possible *in loco parentis*? Respect for the person and the person's essential goodness is the basis for encouraging experimental choice. It is essential to remember that each student is a person in progress, whose concrete choices are made with limited freedom and knowledge, and whose mistakes will ultimately contribute to maturity. It is essential to balance a respect for the person and the fragile reality of where they are with the need to "hold the line" with regard to representing fairly the Catholic perspective.

To accomplish the tasks suggested it is imperative that those people who work with young adults know the teaching of the Church. First, I suggest that personnel acquaint themselves with church teaching by reading *Gaudium et Spes*. This document is a prophetic foundation for helping people to grow. In this chapter we have only scratched the surface of its content. Also, learning the content of the documents of Vatican II can prove helpful.

Second, it is important that those who work with students remember that their professional training in understanding and accepting the normalcy of stages of development is not incompatible with what the Church teaches about growth and development. Third, a vision of how God approaches people might be considered. Perhaps the story of the rich young man as portrayed in Mark's Gospel (10:17–22) is the best example. Jesus is questioned by a young adult who wishes "everlasting life," a desire for the best, for perfection. Building on the young man's goodwill and affirming the knowledge that is already present in him, Jesus suggests that he follow the commandments—a list that Jesus assumes the man knows (already present as part of the content of the man's conscience). The man isn't totally without knowledge or goodwill. Complimented that Jesus assumes the best from him, he tells Jesus that he already obeys the law and has done so since his youth. With that, Jesus goes further: "Sell what you have and give it to the poor. After that come and follow me." Youth is open to challenge, to idealism, to doing the greater good. Jesus simply paints a picture of what that might look like (offers additional content). Now the person has as much knowledge as he needs to decide. The decision to act in a new way is not imposed but left to free choice. But moral decision involves more than knowledge; it demands action as well. The youth must choose and act on the decision to go deeper, to aim higher. At this point in the story everyone is rooting for the rich young man. Do the greater good. In a modern context: yes, join the Peace Corps; help out at the soup kitchen, create a new service program to help underprivileged youths. We are a bit disappointed when the response in the story is a negative one. The man "went away sad," rejecting the challenge of the charismatic preacher. Here, however, is the important key to dealing with students. Jesus does not grab the man by the scruff of the neck, nor does he raise his voice and inflict on him a sermon on the greater good. Jesus allows complete freedom of choice, even a choice that is not apparently the best one.

As those who deal with fragile developing consciences, it is important for student affairs professionals to listen to this message. To respect others' freedom of conscience is to avoid using the power that is part of the office they hold to force conformity, especially when it is not essential that conformity be had. In respecting choices and allowing diversity we go a long way toward helping students form a mature conscience. If choices are not their own, they are not really free choices. If students are coerced to follow the good as defined by another they will not attain true freedom. They will remain merely automatons, clones of their elders. Remember the student majoring in business who wanted to teach Spanish?

A caveat is needed here. To allow freedom is not the same as allowing license. Certainly we should do what must be done to protect the common good. Let us now return to a discussion of what freedom is and is not. Freedom is not doing whatever I please, wish, or think. Simply because I do something in freedom does not make it a right action. I may wish to drop a case of empty beer bottles from my fifth-story room into the hallway below that is filled with students. That seems to be ultimate freedom. Not so.

Freedom, as understood in the Catholic tradition, must be rooted in objective values. Freedom is not properly exercised without a knowledge of the good and a movement toward that good. That is the basis of Catholic teaching and the corrective to the relativism that is decried in such papal pronouncements as *Splendor of Truth*. Conscience, properly exercised, must ground its selective action on real value.

Some Final Thoughts

Let us conclude with some suggestions for those who work with students in Catholic colleges. First, it is essential to know the Catholic tradition, not only in its narrow expression regarding rules, but more appropriately in its anthropology and methodology. This tradition can be studied in its origins in Jesus the Christ, in its documents, and in the living communities of family, *ekklesia* (church), and the nexus of college communities. By affirming the basic goodness of persons and the human characteristics articulated in *Gaudium et Spes*, one creates a positive ground on which to build high moral character. Further, by articulating a moral method that locates choice on a continuum toward one's ultimate choice—God—in a communal world of possibilities, one expands the vision of rightness and wrongness. The tradition is broader than a set of rules, affirming a positive and accepting vision of the human person. Its moral method is aimed at creating whole and free persons suited for life in the community of earth and the kingdom of heaven. It is optimistic, a tradition full of hope.

Second, it is important to recognize the influence of one's own prejudices and needs in dealing with students. Openness to a variety of stances is essential. If bias is present—for example, if one is pro-abortion, anti-gay activity, pro-casual sex, in favor of recreational drug use—such a bias will hinder the ability to allow freedom in the other person, particularly in a person over whom some degree of control is exercised. There is, of course, a power differential in the relationship between students and most persons who work with them. While a person cannot always transcend his or her own biases, if they are named and acknowledged they become a visible part of the equation.

Third, the role played by student affairs must be made clear. While not parents, such persons likely are seen by students as representative of the values and identity of the institutions. To remain silent or non-judgmental in the face of student revelations of destructive choices or values contrary to the values of the institution is to leave with students the impression that the professionals are in agreement with the student perspective. "Well, my counselor didn't say it was wrong, so it must be okay." Those who work with students would do well to think through when and where to clarify or articulate the values of the college that they, whether they like it or not, represent. It is an art to know when to speak out and when to remain silent.

Finally, the formation of conscience is a process that demands that each person is loved and accepted, but also challenged to grow and to appreciate new values. In a sense, those in student affairs in Catholic institutions enflesh the promise of Christian baptism: sin and evil may be present in the world and in each of us, causing a blindness and sometimes inflicting serious damage on persons, but evil is not all there is. The central message of Christ is that sin is not the final answer, rather Christ is. And the love of Christ is stronger than death.

6

Student Affairs and Academic Affairs: Understanding Our History and Exploring New Relationships

Martin F. Larrey

Although originally trained as a historian, for almost thirty years I have worked in academic administration: nine years as a college dean and the remainder as the chief academic officer. All of that service has been in the cause of Catholic higher education, which I believe is the best venue for providing students with strong living and learning principles for a lifetime, as well as high quality skills and knowledge base for entrée into the professions. I will return to this theme later in the chapter. Underlying all of that is my belief that such settings as Catholic colleges and universities are most supportive and congruent with my own personal religious beliefs and aspirations.

In the course of my career I have had the opportunity to work with student affairs personnel, to become familiar with the worlds of student activities and student development, and to appreciate the complementarity and synergistic relationships that exist between academic affairs and student affairs. The reflections that follow are gleaned from the cumulative experience of those relationships and that history.

The chapter has three principal purposes. First, I will trace the relationships between academic affairs and student affairs as they have evolved over the last half-century. Second, I will analyze the two models that have been used to characterize these relationships and why they have proven inadequate. Third, I will summarize some practical activities in campus life and learning that point to a new model to structure the relationships of academic life and student development.

In the last three to five years we have seen increasingly richer conversations concerning the relationship of academic affairs and student affairs than probably at any time in the last century. In the main, two broad streams of thinking and acting have converged to make this possible. On the one hand, the emergence of enrollment management and programmatic marketing have compelled institutions to draw together their human and financial resources to achieve more effective control over the recruitment, admission, and retention of students. Concomitantly, the entire area of student affairs over the last fifty years has gone through a broad and remarkable evolution, emerging from virtual invisibility into a sophisticated profession that can stand in the front rank of the professions along with law, medicine, and the academic disciplines. Let us examine these two streams.

Since the market in higher education is considerably fragmented, being more analogous to jewelers than to automobile makers, competition takes place on many levels: locally, regionally, nationally, by program, by public/private differences, religious/nonreligious commitments, size, location, and perceived status, to name the most obvious. At one time, the very fragmentation of the profession buffered the competitive edge. Private colleges and universities could leisurely count on a significant number of new enrollees coming from traditional catchment areas that had developed and been nurtured slowly over a number of years, and were held together by tissues of alumni, well-recognized areas of study, religious orientation, simple geography, class values, or national recognition. Moreover, this was reenforced by a rather simple conception of education that, *a priori*, separated vast numbers of young citizens from the pool of prospective college students: those destined by class or aspiration or simple financial necessity for the labor market, the trades, stenographic service, and local business careers. For much of their early history, admissions offices served more as intake offices than as high-powered recruiting engines with budgets the size of small corporations.

In the aftermath of World War II, significant changes began in the general composition and outlook of American society. These changes were both wide and deep and, in great part, continue to occur. Higher education, like many other aspects of life, was seriously impinged. A college or university degree moved from being a badge of status, refinement, or completion to being an entrée to a more diversified, and increasingly complex, career market. Catholic colleges and universities, in particular, where motivation was high to move the children of the unskilled immigrant workers into the professions, took the lead in this changing orientation. Colleges and universities perceived that their stability and continued growth depended on providing a broader range of programming with a higher utility factor. We have all witnessed this in the transmutation of the traditional disciplines into their more utilitarian progeny: the English major into communications, economics into business administration, political science and sociology into urban and ethnic studies, art and music into art and music therapy, psychology into mental health counseling.

As higher education became more accessible and as the range of program offerings expanded dramatically, it was necessary to make the college known to broader audiences and to trumpet the particular virtues of one's own institution, hence recruiting a larger and more diversified student body. Today, competition is a key factor of institutional policy from Harvard and Stanford to the most modest Bible college recessed in the Smoky Mountains. As competition moved to the center of campus planning and action, it was quite clear that securing students was simply not the job of admissions staffs alone. What good was it to expend sizable human and material resources to admit students if, after they arrived, they were disappointed by the services, found the college to be something very different from what they were led to believe, or learned that their chosen course of study was staffed, at best, by mediocre faculty? Academic affairs and student affairs have had to come together to create a more coherent experience to assure that admitted students attend and that attending students stay—hence, the need to continued dialogue in how better to work together.

Let us now turn to the remarkable evolution of student affairs from an academic footnote into a fully developed enterprise.

In its nineteenth- and early twentieth-century incarnation, the American college and university, including the large land grant institutions, were primarily conceived as academic enterprises, where professors taught and did research and students learned. That was the formal purpose of going to college. Remembering, as mentioned above, that the environments of such institutions were strikingly homogeneous, social and non-classroom time reflected the particular values and practices of the families from which the students came. Until a long generation ago, successive waves of alumnae and alumni could return to their alma maters, be they Vassar, Iowa State, Santa Clara, or Colgate, and find many familiarities: the setting, the mystique, the faces, the neighborhood, the hangouts, and probably even a number of the faculty and staff.

In this environment, the function of student affairs was almost exclusively instrumental: checking night curfews in the residence halls, organizing the athletic teams, meting out justice for infractions of the rules, sponsoring homecoming events, and perhaps serving as a sympathetic ear for the homesick. In many cases in small schools, members of the faculty performed these functions (and I know of cases in which this perdures). Who has not perused the pages of an alumni magazine and found eulogized some legend of the faculty who, in addition to teaching biology or mathematics or history for half a century, also drove the athletic bus, trained the school band, ran new student orientation, and may have lived in one of the residence halls? For the skeptical, permit me to adduce the following. Yesterday I received an alumni publication from a private, Midwestern college, well passed its centenary, from which I lifted this exact description. To the extent that there was a student affairs "world," it was a modest appendage to the main work of the college, which was done exclusively in the classroom.

However, the very transformations, which rocketed through the academy in the post-1945 world, ushered in the adolescence of student affairs. Campus homogeneity began to dissolve, reflecting the growing heterogeneity of the larger society. The new students on campus brought with them problems and issues with which faculty members were unfamiliar and often found off-putting. The first applications of developmental psychology also began to hint that college consisted of more than knowing the principal parts of *sum, esse, fui* or the rituals of fraternity life or what the win/loss record was against the college's arch rival. Athletics, on many large campuses, had already matured into a full-blown enterprise (with welcomed and unwelcomed consequences) requiring segmentation and expertise. Neither could the cozy framework of student activities in the classical college model—glee club, debating and literary societies, intramural sports, the yearbook, program-specific clubs—contain the new spate of student activities, reflecting the new interests of new members of the college population. Student activities and student development—the lungs of student affairs—grew more complicated and diverse, calling for persons experienced with these new realities. A new generation of student affairs professionals began to emerge, many combining on-the-job training with instruction in psychology or human relations or a similar discipline.

By the 1960s two further developments accelerated the maturation of student affairs; one dramatic, the other incremental. Combined, they have revolutionized the very fabric of collegiate life. These developments are, first, the abolition of *in locus parentis* and, second, the presence on hundreds of campuses of the adult learner (ironically, often the most traditional and homogeneous). I would maintain that even more than the distension and expansion of the curriculum, the abolition of surrogate parental supervision and the mass ingress of adult learners irrevocably altered all dimensions of college life.

Students were not only liberated from all the old rules and regulations, which attempted to mimic home life, but their independence was enshrined in state and federal legislation. Suddenly colleges were expected to deal with students as equals while at the same time working out ways to fulfill their responsibilities to the students and, to some degree, their parents. These were new and turbulent seas for which traditional faculty were even less comfortable (or able) to navigate than those they encountered with the returning soldiers of World War II. Whereas in earlier days, student development was taken as something that simply happened by osmosis in a settled environment where faces and places and rules stayed the same year after year, now it was a conscious activity that could as easily be done badly or well, depending on the knowledge and skills of the practitioners. It had to deal with students who were as strangers to the college, unversed— and uninterested—in its hoary past and legendary founders. These students brought their own agendas and their own pasts and their own wounds for marking their lives and shaping their aspirations. Colleges actively began to recruit personnel adept in student development with all its new amplitudes.

Fortunately, as student affairs was reaching its early adulthood, a generation of groundbreaking thinkers articulated a theoretical framework for the discipline. Tracing its course can be found in another part of this book.

At the same time, thousands of adult learners—most of them women—flooded into first evening and weekend classes, and then into the very heart of the academy. They brought with them concerns, issues, and attitudes not seen before on college campuses: day care needs, perhaps having to redefine their lives after divorce, a profound disinterest in the traditional activities of college life, and a lack of patience for mediocre teaching or administrative runaround. They heightened the college's consciousness that education could be an on-again-off-again, part-time venture with an end point in an undefinable future that did not often fit smoothly with the neat, four-year curriculum. They challenged the pedagogy of college professors who had to address different audiences at the same time and in the same place. The entry of many new traditional-age students and the reentry of an equal number of non-traditional-age students into university life became fragile events, requiring people who knew how to manage them.

The irony of all this was poetic. At the very time colleges began to accelerate their need for effective and sophisticated recruitment plans and strategies and augment their staffs to face new levels of competition, they were also acquiring an immensely diverse population with multiple and often mutually exclusive needs. Traditional students wanted more enriching and varied student life and accommodations; adult learners wanted more flexible and accessible curricula and customized programming. They also didn't want to pay for more activities and services they didn't use and they didn't see the reason to pay increasing tuition for more elegant residence halls they never lived in.

All this change profoundly exacerbated a growing tension between academic affairs and student affairs. The issues and learning in student affairs had grown explosively over fifty years. In practice if not in theory, the abiding belief and theoretical framework that student affairs was the handmaiden or warm and fuzzy stepsister of the academicians, "taking care of the details" of college life outside the classroom, was increasingly uncreditable.

In academic affairs, change evolved slowly over time; in student affairs, change was revolutionary. Most of the change in academic affairs had come in regard to the curriculum or degree expectations. For example, an advanced degree was expected as a condition for membership in the academy in 1910. It still is; we just ratcheted up the degree from the masters to the doctorate—with some wholesale exceptions. We accord to the ranked instructor of organizational development or sports medicine the identical status we do to the senior historian or philosopher on the faculty.

However, attitudinally, change was hardly perceptible in the heart of the academy. We academicians believed—and still believe—that the classroom and what occurs there is the heart of the collegiate endeavor. This position, hallowed by custom and inertia, has been doubly strengthened by the dogma of academic freedom. The professoriate is conceived as an autonomous class of colleagues who work and decide things collegially, which has calcified for many academicians into a type of patrician outlook that everyone else on the campus is there to take care of "secondary" issues. This posture is sufficiently widespread, unfortunately, to have internalized in many student affairs personnel a feeling of inferiority, giving us a type of collegiate apartheid. Unfortunately, in the evolution taking place on the American campus, no provision or even attempt was made to frame a conversation about the changing nature of student affairs and its impact on campus and its ever-changing relationship to academic affairs.

We can identify two principal stages in the evolutionary relationship between academic affairs and student affairs. From the times of their foundations until the postwar era, on most campuses the relationship was one of undifferentiated subordination in which clearly identifiable student "services" were simply less classroom-centered aspects of academic life. In the heady 60s and 70s, with the maturation of student affairs, campuses—still not engaging these new realities on a theoretical plane—lazily defaulted to the standard American model: *laissez-faire* autonomy.

In its classical form, the typical college modeled the *laissez-faire* principles that Adam Smith illuminated for economic activities; namely, that if each area did its part well—as autonomously and as professionally as possible—the result (of the invisible hand) would be a well-educated graduate. This succeeded only in special circumstances and at a very limited number of institutions; principally those in which a homogeneous culture pervaded all aspects of personnel and institutional life, such as small, richly denominational schools or elite, highly selective liberal arts colleges. But the Bereas and Sweetbriars of this world could only exist under unique conditions, conditions that were not common throughout society nor exportable as models. Most of us found ourselves in the midst of very heterogeneous cultures re-enforced by the varied outlooks of our students, their parents, the communities we found ourselves in, and the various other audiences to which we had to relate. Moreover, the autonomy of the several parts in our institutions were themselves structured by varying values, aspirations, and benchmarks of professionalism. This most often led to working at cross-purposes rather than in a cooperative manner.

In a word, the old *laissez-faire* model has not succeeded in assuring quality educational outcomes. More likely it has led to inefficiency, frustration, and a waste of time and resources.

Matured student affairs offices became more alienated from the academic enterprise. An inchoate dialectic between the two areas became more dolefully common. It could be witnessed in the "interventions" on behalf of students who wished academic rigor to be mitigated. It was replayed in the sterile and frustrating struggles of college budget committees where academic and student vice presidents arm wrestled over modest discretionary funds. One found it in the rigidity of college faculty who were loath to make accommodation to diverse populations, zealously championed by student affairs personnel.

Yet, across the quad or down the hall, swelling battalions of student affairs professionals, now often well degreed and with seasoned experience, found themselves deeply immersed in teaching and learning.

They have developed wellness programs, taught transition-to-college courses, held value clarification sessions, mentored students for career placements, coordinated large internship programs. They have taught their college colleagues about crisis intervention and how to prioritize life choices and challenges, engage in personal conflict, mentor roles for success, learn the value of diversity, and appreciate the role of spirituality in human maturity. Most evident of all, they have established themselves as an independent entity with a recognizable theoretical framework, a body of literature, a panoply of national and regional organizations, and programs of advanced study for aspiring practitioners that hold an integral part of the new configuration of collegiate life.

This state of affairs requires that a new paradigm be structured in which academic affairs and student affairs can work in an integrated manner, holistically committed to teaching and learning on the campus as a unitary experience. They must become equal partners in a common cause so that the often dysfunctional personal and professional relationships will disappear and the seemingly eternal and frustrating competition for scarce dollars in dispiriting budget meetings will likewise vanish. This new paradigm requires that academic affairs eschew its clubby and often tacit mandarin posture, replacing it with a stance more refreshingly latitudinarian and inclusive. All college professors, not simply self-selected ones, need to be actively involved in issues related to residence life, student activities, and student development, assuming a collaborative rather than a gate-keeping position.

Reciprocally, student affairs professionals have tasks ahead for themselves in order to actuate this new paradigm. Risking the scorn of my academic colleagues, I believe that student development theorists need to take the lead in articulating it. The new realities of student life have transformed every college campus; therefore, it would seem logical that student development theorists are more familiar with the lines for further development. At the same time, they need, frankly, to shed their "second class" status and victim mentality and mute their advocacy role, as if only they took student interests to heart. They need to accelerate and deepen their programs of advanced studies so as to assure that future student affairs professionals are academically equipped to enter the academy as peers, no less interested in research and publications than traditional academicians. This is simply to acknowledge that degrees and advanced studies remain—and will remain—the essential criteria for admission to the new academy, just as it was to the old academy.

Some institutions in recent years have become sensitive to these issues and have sought ways to overcome the problems inherent in the conventional relationship between academic affairs and student affairs. This new model calls for a fusion of the two areas under the leadership of a vice president for academic and student affairs. Heartening as this move may be in acknowledging the bankruptcy of the old model, I fear that it is stillborn at best and pernicious at worst; basically, for three reasons. First, no significant theoretical foundations have been adumbrated for this model so participants cannot reconceptualize the entire enterprise in a new way for new purposes and with new mechanics to succeed. Without a radically new framework from which everyone can see his or her work anew, the theoretical lens will remain what it has always been. In addition, educational activities will not be able to benefit from new modes unearthed by a new model of relationships.

Second, all the old attitudes, postures, and rivalries remain intact so a genuine metanoia, prompted by a new paradigm, is impossible. The struggles between academic affairs and student affairs continue unabated, only now they are similar more to domestic violence rather than to street gangs contending over rival territory. Organizational redesign has only modest impact in changing attitudes; especially, ones that have become ingrained as a matter of survival and resource raiding. What is most likely to happen is that where the principal vice president is drawn from academic affairs, the effective apartheid of student affairs will continue. If the case is reversed, the faculty and academic staff will probably engage in a guerrilla war of effective secession shrouded in haughty ignorance.

Third, such a model creates an unbalanced organizational world in which an overwhelming number of employees and overwhelming amounts of resources are concentrated in one unit. Advancement and business affairs are, per force, diminished in the eyes of the entire collegiate community, becoming like mice around the feet of an elephant. This could hardly contribute to healthy institutional morale.

We need to formulate a new conception of the learning experience of the college student. This conception must be a seamless continuum of living/learning wherein there is no formal separation of the work inside and outside of the classroom. We must recognize that the "departmentalisms" of collegiate activities are purely instrumental. There has to be a housing officer to track students in the residence halls, a career counseling office to keep inventories of job placements, and an English department chair to schedule classes, and so on, but the work of education is comprehensive and should be done by teams of college personnel with high levels of interaction and varied tasks.

Our thinking has to move away from "I am going to be a biology professor" or "I am going to be a student activities director." People contemplating entrance into higher education as practitioners have to think more globally and interactively; that is, they are going to be college educators primarily and biology teachers or residence hall directors secondarily. What in the past were discrete, occasional, and unrelated activities (as if a college was a large holding company akin to ITT) have to be brought front and center as the main endeavors of the entire college community and reconceived as an organic whole. This requires a two-step process.

First, a sophisticated theoretical framework has to be devised for this new paradigm. It is a hope that out of graduate schools for educational administration or newer ones that focus on educating student affairs professionals, a new theory will emerge, a theory that conceptualizes the educational enterprise as a unity containing interrelated subsets, interrelated as much to each other as to the overall unity. Second, we must conduct an inventory of activities that strengthen the unity of a college experience, recognizing at the same time that "teaching" and "co-curricular" are far broader terms than we have heretofore meant them to be. I might suggest even that these terms have become so established that we can no longer redefine them and that the best course would be to abolish them altogether.

This is a daunting task; however, in this enterprise I believe that Catholic higher education has a unique mandate and a distinct advantage.

One of the most incisive and creative initiatives that illuminates this new orientation is the document *Ex Corde Ecclesiae*, offered as a broad vision of Catholic education in the contemporary world. According to the document, the Church affirms the work of the university as a center for the pursuit of truth in all its forms and amplitudes. Focused on inquiry into all of the arts and sciences, it quickly centers this activity in the holistic nature of the university experience as that of a *community*. Moreover, the norms clearly demand that service to the larger community, interaction with the larger culture, and an institutional commitment to social justice are *equally* goals of the educational experience.

From its very beginning the document conceives of the Catholic university as a center for the whole person where knowledge is affirmed to have several ends that are to be simultaneously pursued, no one of which is more important or "truer" than any of the others. Among those is "service to the people of God," an "obligation to communicate to the whole society those *ethical and religious principles which give full meaning to human life*" and "*to give a practical demonstration of its faith in its daily life*" (italics in original).

Perhaps the most explicit statement of the Church's position on the integrative and holistic nature of Catholic education can be found in Article 4, sec. 5 of the document. It is important enough in my opinion to be cited intact:

> The education of students is to combine academic and professional development with formation in moral and religious principles and the social teachings of the Church; the program of studies for each of the various professions is to include an appropriate ethical formation in that profession. Courses in Catholic doctrine are to be made available to all students.

While this language deals with ostensibly traditional academic matter, the entire outcome is to prepare students for a life of action in the larger culture as particular kinds of people. The critical component is fundamentally formative, something that comes much more directly from the area of student affairs than from academic affairs. If indeed we are in need of a new theoretical framework with a new paradigm and if, as I believe, it should probably be significantly shaped by persons from student affairs, we can hardly do better than take the Apostolic Constitution on Catholic Universities as a comprehensive starting point. It's inclusive and integrative nature, relating intellectual to spiritual realities and both to social responsibilities, offers us an excellent opportunity to reconceptualize the educational venture as well as helps us avoid unresolvable dilemmas created by the older model. I would commend it as foundational to all future conversations on this topic.

In the remaining space, I would like to describe at least a dozen collegiate activities that mirror this new concept of collaborative efforts. These are ways in which academic and student affairs personnel can share equally in the learning/living enterprise that is the new model for collegiate education.

The first major step would be to extend faculty rank to all student affairs professionals with appropriate degrees. Rank is the defining method of identifying members of the collegiate community. An anecdote about Dwight Eisenhower's tenure as president of Columbia University in the late 1940s illuminates the point. On the occasion of addressing the faculty of the university, then General Eisenhower repeatedly spoke about the "employees" of the university. After several iterations of this statement, he was interrupted by a white-haired doyen from the back of the auditorium who rose and said, "General Eisenhower, we are *not employees* of Columbia University, we *are* Columbia

University." From the largest and most prestigious university to the humblest Bible college, university personnel—and the public at large—acknowledge and affirm that professorial rank is the badge of membership, the claim to authority, and the *sine qua non* of legitimacy. Therefore, those who have completed advanced studies, be it in Greek or in student affairs personnel administration, should be accorded academic rank. This step would immediately establish parity among all professionals on a college campus and go far in strengthening the "team" model of education.

There is a clutch of college activities already found on many campuses that can be fruitful arenas for cooperation between academic and student affairs. While they are similar, there are different ways in which the interaction between these two parts of a campus community can happen.

For some time, many colleges have been utilizing an intern system to complement a student's education with "in the field" tasks. Interestingly, the management of internships is as commonly found under the supervision of student affairs as it is found in the academic departments of the college. Internships aim to enrich a student's experience by putting her/him in a setting in which the learning that took place in the classroom can be applied to real-life situations. There are learning outcomes and often prescribed debriefing seminars where students in similar career paths compare and discuss their respective experiences. But far more than mere book learning or rote applications take place in these work settings. Time management and "people" skills are equally important to success. Solving real problems not anticipated in the textbooks and notes also become important. Learning whether to "do this" for the rest of one's life emerges as a real choice, with pluses and minuses often not mentioned in class. Working with an on-site supervisor unversed in college lore or learning requires adjustments in style, language, and tone. In a word, a whole lot of learning takes place that isn't "academic." Often, to process this learning, the skills of student affairs personnel are more appropriate than those of the classroom professor. It would be better yet if both were brought together to assist the student along another path of maturation.

Volunteerism has been growing apace on college campuses in recent years. This often takes the form of "service learning." Especially for faith-based institutions, this is a premium of the educational experience because it affords the institution an opportunity to express its mission in a visible, practical way. Assisting the disabled, being a companion to shut-ins, providing catechetical work for children, cleaning trash out of parks, using a spring break for missionary work in rural areas—all make demands on students whose classroom experience may not have prepared them adequately for such tasks. While in the classroom they are habituated to be the focal point of the activity, expecting presentations and materials to be adjusted to their horizons and knowledge base, in-service learning experiences, other people, often at a disadvantage, are the focuses of activity. Here students can encounter disinterestedness, antagonism, limited understanding, uncomfortable and alien settings, and downright failure. Once again, out-of-the-classroom skills and knowledge can be more helpful. Knitting the meaning of the mission of the college to one's actual activities is not even primarily an "academic" matter, although it can have that component. Student affairs professionals can facilitate a better understanding of the situation in which one finds oneself and can help clarify the issues that often leave students bewildered when they venture off campus to live out their beliefs and commitments, especially to others.

I have seen some excellent models for this type of collaboration. At one college at which I worked, a ministry in nursing course, the capstone course of a BSN curriculum, actually was taught in the barrios of Sucre, Bolivia, by a team of nursing faculty, campus ministry personnel, and student affairs professionals. Not only did the students practice the nursing skills and utilize the nursing knowledge they had acquired over four years (and thus complete the knowledge outcomes of the course), but they also experienced living in a radically dissimilar culture from which they came, dealing with people of vastly different expectations and aspirations, and encountering obstacles that they never could have imagined let alone experienced in their suburban settings. These again were realities that they had to absorb for which nothing in the classroom prepared them. These realities were more akin to the typically "human" issues with which student affairs professionals deal on a daily basis and are therefore better suited to facilitate learning.

This collaborative model could be applied to other academic programs, such as student teaching. Unlike an internship, here the student leaves the college setting entirely for a period of time and works full time. Much of the learning that takes place in this experience is academic; that is, learning to apply pedagogical methods in real-life classroom settings. However, much of the learning is more personal, such as learning to manage one's time in new ways, working with co-teachers and others in the work environment, and processing new ways of being and relating as one moves from being a student to being a professional. An academic-student affairs team can be excellent mentors in walking a student through these difficulties, helping her/him see new relationships between the classroom and the workplace, clarifying priorities, and envisioning all the aspects and consequences of difficult choices.

Over the last couple of decades, faculty at all kinds of colleges and universities has been lamenting the lack of preparation of incoming college students. Apart from what is perceived as a general "dumbing-down" of secondary education so that what were once expected bases of knowledge and groups of learning skills are only fitfully present, there has also taken place an increased diversification of our student bodies. Not only do they know or not know things they should have learned; their trajectories of learning are all over the map. A simple case is that at one time we could reasonably assume that every college-bound student had probably read a Shakespearean play, perhaps two or three. Now, we need to be prepared for college students who do not even know Shakespeare. Where once college students came, by and large, from stable, middle-class families with two parents and a complement of siblings, now hybrid families are common and students bring life experiences to the classroom that were once unheard of.

For schools that are critically dependent on enrollments (and that in fact, is all of us), various responses have been devised. The most widespread is the Freshman Year experience in all its permutations. We have acknowledged that students need an "orientation" to a college experience, not just a two-to-three-day set of ice breakers, placement tests, residence hall klatches, or the like, but rather extensive, formal engagement of life and living issues so that the chances of success in college are enhanced. This blended "living-and-learning" is perhaps the quintessential arena in which faculty and student affairs personnel can best exemplify the team model of education.

I am sure that others can adduce similar and perhaps more germane cases to give form and substance to this new model of collaborative teambuilding and acting. In any case, I am convinced that the present status of the relationship of academic affairs and student affairs is not as productive as it could be. This is not to say that many colleges and universities won't continue to use the shopworn model of autonomous and competing units. Some may even opt for the newfangled "fusion" model. Neither in my opinion has a promising future. Neither certainly has any charm or effectiveness in advancing the unified purpose of collegiate life espoused in *Ex Corde Ecclesiae*: teaching students across the range of all their experience—intellectually, socially, emotionally, physically, and spiritually—for lifelong learning.

7

How a Student Affairs Team Helped Shape and Advance the Catholic Identity of a Catholic University: St. Mary's University, San Antonio, Texas

Andrew J. Hill

This case study centers on how a small team of student affairs professionals from St. Mary's University, San Antonio, Texas, returned from the 1999 Institute for Student Affairs at Catholic Colleges (ISACC) to help shape and advance their institution's conversation concerning its Catholic identity. Currently, this conversation is flourishing, due in part to the efforts of the St. Mary's ISACC team based upon their training at the 1999 institute. At that institute, the curriculum centered around two key documents in the Catholic intellectual tradition: *Gaudium et Spes* and *Ex Corde Ecclesiae*.

The institute employed a team approach to immerse groups of student affairs colleagues into a process of critical reading, reflection, and conversation about these key documents so that they could in turn implant the ISACC experience into their respective institutional cultures. This is precisely what happened for the St. Mary's ISACC team who experienced the institute as a vehicle for personal growth as well as professional development. The team consisted of three members of the student affairs staff, including the new vice president. The team returned to its institution with a plan to implant the spirit of ISACC into not only the student development division but into the university as a whole. The following is the story of how one ISACC team's transformative experience has emerged as a pivotal point in the history of Catholic identity for an entire university community.

St. Mary's University: A Catholic School, a Marianist Mission

St. Mary's University is an independent Catholic institution inspired by the Gospels and shaped by the rich tradition of the Society of Mary (Marianists). Founded and fostered as a community of faith for the advancement of the human family, the university gives Christian purpose and dynamism to a pursuit in which people of varied traditions and experiences unite in commitment to an educational venture, in dedication to a life of scholarship, and in the extension of service to society.

— Mission Statement

To understand the ISACC team's impact upon St. Mary's University, it is necessary to review briefly the institution's history, particularly those moments and events that have prompted a new, intentional conversation about the Catholic and Marianist nature of the university. Like many of the 235 Catholic colleges and universities in the United States, St. Mary's was founded by a religious order, the Society of Mary (Marianists), which today has 1,505 members. The Marianists founded the university in 1852 as an apostolic mission, infusing the institution with the Marianist spirit, or charism. For the next hundred years, as an apostolic mission, the Marianist character of the university was inseparable from the priests and brothers of the Society of Mary. The Marianists, through their active presence and lifestyle, were the sole shapers of the university's institutional culture.

> For most of its history, the culture of St. Mary's was determined by the presence of Marianists at all levels and in most of the principal roles. That culture was maintained primarily through a socialization process which formed personnel into the world of everyday life of the Marianists and their educational practice.[1]

The contemporary history of the university centers, in part, 1) on a destabilization of that inseparability of the identity of the university with the identity of the Society of Mary that flourished for over a century, and 2) the present, ongoing effort to sustain a Catholic and Marianist identity in the aftermath of this destabilization.

This historical shift of destabilization began after the first four decades of the twentieth century. From the 1920s through the 1940s, "the institution's values and purposes were implicit in the religious community whose members, formed in the Marianist tradition during studies both in American and Europe, made up entirely the board of trustees, the administration, and eighty percent of the faculty. In consequence, a consensus on basic policies was present as a kind of social given, and it is not surprising that chapters (legislative sessions) on 'education' and 'instruction' from the Constitutions of the Society of Mary provided the shared meanings and values from which the work was pursued."[2] However, in the period between the 1950s and the 1970s, the university experienced rapid growth, doubling in enrollment. This dramatic growth necessitated the hiring of many new lay faculty and staff, prompting the destabilization process as lay faculty began to outnumber Marianist faculty.

> By the end of the seventies, the Marianists were becoming aware . . . that the conditions that had assured the preeminence of Marianist values in the past would not be present in the future. Community up to this historical moment had been realized as lay men and women collaborators were acculturated into the University through their daily interaction with the Marianists. Community of this kind—as the principal "instrument of educational practice"—had been sustained by the presence of the Marianists throughout the University in administrative posts, in the chairs of many departments, and as a majority in the faculty . . . To many in the University then, it seemed the University as a Marianist apostolic mission was clearly at risk.[3]

In the 1980s, with these growing demographic changes at hand, intentional efforts were initiated to identify and describe core Marianist values that shaped the university. The priests and brothers created the Marianist Forum to tackle this task. The Marianists then extended the invitation to participate in the forum's dialogue to the wider university community. The central questions pursued were definitional ones: What is meant by the term *Marianist charism*? What are the core values of the Society of Mary that fostered the identity of the university? Though often difficult to sustain the dialogue, some common ground was reached, and while it remains true that consensus on certain issues has never emerged, some shared concepts developed. Through this dialogue, the university community, professed and lay members together, for the first time, began actively, intentionally, and explicitly to examine itself as a Marianist institution—the days of taking that identity for granted were over.

During these conversations in the 1980s, the university community intentionally recognized the Marianist spirit of the school as a gift of the Holy Spirit to the People of God. The charism was not "owned" by any individual or single group, not even the Society of Mary, but rather it was a set of shared meanings and values with a corresponding responsibility to sustain it as it sustained the university.

In the 1990s, the Marianist Forum moved from exploring definitional questions to ones of implementation: How are Marianist values shared with all members of the university community? Through what ways can the university shape the roles and activities of the members of the community to reflect Marianist values? How can the university maintain its Catholic and Marianist identity when the number of Marianists within the community is shrinking rapidly? With a base of knowledge surrounding the definitional questions, a new emphasis on praxis emerged in *The St. Mary's University Strategic Plan, 1995–2000*. This plan named the maintenance and promotion of the university's Catholic and Marianist character as the institution's chief strategic priority.

This strategic priority was rooted in the 1991 General Chapter of the Society of Mary's call for the "articulation of the common elements of the Marianist educational philosophy and spirit." This call culminated in the publication of the *Characteristics of Marianist Education* (for Marianist grammar and high schools) and the *Characteristics of Marianist Universities* (CMU). The CMU outlines five common characteristics that ideally permeate a Marianist institution of higher education:

- Education for formation in faith
- Education in a family spirit
- Education for service, justice, and peace
- Education for adaptation and change
- Provision of an integral quality education

As the Marianists and their lay collaborators dialogued and strategized about Catholic and Marianist identity, Pope John Paul II initiated a global dialogue about the nature of Catholic colleges and universities with the release of the apostolic constitution, *Ex Corde Ecclesiae*, the Vatican document that guides Catholic institutions of higher education. After much consultation with college presidents, and the rejection of several drafts between 1996 and 1998, the National Conference of Catholic Bishops approved a version of the application document of this constitution in 1999.

Internal and external conversations regarding *Ex Corde Ecclesiae* and the *Characteristics of Marianist Education* have served as the larger context within which St. Mary's has wrestled with the questions of its Catholic and Marianist identity. These two documents also served as a backdrop and a resource for a study undertaken at St. Mary's in late 1998. Although the campus environment reflected the long-standing values of the Society of Mary, the 1998 study and subsequent report quantified the changing demographics of the decline in professed Marianists working at the university. The day that so many had feared was at hand.

The 1998 Report: The Day of Reckoning

By the fall semester of 1998, the Marianist Forum was effectively facilitating ongoing conversations about the Catholic and Marianist character of the university with various parts of the university, including the student development division. Up to this time, the student development division had not specifically addressed the role and impact of these identity questions in student affairs work, due in part because at St. Mary's this division houses campus ministry whose good work reflected positively on the entire division. However, the structural arrangement also made it easy for other divisional areas to avoid addressing these questions directly.

The vice president for student development in 1998 was Ruth Rogers. Ms. Rogers actively worked with Rev. John Moder, S.M., the university's president at the time, the Marianist Forum, as well as others concerned with the identity question. She cultivated support throughout the division for a new, sustained initiative regarding the division's identity as an integral part of a Catholic and Marianist institution. For the first time, the student development division responded to the Marianist Forum's praxis question of "How do we sustain and integrate the Catholic tradition and the Marianist charism into the life of the university?" by constructing a process for examining how to answer the question within the work of student affairs. To begin, Ms. Rogers commissioned a study of the number of priests and brothers currently working at the university. The results were staggering.

The report noted that in the university's recent history (that is, the last thirty years), the challenge of maintaining institutional culture and identity along with the university's system for addressing this challenge had changed dramatically. As recently as the 1960s, the university had been an all-male school staffed primarily by professed religious. These professed religious, who occupied the vast majority of teaching and administrative positions, maintained institutional culture and identity through their presence and activities. However, while the university was still led in 1998 by a Marianist priest, Fr. Moder, the resignation of Rev. Charles H. Miller, S.M., as dean of the School of Humanities and Social Sciences, left no other members of the Society of Mary in the ranks of the senior administration for the first time in the university's history. In terms of the administrative structure, this meant the following:

- There were no vice presidents (5), academic deans (5), academic associate deans (3), dean of students (1), associate deans of students (2), or other associate deans (2) who were members of the Society of Mary.

- With the exception of the president, no member of the executive council was a member of the Society of Mary.

- No member of the academic council was a member of the Society of Mary.

- No member of the administration and finance council was a member of the Society of Mary.

Of the entire administrative staff across five university divisions, only two full-time employees were members of the Society of Mary, one each in student development and academic affairs. This was 0.5 percent of the total staff. However, one Marianist sister was the campus minister for the School of Law. Her inclusion raised the total number of professed, Marianist religious on the staff to three or 0.7 percent.

The representation of the society among the ranks of the faculty had also dramatically declined. Of the university's 240 full-time faculty members listed in the 1998 catalogs, 23 were members of the Society of Mary, or 9.6 percent. One Marianist sister was also listed but she was officially retired. Nevertheless, this figure was slightly misleading for the following reasons:

- Of the 23 members of the Society of Mary who were listed, four were officially retired.

- Of the 23 members of the Society of Mary who were listed, three were officially on leave.

- Of the 23 members of the Society of Mary who were listed, one was on sabbatical.

- Of the 23 members of the Society of Mary who were listed, one taught only part-time (one course per semester), due to administrative duties as president.

That left only 14 members of the Society of Mary who were full-time faculty members, lowering the percentage to 5.8 percent of the group. At the time, *these 14 members had an average age of 65*. Nevertheless, even using the original number of 23 plus 2 staff members, the members of the Society of Mary only make up a total working presence of 3.9 percent of the university community.

St. Mary's University, which had seen itself as an institution with a declining but critical mass of professed religious, realized that the changes for which it had been preparing were at hand. The professed religious were nearly gone from the university workforce. The 1998 report starkly detailed the reality of the declining number of Marianists while discussing generally the challenge of maintaining institutional culture and identity in this brave new world. It also offered several recommendations about how to engage the student development division in conversations and activities linked to the Marianist Forum's identity questions as well as those raised by the CMU and *Ex Corde*. The first recommendation of the report was that the student development division needed to send a team to the 1999 Institute for Student Affairs at Catholic Colleges.

The 1998 Report:
ISACC as a Response and Turning Point

In the spring semester of 1999, a new vice president for student development was named at St. Mary's University, and Katherine M. Sisoian took over the division. Ms. Sisoian was an internal candidate with many years of experience at St. Mary's, and she quickly applied that knowledge base, and her personal example, to the issue of building a Catholic and Marianist identity. In her articulation of a new, strategic plan for the division, she announced that the identity initiative begun by

Ruth Rogers would be carried forward, and that she would personally lead the team to the 1999 Institute for Student Affairs at Catholic Colleges (ISACC).

From July 27 to August 1, 1999, the St. Mary's University ISACC team attended the training institute at John Carroll University in Cleveland, Ohio. The goal of ISACC is to help create at Catholic colleges and universities an environment that is grounded in Catholic values, and although there are many groups within the modern Catholic university that can help to build such an environment, ISACC focused on how student affairs professionals could best contribute. The means for accomplishing this goal was the transformation of small teams of student affairs professionals from Catholic colleges.

The 1999 institute was the fourth and final annual meeting, and fifteen universities sent sixteen teams (John Carroll University sent two teams) through the weeklong training. Inspired and energized by this experience, the St. Mary's University ISACC team returned to campus to make plans for the fulfillment of the implementation goal, within student development as well as the entire university. The group quickly realized how fortuitous their timing had been, when that fall semester of 1999 the university turned an unprecedented corner.

On September 10, 1999, Rev. John Moder, S.M., Ph.D., the eleventh president of St. Mary's University, announced that he would not seek re-appointment for a fifth term. Fr. Moder's tenure, the longest continuous tenure of any St. Mary's president, had been a source of reassurance and stability for well over a decade. Charles L. Cotrell, Ph.D., vice president for academic affairs, assumed the duties of acting president on October 27, 1999. As of that date, Dr. Cotrell became the first person who was not a member of the Society of Mary to lead the university, leaving the top ranks of the university's administration devoid of Marianists.

This transition to the university's first lay president, which became official when Dr. Cotrell was named to the permanent position the following spring semester, meant a year of major changes. However, it was during this next year that the ISACC team returned to St. Mary's to implement their plan for training and transforming the student development division and the larger university community. During that first year, the team either hosted, participated in, or inspired and shaped the following events:

- During the fall 1999 semester, members of the ISACC team presented a three-part series on the history of the Catholic Church and the Society of Mary to the Student Development Council, the chief policy-making body for student affairs.

    | September 15, 1999 | History of the Marianists |
    | October 20, 1999 | Vatican Council II |
    | November 17, 1999 | The Journey of Community |

- On September 18, 1999, members of the ISACC team attended a national conference about *Ex Corde Ecclesiae*, at the Catholic University of America (CUA) in Washington, D.C. One of the main speakers, Gerard Bradley of the University of Notre Dame, spoke at St. Mary's University two days later, upon the request of the theology department.

- On October 15, 1999, the Marianist Forum and the faculty senate held their first joint convocation, and the topic was the CMU. The ISACC team was part of the planning committee for the event. In fact, one of the most productive things that the ISACC team did throughout the year was simply to help spark conversations between various stake-holders in the community.

- On November 18, 1999, Charles Cotrell, the university president, convened a meeting of the university's executive leadership and the theology department to discuss the potential impact of the National Conference of Catholic Bishops (NCCB) vote that resulted in the approval of the application document for *Ex Corde Ecclesiae*.

- On December 13, 1999, the ISACC team released *St. Mary's University: A Marianist Apostolic Mission*, which was described as a "A Reflection on the History and Future of the Marianist Charism at St. Mary's University: A Call to Gather in Retreat to Discuss Our Identity as a Catholic and Marianist University." The well-received proposal helped, in part, to launch a university retreat that was held two months later.

- On February 18, 2000, Charles Cotrell convened a daylong retreat of the university's executive leadership, along with a broad cross section of the faculty, to discuss the Catholic and Marianist identity of the university. The retreat, held at La Mansion del Rio Hotel (the former site of the university), was

led by Carol Quinn, the director of the North American Center
for Marianist Studies, in Dayton, Ohio.

- On June 25, 2000, a member of the ISACC team attended a
  special session of the annual meeting of the National Association of College and University Attorneys (NACUA) in Washington, D.C., regarding the civil law aspects of *Ex Corde
  Ecclesiae*.

- July 9–29, 2000, St. Mary's hosted the Marianist International
  Institute of Language. The participants, educators at Marianist
  schools from around the world, shared a common commitment
  to education in the Marianist tradition. Members of the ISACC
  team were instrumental in every aspect of this unique Marianist experience, including developing and teaching the course
  curriculum.

- July 20–23, 2000, St. Mary's University sent a large delegation
  (40+) to Assembly 2000: A Passion for Faith and Justice, the
  first joint assembly of the Marianist sisters, Society of Mary,
  and lay Marianists of North America. The event occurred at the
  University of Dayton in Dayton, Ohio. Again, members of the
  ISACC team were instrumental in organizing the university's
  participation.

- July 27–29, 2000, the ISACC team attended the first annual
  conference of the Association for Student Affairs at Catholic
  Colleges and Universities (ASACCU), at the Catholic University of America in Washington, D.C. St. Mary's University's
  ISACC team offered to host the 2001 conference. The proposal
  was enthusiastically accepted.

In addition to the initiatives of the ISACC team as a whole during this year, individual members have also brought back to their areas
of campus life a renewed sense of attention and enthusiasm for concerns about the Catholic and Marianist identity of the community. Put
simply, because of the ISACC experience, people in the division do
their jobs differently now. One small, practical example: Karen Johnson, the dean of students, changed the front cover of the new student
handbook for the 2000–2001 academic year. The cover displayed a portrait of the "Marianist Cross," a rendition of Mary at the foot of the
cross that graces the offices of the General Administration of the Society of Mary in Rome.

The ISACC Team Engaged and Leading the Discussion

Following their return from the first annual conference of the Association for Student Affairs at Catholic Colleges and Universities, the members of the ISACC team created their strategy for the future. With much of the groundwork laid within the division during the previous calendar year, the team was positioned to take leadership roles at the university level during the 2000–2001 academic year. The year was marked by much work around four key events:

- On July 17, 2000, the chairman of the board of trustees and the corporation of St. Mary's University charged President Cotrell to create and chair the "Task Force on an Enduring Marianist Presence and Perspective within St. Mary's University." The stated goal of the task force was to find ways to preserve and maintain the Marianist charism and character at the university. Three of the four members of the ISACC team were chosen to be on the small task force of a dozen lay and professed members of the university community that met throughout the academic year.

- On September 3, 2000, the founder of the Society of Mary, William Joseph Chaminade, was beatified in Vatican City by Pope John Paul II. This was a cause for celebration by Marianists around the globe, and the local observance at the university was a major event; two members of the ISACC team co-chaired the important and festive commemorations during November of 2000.

- Between June 5 and June 8, 2001, St. Mary's University hosted the 2001 Marianist Universities Meeting (MUM), the annual gathering of the three universities that are sponsored by the Society of Mary: Chaminade University, St. Mary's University, and the University of Dayton. One of the members of ISACC was a member of the planning team, and ISACC presented the opening session of the gathering.

- Between July 2 and 29, 2001, St. Mary's University hosted the second annual meeting of the Association for Student Affairs at Catholic Colleges and Universities. One of the members of the ISACC team was the conference chair, and the entire team helped to prepare and conduct this important annual meeting.

The three events related to the Catholic and Marianist identity of the university listed here, the beatification celebration, the annual MUM gathering, and the ASACCU conference—all required significant time to plan properly; the success of these programs has been rooted, in part, in the dedication and specialized training of the members of the ISACC team. However, the task force, with its strong student affairs voice, is most likely to have the greatest long-term impact on the university's institutional culture.

After meeting throughout the 2000–2001 academic year, the task force proposed a restructuring of the university through the creation of a new executive level position to address the university's Catholic and Marianist identity. The proposal calls for a Marianist to fill the new position, and for campus ministry and the Marianist Forum to report to this new officer. He or she will have full voice and vote on the executive council of the university, along with the vice presidents of the five existing divisions.

Such a significant structural change will dramatically affect the entire university and its institutional culture for years to come. It was a blessing that the student development division was so well prepared for this conversation, and that it was positioned to play the role that it did within the task force. This is perhaps the most significant and clearest example of the success of the ISACC team as a vehicle for education and transformation. At St. Mary's University, the ISACC team model was used to help build the Catholic and Marianist identity of the division, and in turn, of the university. By all accounts, it has been a successful run over the last two years.

However, even as the student development division reflects on the success of the recent past, it is planning to evolve beyond the ISACC team model, just as the institute (ISACC) is evolving into the professional association (ASACCU). Because of this impending evolution, the division is again explicitly asking: What will the future look like?

Fortunately, the university has been conducting a number of activities over the years, under the guidance of the Marianists, that directly and indirectly have helped to maintain its Catholic and Marianist character. The ISACC team's efforts to bring the conversation alive within student affairs reflects this long tradition. However, in the future it may be necessary to abandon the model in order to drive the message throughout all levels of the division. Although the ISACC team helped move the conversation from the university level to the divisional level, a new model may be needed for moving the conversation down to the departmental level.

At the same time as new efforts are being made to reach deeper within the division, it is also necessary to find new ways to help spread the conversation across campus. The Marianist Forum has led these pan-campus efforts by collaborating with an impressive array of individuals and groups, such as the faculty senate. However, because there are many stakeholders involved, there needs to be a clear understanding of their respective roles. For example, the Marianist Forum ideally operates independent of, but in conjunction with, both the theology department's academic role and the Office of Campus Ministry's sacramental, liturgical, and spiritual formation roles. In the spirit of collaboration, these three respect each other's autonomy while working together to build interdependence.

The student development division needs to stay engaged in these larger conversations, either as the ISACC team, or some new variation that can work effectively with the new executive officer. The division is significantly impacted by the proposed restructuring, especially with the movement of campus ministry to a new division, but the important consideration is adapting so that there is always a vehicle for defining, building, and sustaining the charism.

However, to ensure the continuation of the university's Catholic and Marianist identity, the conversation needs to be deepened within the division and expanded throughout the university. The explicit call at St. Mary's is to ensure that even greater efforts be made to draw everyone—faculty, staff, and students—into contributing in appropriate ways to the Catholic and Marianist character of the university. These steps have the potential to guarantee its sustenance. Like the priests and brothers who founded and shaped the school from its early days, the contemporary community must work hard, place their trust in one another, and keep their faith in God. If these things are done, the identity efforts, grounded in the ISACC team experience, will undoubtedly continue to prove successful in the future.

8

Redefining Student Affairs at a Catholic University: John Carroll University, Cleveland, Ohio

Patrick Rombalski

In 1997, John Carroll University, a midsized Catholic and Jesuit university located in the suburbs of Cleveland, Ohio, implemented an internal evaluation of the student life area with the goals of redefining student affairs work within the institution and establishing connections with faculty and other departments in order to maximize student learning and improve student services. This chapter explores this process and makes recommendations for application on other campuses.

Setting and Background

Leadership for the Division of Student Affairs at John Carroll is through the vice president for student affairs. Reporting to the vice president of student affairs is the dean of students, who supervises six functional areas which will be referred to as student life: commuter and off-campus affairs, counseling, health services, judicial affairs and orientation, residence life, and student activities. (Note: In 1997, two of these areas, both commuter/off-campus affairs and judicial affairs/orientation, did not exist.)

In the summer of 1997, all department heads met with the dean of students for a one-day conference to begin to articulate the process that would redefine the work within the student life areas. The dean had the advantage of being new to the university so there was certainly some openness and receptivity to a new direction. The meeting set forth the guidelines that all departments would pursue in reshaping their work to best complement the mission. The plan called for each department to develop its own mission statement; complete the self-evaluation provided by the Council for the Advancement of Standards in Higher Education (CAS); establish goals and objectives; and develop an assessment plan. The final product was to establish teams that would carry on the educational work of the division. These teams were either to work closely with or include members from the faculty, campus ministry, and student body.

Certainly new leadership is one reason to begin to assess divisional purpose and effectiveness. But what are others? Why else might a vice president, dean, or department head choose this path? After all, we are all quite busy with our work and consciously asking for more work might appear to be unwise. First, it is professionally healthy to evaluate the work of a division in light of the institution's mission. The question to ask is, Are we going in the direction we should be when considering the principles of the institution? Second, there have been several major developments over the past ten years in Catholic higher education that require deliberation. One approach would be to try to fit them or add them to the existing approach. The second approach, and the one John Carroll adopted, is to start from the beginning, to reevaluate the work of student affairs according to a set of principles and good practices, and then to make conscious choices about the work that staff will engage in at the institution. Thus, there needed to be lenses through which their work was to be considered. Four lenses were especially important in determining the direction taken by the John Carroll student life staff: the student learning movement, assessment, generational changes in students, and *Ex Corde Ecclesiae*. Each of these four represents a major shift in Catholic higher education over the past ten years.

Student learning movement. While student learning has always been a concern of educators, the Wingspread Group on Higher Education gave a new life to the discussion.[1] Since their report was written in 1993, higher education has seen a proliferation in the student learning movement. One concrete example is learning communities. Approximately 150 colleges and universities have developed some form of learning communities over the past ten years. In 1996, the American College Personnel Association (ACPA) published the *Student Learning Imperative: Implications for Student Affairs* to address the interrelatedness of learning and how learning should be a primary concern of student affairs administrators.[2] The question for administrators is how has this movement impacted the way we do our work on our campus. Have we appropriately adjusted our philosophy and thinking to recognize this initiative? Have we had ongoing dialogue with faculty on how we can work together to create communities of learning?

Assessment. Assessment initiatives begin on a campus for many different reasons. Some campuses begin only because it is part of an accreditation process. Student affairs divisions often develop an assessment plan in response to cost cutting and downsizing. Whatever the reason, there is no doubt that assessment and evaluation is a necessary and crucial part of the work of student affairs professionals. If student affairs administrators are to be seen as the experts on students, assessment serves as the vehicle for gathering the information. Otherwise, student information may appear anecdotal or not relevant. If a student affairs division does not have an assessment plan, then what serves as the foundation for change? What course are we on without systematically evaluating and assessing our students? How are programs determined without accurate information about the students on campus?

Generational changes in students. Simply put, students are changing. Whether or not we agree with what some of the literature is suggesting about our students, there is little doubt we need to approach this coming generation of students with our eyes open.[3] Assessment can certainly assist in the process of getting to know our students but it is no replacement for maintaining a one-on-one relationship with them. And, most important, we must guard against assumptions made about students, whether these assumptions precipitate from our own experiences, over generalized research conclusions, or from limited exposure. We must ask ourselves on a regular basis, What do we know about the students who are on our campus? What is it based upon? Do we have conversations with people across campus on what they have learned about students? What does the demographic makeup of our campus tell us? Do we allow and reward staff for building purposeful relationships with students? Do we reward staff for making a difference in the lives of students?

Ex Corde Ecclesiae. What the *Student Learning Imperative* has done for student learning discussions, *Ex Corde Ecclesiae* has done for conversations on Catholic identity. While most student affairs administrators may not be currently caught up in the web of conversation on the specifics of the document, *Ex Corde* has undoubtedly made us all aware of the ongoing questions about what role we have as administrators at Catholic universities. How are our programs and services different because we work at a Catholic university? Are our students aware of the implications of their attending a Catholic school? In determining the direction for our units, how mindful are we of our responsibilities as being part of a mission that is Catholic?

These four developments served as an impetus for change at John Carroll because we saw that our work did not represent the developments in each of these areas. While there certainly may be other areas of focus for student affairs professionals, the staff at John Carroll regarded these as being most relevant to our work with the students. Even before proceeding with the process described below, it was important to make sure the reasons for initiating it were grounded in the current developments in the field of Catholic higher education. Once there was confidence in the rationale, the movement from step to step in the evaluation process was fluid.

Process

The first step in the process for the student life department heads was to create a mission statement. The mission statement had to complement the university's mission statement as well as set forth the work of the functional area. Next, an internal method of evaluation was used that allowed all staff in the functional areas to participate in the discussion and evaluation. Third, based upon the results of the evaluation, goals and objectives were defined in order to reach compliance with CAS and with the departmental mission statement. Fourth, each department submitted an assessment plan to be used for external evaluation of programs and services. Last, one year later, groups were formed within the division in order to accomplish specific outcomes for students. Each of these steps and the philosophical and practical background is described below.

Mission

The only barometer in the university environment for measuring effectiveness is mission. Robert Birnbaum states, "There is no metric in higher education comparable to money in business, and no goal comparable to 'profits.'"[4] The mission statement then, especially a well-defined one, takes on increased gravity in institutions of higher education where typically the product of our work is so general that many people might claim to be working toward the good or the goal of the university when in reality they may very well be off track. Indeed, "As colleges and universities become more diverse, fragmented, specialized, and connected with other social systems, institutional missions do not become clearer; rather, they multiply and become sources of stress and conflict rather than integration."[5] While true at many levels of the institution, the problem can be remedied with ongoing discussion and collaborative decision making within each unit regarding the interpretation and the application of the mission. If an institution does not regularly visit the mission with all of the constituencies of the university, there could be an increase in the factions of understanding. This does not imply that regular discussions of mission are all that is required to overcome fragmentation. Certainly, leadership and vision within an institution are also critical components.

Catholic universities are no strangers to the call to live the mission and to identify more closely with mission. Indeed, since the mid 1960s when well-known Catholic universities began to increase the membership of laypeople on the boards of trustees, there has been a rise in mission activity on most campuses. This suggests the majority of Catholic universities wanted to reaffirm their identity amidst declining numbers of religious and clerics in key positions. Many Catholic universities have established "mission and identity" offices to symbolize a long-term commitment to the Catholic in Catholic university.

Jesuit universities have also heard the clarion call for mission identification. Jesuit universities, and other Catholic universities that are part of a particular religious order, have the additional responsibility of defining themselves as both Catholic and Jesuit. At least a few Jesuit universities have offices for mission and identity or even a person responsible for carrying out mission activity, such as lectures, retreats, and other educational or spiritual efforts aimed at aligning the university with its distinct character.

J. A. Appleyard, S.J., and Howard Gray, S.J., suggest that the conversation about mission over the past thirty years at Jesuit universities involves four models of education, the Control Model, the Professional Model, the Permissive Model, and the Mission Model.[6] The Mission Model attempts to address the causes of friction in an academic institution over mission. Many have dared but few have succeeded in completely bridging the drive for academic excellence, integrity, and freedom with the desire for a religious, spiritual, and ethical focus. Central to this model is the active dialogue on the different components of Catholic, Jesuit, and university. The interrelation of the three can begin to occur if we ask critical questions such as, "How do faith and learning mutually challenge and enrich each other?"[7]

In the field of student affairs, there also can be difficulty in exploring mission, especially at a Catholic university. Our staff members come from varying perspectives, many from different religious backgrounds. Second, there is often a misperception by some staff on the critical understandings and underpinnings of a Catholic university. Too often, "Catholic" is reduced to how the Church stands on one particular issue such as premarital sex. Some non-Catholics and Catholics, not properly oriented to a Catholic university, can quickly become disenfranchised if the only occasion for mission discussion is when a controversial program is refused. Each Catholic university defines itself distinctively on these issues. One good example in today's culture is the recognition of student groups who work against homophobia, commonly referred to as ally groups for gay, lesbian, and bisexual students. Where one campus is against the recognition and support of these groups, another is clearly for their advocacy. Often, then, what gets labeled as "Catholic" may sometimes be more accurately understood as how a particular institution chooses to define itself as Catholic. So, in the absence of proper orientation, education, and discussion, staff might begin to form less informed definitions of the Catholic mission of the university.

Both the National Association of Student Personnel Administrators (NASPA) and the American College Personnel Association (ACPA) promulgated *Principles of Good Practice in Student Affairs* in 1997.[8] As part of the introduction to the original document, the authors address mission: "The choice of student affairs educators is simple: We can pursue a course that engages us in the central mission of our institutions or retreat to the margins in the hope that we will avoid the inconvenience of change."[9] It is clear from a professional perspective within student affairs that we must look to the driving force, the mission, of the university. "For departments within student affairs to survive and prosper, they must identify how they contribute to the mission of the university."[10]

One significant internal hurdle to examining the university mission and writing departmental mission statements is what is referred to as a "heresy" by Dudley Woodward, Patrick Love, and Susan Komives: "Student affairs practitioners believe that rethinking or restructuring an organization, division, or department is not productive and is a waste of time."[11] If this suggestion is correct, even if only among some staff members, then undertaking the process of redefining mission is more than assigning tasks; it is also empowering people to believe that the process does make a difference.

The staff at John Carroll responded favorably to the conversation on mission due to the fact that some downsizing had just been completed and many staff members were looking for a renewed sense of direction. Their experience over the previous five years had left many of them wondering about their purpose. In addition, they had been without a dean for several months, so there was also a vacuum in leadership. Although there were the significant philosophical reasons to redefine the work in student life, it helped a great deal that the mood of staff members was also agreeable. In short, the time was right for a complete overhaul.

What cannot be underscored enough is that staff members need to be participative partners in writing mission statements. Since one of the reasons to even embark in this endeavor is to bring a connectedness within the division, all barriers must be removed that do not encourage collaboration. The dean or vice president must guard against people who would rather not have open dialogue. Several critical questions need to be asked: Do staff members feel connected and aligned to the university's mission? If individual departments do not have missions, what statement guides their work and what principles do they adhere to? If mission statements do exist, when was the last time they were reviewed? Are they still a living document in the work of the professional staff?

Although certainly not a new development in the field, one last consideration for each department was its current state of performance. Thus, performance was added as a consideration in addition to the university mission and the four lenses described above. While some departments were allowed to consider higher order issues related to learning, others were forced to secure their foundation before moving to higher ground. One such area was residence life. The university knew back in 1997 that there were many factors that needed improvement, as evidenced by the results of an internal residence satisfaction survey, not unlike the one currently used as one of the EBI benchmarking projects in collaboration with the Association of College and University Housing Officers (ACUHO). The survey revealed a high level of dissatisfaction with housing services. Therefore, residence life was asked to resolve this problem before moving into other areas of residence life and living and learning.

A critical question one might ask is, "Why does a university need mission statements at the departmental level or even the divisional level?" In reflecting back on writing the mission statement, the director of residence life said she felt it legitimized her work and provided a link between the university's global vision and the specific work of her department. In fact, she found drafting the statement to be a way of renewing her commitment to the profession and to her department. What was once a little-read document now became a document that was read and re-read in order to understand its implications for residence life.

The mission statement for residence life, stated below, reflects what was considered a "new" vision:

> The mission of the Office of Residence Life at John Carroll University is to advance the mission of the university by fostering an environment for academic success, facilitating the creation of a caring community which values each individual member, and promoting growth in human development through participation in both formal and informal programs. In addition, we strive to provide clean, well-maintained buildings with attention to utility, comfort and safety in order to structure environments conducive to the success of this unique living/learning experience.

This mission statement reflects the greater mission of the university and possesses key components important to the student affairs division at the time it was written. Before it was drafted, residence life lacked purpose and direction. Staff members found themselves immersed in the daily regiment without paying attention to what lay beyond the horizon. This initial document served as a foundation for the important work ahead.

A key component in writing the mission statement was to make every attempt to identify areas that were unique because of our Catholic heritage. The counseling center revised their mission statement to include the following:

> The mission of the John Carroll University Counseling Center is to facilitate the growth of our clients within the context of the whole person—enhancing their emotional, physical, spiritual, intellectual, social and occupational development.

It further states:

> The mission of the UCC [University Counseling Center] is consistent with that of the larger University in its concern for the human and spiritual developmental needs of our students along with a deep respect for the freedom and dignity of the whole person.

Therefore, the task of rewriting mission statements also allowed the student life staff to examine its work in light of the Catholic and Jesuit nature of the university. Each department took on the responsibility of researching the potential implications of being at a Catholic school and then incorporated these into the fabric of the process. No assumptions were made about the knowledge base of the staff, whether non-Catholic or Catholic. Therefore, all staff participated either in training, education, or discussions about the meaning of student affairs work at a Catholic university.

These ongoing conversations on the integration of student affairs work and the mission of a Catholic university served as the foundation for defining student life work at John Carroll. Some staff participated in the Institute for Student Affairs at Catholic Colleges (ISACC) that addressed a variety of important topics, such as the Catholic intellectual tradition, *Ex Corde Ecclesiae*, and Catholic moral teaching. Other staff attended the five-year Jesuit Association of Student Personnel Administrators (JASPA) conference that examined student affairs work in light of the Jesuit model of education. These two opportunities as well as several local conversations and conferences deepened the understanding and sensitivity of the staff to John Carroll's Catholic and Jesuit mission. Overall, these important learning experiences have molded the way the student life staff understood their work that, in turn, changed the nature of what we did.

Self-Evaluation, Goals, and Objectives

The process began with the mission statements in order to develop a sense of direction for each department before moving on to the next process of self-evaluation. Once each department wrote their mission statement and shared it with the student life staff, they proceeded to the next step, an internal evaluation. Many methods were explored to engage the staff and it was decided that CAS standards and guidelines would influence our work.[12] CAS ". . . was established nearly two decades ago to develop and promulgate standards of professional practice to guide practitioners in their institutions, especially in their work with college students."[13] It seemed, then, that the CAS standards were the natural step to take given the fact they were aimed as just the type of self-evaluation for which we were preparing. The CAS standards are a set of standards (essential criteria) and guidelines (desirable characteristics) for most every department within student affairs. The areas assessed by John Carroll University were campus activities, commuter programs, counseling services, housing programs, judicial programs, leadership programs, and student orientation.

The staff decided to embark in the self-study using most of the steps recommended by CAS.[14] The first step was to determine the type of self-study and who would be involved. This was particularly an important component for staff members, as they wanted it understood from the beginning that every staff person would be allowed to help shape each department. Next, each department had a meeting to discuss their standards as outlined by CAS. Once each area had a general understanding as to the meaning and intention of a standard, the staff (and students) then individually wrote their judgments. The department heads collected all of the individual statements and compiled a list according to each category. What proved to be one of the most rewarding pieces of the entire process is what occurred next, mainly the discussions within the departments. The standards ask for one mark regarding compliance; thus, people had to essentially agree as to the level of compliance or non-compliance. Since the CAS standards are so thorough, it allowed staff to have a comprehensive conversation on departmental effectiveness and direction. As part of the departmental evaluation, CAS calls for identifying and summarizing evidence, which is a way of documentation. Since the departments at John Carroll are relatively small, this evidence could be mostly examined without actually collecting each piece of information. The collective knowledge of each department made this phase go quickly and smoothly.

Next, each department identified discrepancies between the standards and the actual performance. In the estimation of the staff, there were only a very few instances where CAS did not have a standard identified that the department thought was important. But, there were certainly some aspects of the CAS standards not relevant, such as when another department at John Carroll held that responsibility. Although the standard applied to the whole institution, it did not apply to the department identified by CAS. Another integral conversation came when the departments prioritized the corrective actions to address any discrepancies. These actions developed into the goals and objectives that served as the action steps for a five-year plan.

Writing the mission statement and completing the self-evaluation were relatively easy compared to the task of integrating the recommendations (goals and objectives) into the daily actions of the department. Now that each department knew what the definition of their mission was and knew how they compared to the standards of the field, they asked, How could we align our department to begin the work of overcoming weaknesses, maintaining strengths, and addressing the mission? Some departments had to be warned to proceed slowly since too many goals could only overwhelm them and lead to a sense of failure. It was in the articulation of these realistic goals and objectives where the real work began to shape student life. For example, the Dean of

Students office began offering an international immersion trip to Duran, Ecuador, through a program called Rostro de Cristo. Prior to this decision, it was decided that the student life area was not offering viable programs that helped students broaden their worldview in a Catholic context of prayer and reflection. This realization of a pronounced weakness *vis-à-vis* the mission led to the development of a program that has grown substantially since its inception. Would this have happened without the commitment to mission, evaluation, and action? Perhaps not.

Goals and objectives, then, are the actual plan a department commits itself to in order to improve services and programs. These goals should be clear and easily understood, and the objectives oriented toward a specific action. Together, the goals and objectives act as a beacon for the department to follow. How do we know we are being successful? Are we making the difference we hoped when we set forth the plan? These questions are answered in the next section.

Assessment

M. Lee Upcraft and John H. Schuh's book, *Assessment in Student Affairs,* has served as an excellent resource to help the student life staff map out a plan for assessment and evaluation.[15] This by far was the most difficult part of the process for the staff. First, staff did not consider themselves experts in assessment. In fact, they had little to no experience or background in this area. Second, assessment is almost countercultural with staff members who work by moving from one task to the next in little time. Student life staff members at John Carroll were doers and did not value sitting for long periods of time reflecting back on programs or services. Last, we had a small staff with overcommitted calendars. Asking staff to take on a new way of thinking with little more assistance seemed unreasonable.

What seemed to win staff over was the argument that student affairs staff members should be the experts on campus on what students thought and who students were. The fact that staff could carve out a niche for themselves on campus was more empowering than first perceived. They saw the positive impact given by the dean of students on "Who Are Our Students?" to approximately 200 faculty early in the process. If assessment could assist all departments in gaining collaborative work opportunities with faculty, it seemed to be well worth everyone's time. In addition, staff realized the weakness in only having anecdotal information available on students. They knew they had to have better and more thorough information, especially in an academic setting.

Since 1997, the assessment movement has taken off to the point that it is a key function of the Dean of Students office. Regular publications are printed every two months entitled *What We Know about Our Students*. Each of these publications takes an in-depth look at one particular component of an assessment tool. For example, one of the spring 2001 issues looked specifically at what student attitudes were on the topic of diversity. *What We Know about Our Students* has become a conversation piece on campus among faculty, administrators, and students. What began as an assessment tool for a particular department has taken on a life of its own.

Upcraft and Schuh offer seven components to a comprehensive student affairs assessment model.[16] The first tracks users of student programs, services, and facilities. The second assesses student needs. The third is user satisfaction of our services, programs, and facilities. The fourth assesses campus environment and student culture. The fifth assesses the outcomes of the persons who use our programs, services, and facilities. The sixth shares assessment with comparable institutions, something many national tools now do. The seventh compares a particular institution's assessment with nationally accepted standards.

After carefully reviewing this model, it was decided that the Dean of Students office would initiate the assessment process for student life. Each department, based on the CAS findings, decided which components of the model were needed. Then, after consulting with universities with developed models, instruments were chosen to obtain the information needed for that department. For example, in residence life there was substantial concern over staffing and facilities. At that point, since there was no known instrument, the university used a survey developed by the dean of students. One year later, ACUHO instituted the resident satisfaction survey. Since the two surveys were very similar, the ACUHO resident satisfaction survey became the survey instrument.

After reviewing the needs of all the departments, student life also made the decision to begin the Higher Education Research Institute (HERI) College Student Survey and to participate in the National Survey on Student Engagement (NSSE). The point is that assessment tools were chosen based on the areas we wanted to assess; these assessment areas were all stated in the goals and objectives for a particular department. This may appear simple but it is, in fact, fundamental. It is easy to collect information but it is quite another thing to use the data in productive ways to improve services, programs, or facilities. It is true that not all of the information is used from the surveys, but an attempt is made to at least make the information available to the campus community. In addition, reviewing data on an ongoing and regular basis does produce unpredictable benefits.

As stated earlier, assessment is not always the most welcome process for professionals in student affairs. However, the student life staff members at John Carroll were able to reap the benefits of a planned and reasonable assessment plan. Collaboration with faculty and other offices became much easier because the departments had something substantive to share. After several presentations and the publication of *What We Know about Our Students*, more and more faculty and administrators began to call on student affairs staff members to visit classes, give presentations, and consult at meetings. Most important is the benefit seen by students in improved productivity through programs, services, and facilities. Residence hall renovations, student activity programming, leadership development, Greek life, and, yes, even classroom instruction have all been impacted by the assessment movement on our campus. While the current plan is certainly not as comprehensive as the model suggested by Upcraft and Schuh, it does contain all of the components important to the John Carroll University campus at this point in our history.

Educational Groups

An unpredicted outcome was the formation of cross-departmental educational groups. A cross-departmental group consisted of a group of professional staff and faculty who met in order to advance a particular educational area on the John Carroll campus. This emerged from the desire of the professional staff to see the quality of psychosocial programming rise to a new level. In the past, students had created many of these programs; thus, the student life staff wanted to create a more professional approach. Another motivation was that most of the programming up to that point had been done independently, sometimes without the knowledge of another department. In a small staff, this seemed inappropriate and not educationally sound.

The first task of creating these groups was to formulate a mission for the entire student life staff, something that represented all of the departments within student life. Once this was done, the ideas for the educational groups came easily. The topic areas for the first year were eating concerns and body image, healthy relationships and sexual assault, high-risk drinking prevention, and diversity. The idea was to form a think tank around a topic and meet regularly to discuss the university's progress. Faculty and campus ministry staff members were invited to participate in some of the groups in order to have a well-rounded approach to each topic. These groups were not given parameters within which to work, therefore, some of the programming from the committees reached across the entire campus.

The work of these groups developed into several other projects. For example, the high-risk drinking prevention team helped create a cross-constituent group of faculty, staff, administrators, parents, and alumni that now addresses the problem of alcohol use and abuse across the entire John Carroll community. The president commissioned the group, and we now await recommendations. The eating concerns group created a professional consulting team consisting of a dietician, a counselor, and a nurse who meet to discuss specific students who have eating disorders. These and many other programs would not have been created without the ingenuity of the staff members. Asking professionals to respond professionally has made all of the difference on our campus.

Conclusion

In preparation for this chapter, I met with several of my staff to review the last several years to gain their insights on what we had accomplished and where we had stumbled. The most significant critique was that some staff members wished that I had gone a little more slowly and that my desire to "fix" things was sometimes overwhelming in terms of workload. But the vast majority agreed that the whole process helped define the work of our area and that the reputation of the staff and the quality of their work had risen substantially. This is all due to a clear vision, stated outcomes, shared responsibility, and measured results. Surely, this work can be done on any campus.

I think we are like so many other Catholic colleges and universities with limited resources but a very resourceful staff. If it were not for the openness of my staff throughout these past few years, this would have been an arduous task. Instead, each of the steps described above has given birth to new programs, processes, services and, thankfully, resources.

9

Developing Policies to Address Controversial Issues: University of St. Thomas, Saint Paul, Minnesota

Gregory Roberts

Introduction

> Today, the human race is involved in a new stage of history. Profound and rapid changes are spreading by degrees around the whole world. Triggered by the intelligence and creative energies of man, these changes recoil upon him, upon his decisions and desires, both individual and collective, and upon his manner of thinking and acting with respect to things and to people. Hence we can already speak of a true cultural and social transformation, one which has repercussions on man's religious life as well.[1]

The changes written about in the above statement from the Vatican II document, *Gaudium et Spes*, have had significant ramifications on the Catholic college campus during the past forty years. Catholic colleges are composed of a diverse community of individuals who come from different social and cultural backgrounds and perspectives. It is the responsibility of the Catholic college or university to provide for an expression of this diversity while at the same time providing for the expression of the institution's Catholic identity. Difficulties often arise in balancing these priorities, and are often expressed in controversies surrounding organizations and speakers on campus. Having guidelines for addressing controversial issues on campus can be very helpful in assisting the community in managing these conflicts constructively.

This chapter will discuss the development of such guidelines at the University of St. Thomas, in Saint Paul, Minnesota, and how these guidelines have helped the St. Thomas community address specific controversies that have arisen. In 1994, the efforts of many members of the campus community culminated in a document designed to guide us through the difficulty of trying to accommodate all segments of the community while ensuring our students have the greatest opportunity for learning the truth about issues so commonly a part of today's young adult life. Perhaps such a statement can help other university communities address similar issues that arise on their campuses.

Developing the Statement

The impetus for this document was "multifaceted." According to Dr. Charles Keffer, provost of the University of St. Thomas in 1994, one impetus came from the board of trustees. In the summer of 1992, at the board's annual review of the performance of the university president, there was discussion about controversies on other Catholic college campuses, and "the question was raised as to whether St. Thomas had a policy statement related to these questions/issues/situations."[2] A second impetus, Dr. Keffer said, arose from members of our student affairs staff who were concerned about how they "could/should handle issues that were/are controversial from a Catholic perspective."[3] Dr. Keffer's role at the time was serving as the unofficial vice president for student affairs, due to the vacancy created by the departure of the incumbent.

Dr. Keffer said, "I was concerned about dealing with this subject in some direct and proactive way. It was agreed that a major training activity or professional development experience for student affairs staff should focus on this subject of controversial issues at St. Thomas."[4] As provost, Dr. Keffer also felt "there was a need for the university to make a public statement about what it means to be a university and a Catholic university because both our internal and external publics need to know what we think that means and because there are too many people associated with the university internally who feel that there is a repressive atmosphere about controversial issues."[5]

The student affairs retreat was held on the University of St. Thomas campus in Chaska, Minnesota, in late fall 1992. At this retreat, many members of the UST student affairs staff and Dr. Keffer participated in the creation of a draft policy statement that outlined how the university would address controversial issues and organizations. After more than five revisions, the draft statement was made public to the campus. This draft began to move through many groups on the campus and was revised, amended, and reviewed. These groups included faculty, staff, students, and select members of the clergy. Groups were identified by the provost and were self-selected through their participation in open forums.

As the new vice president for student affairs, I arrived on campus in February 1993, and the discussion continued. As was customary at that time, any topic of importance to the entire university community came before a campus-wide provost's forum, and such a forum was held in March 1993 to discuss the statement. According to student affairs staff, this was the most widely attended provost's forum in history.

Following the forum, the president's staff reviewed and contributed to the document, as did the priests of the university. The "final" draft was published in the university's official publication, *The Bulletin*, and subsequently was shared with the executive committee of the board of trustees and accepted by the full board at their spring meeting in 1994.

Bringing closure to this process and gaining the ultimate acceptance and approval of this statement was empowering and relieved a great deal of stress for the student affairs staffs. One challenge of our profession is being placed in the complex position of working with students and accepting them where they are while moving them where the institution believes they should be. Given the modern-day behavioral norms of young adults, they must be nurtured and challenged to gain a greater appreciation for the importance of each human person and the dignity and respect deserved by all, the basic teaching of the Church.

Since 1994, the statement has been used many times as a framework for discussion on various issues believed, by some, to be in "conflict" with the Church's teachings. All too often the "sexual" topics, such as premarital sex, homosexuality, condom use, AIDS, and other sexually transmitted diseases, are the sole focus of external attention. However, it is the process of moving a student from inward focus to community focus that integrates all aspects of our Catholic and Christian traditions. The end result is usually something any parent, pastor, or friend would find refreshing, responsible, and respectful. As stated in the mission of the University of St. Thomas, the goal of the educational process is to mold "an educated citizen, morally developed, with career competency and having intellectual curiosity." If we are to remain true to our mission of "educating morally developed citizens who have the skills to achieve competency in a career as well as being challenged with intellectual curiosity," it is imperative for students to be exposed to an academically sophisticated discussion on worldly topics. The statement established a level playing field on which this discussion may occur.

The impetus for creating the draft statement was multifaceted with deep roots in the university's past. More than one hundred years ago founder, Archbishop John Ireland, made several key statements:

- "Let Christians act out their religion and there is no more race problem."[6]

- "I know no color line, I will acknowledge none."[7]

- "No church is a fit temple of God where a man because of his color is made to occupy a corner."[8]

- "The colored students will be cared for in company with and in the same manner as the white students. They will be ordained at the same altar."[9]

It was highly uncommon for a person of national prominence such as Archbishop Ireland to speak so publicly about an issue so controversial during his time. He had a great appreciation for the struggle that Irish immigrants made to come to this country and the limitations and discrimination put upon his fellow Irishmen, making a "higher education" impossible for most. He went on to be one of the early individuals to speak out on civil rights in the United States.

Although the issues of the day were related to race, Archbishop Ireland's comments echo the ongoing complex challenges of our own time, including those surrounding race and gender. Our challenges today are equally complex, compounded with the continuation of issues around race and gender as well as sexual orientation, birth control, and human rights.

The post-Vatican II Catholic Church continues to issue modern-day statements that resonate with John Ireland's statements on issues of race. One such statement of recent vintage is taken from *Gaudium et Spes*, article 28, "Respect and love ought to be extended also to those who think or act differently than we do in social, political and even religious matters. In fact, the more deeply we come to understand their ways of thinking through such courtesy and love, the more easily will be able to enter into dialogue with them."[10]

Let's take a look at the actual statement as drafted primarily by the student affairs staff in conjunction with others on the campus:

The Statement

The final statement as approved by the board of trustees on May 19, 1994 is as follows:

The Addressing of Controversial Issues at the University of St. Thomas:

In its undergraduate programs the university is committed to the development of the student through a liberal arts education within the living Catholic tradition and through a high degree of personal attention in a spiritually and intellectually stimulating campus environment . . . In all of its academic programs and other educational enterprises the university is committed to meeting the diverse, changing needs of the community. . . . The university fosters in the student an energetic, thoughtful approach to the challenges of contemporary life [from the University of St. Thomas' Mission Statement].

The university's education program . . . strives to give a student a foundation for clear thinking and expression [from the University of St.Thomas Convictions]. ". . . it is evident that besides the teaching, research and services common to all universities, a Catholic university, by institutional commitment, brings to its task the inspiration and light of the Christian message. In a Catholic university, therefore, Catholic ideals, attitudes and principles penetrate and inform university activities in accordance with the proper nature and autonomy of these activities. In a word, being a university and Catholic, it must be both a community of scholars representing various branches of human knowledge and an academic institution in which Catholicism is vitally present and operative" [from *Ex Corde Ecclesiae*, Pope John Paul II's Apostolic Constitution on Catholic Universities, paragraph 14].

By its very nature, a university develops culture through its research, helps to transmit the local culture to each succeeding generation through its teaching and assists cultural activities through its educational services. It is open to all human experience and is ready to dialogue with and learn from any culture. A Catholic university shares in this, offering the rich experience of the Church's own culture. In addition, a Catholic university, aware that human culture is open to revelation and transcendence, is also a primary and privi-leged place for a fruitful dialogue between the Gospel and culture [from *Ex Corde Ecclesiae*, Pope John II's Apos-tolic Constitution on Catholic Universities, paragraph 13].

In its Mission Statement and supporting documents, the University of St. Thomas commits itself to its Catholic char-acter and to valuing the diversity of viewpoints reflective of a larger society. Diversity is complex, and is best achieved through intentional planning, listening, reflecting and inter-acting.

St. Thomas values its role as a diocesan, Catholic uni-versity. The university also recognizes and accepts its responsibility to respond to the dynamic tension that exists between the challenges of contemporary living and educat-ing within the living Catholic tradition.

The university exists as an environment, which not only allows but also encourages members of its community to ask questions and openly explore challenging ideas in their per-sonal search for truth. Open forums through which contro-versial issues may be addressed in a responsible and educative manner will be available. More important, the uni-versity will ensure that these dialogues occur in an arena free of fear of reproach or reprisal.

While the university cherishes free expression, it recog-nizes the difference between freedom of ideas and freedom of behavior. In discussion and debate, members and guests of the university community are expected to treat one another with respect and dignity.

Some of the implications of this statement are:

1. The University of St. Thomas is committed to open dia-logue about controversial issues.

2. The University will provide in-class and co-curricular opportunities for discussion and debate about contro-versial issues.

3. The University believes that public dialogue around challenging issues does not diminish its fundamental commitment as a Catholic university.

4. The University has the responsibility to educate mem-bers of this community about the beliefs and moral val-ues that make us Catholic.

5. The University will refuse official recognition to any group or organization which promotes a position contrary to the teachings of the Catholic Church.

6. The University welcomes to the campus students, faculty, and staff from diverse cultural, religious, and ethnic backgrounds. It values the perspectives they can provide on issues of common interest.

7. The University will strive to ensure that each member of this community receives respect.

8. The University employs individuals who are committed to the ideals stated in this document.

As one can see, the statement calls upon the richness of Catholic Church documents, reflection on the philosophical traditions and beliefs of our founder, Archbishop John Ireland, and the tenants of a quality liberal arts education. The statement is grounded in civil and respectful discussions that have been valuable in helping frame responses to controversial issues.

Implementation

The following section of this chapter will compare two case studies describing controversies at the University of St. Thomas. The first case study concerned hanging of a poster in the main library, depicting Margaret Sanger, a leader whose actions had a profound impact on the twentieth century through her views on family planning and the issues leading up to the creation of Planned Parenthood. This incident occurred prior to the development of the controversial issues statement.

The second controversy involved the selection and use of the book *Heaven's Coast* as the common text for all first-year English classes. This controversy occurred after the development of the controversial issues statement.

What makes the statement valuable to Catholic campuses facing controversial issues is that it calls upon the richness of known documents and beliefs from the university's Catholic heritage and founders. Often controversies on Catholic colleges and universities stem from critics' views that faculty, staff, and administration turn away from church teachings and historical precedents to deal with new challenges. The beauty of the controversial issues statement is that it is based on the university's mission statement, *Ex Corde Ecclesiae*, and founder John Ireland's valuing of diversity.

Case #1: Library Poster Series, Including Margaret Sanger
(a campus issue that occurred prior to the development of the controversial issues statement)

Prior to completion of the controversial issues statement in 1993, we were faced with an issue on campus. An auxiliary bishop raised concern about a poster series hanging in the university library that included a poster of Margaret Sanger, "the mother of Planned Parenthood." Many from the external community and some from the internal community felt it to be inappropriate for a Catholic university to display the image of someone known to advocate Planned Parenthood. Given the strong opinions about family planning methodology, the external community focused their intensity on the topic. It was extremely painful and hurtful to the campus and our extended family of alumni and friends. The realization that we are a university rather than a parish in the community was not clear to some. Unfortunately, the statement was not yet completed, and therefore we had no agreed-upon method to address issues of this magnitude with the internal or external community. Most of the faculty, administrators, and students felt the poster series should remain in the library, including the Sanger poster. The library subscribed to the poster series for several years. This particular series had been on display for quite some time before the issue was raised.

This issue was very divisive for some of our external constituents, and many threatened to abandon their support for the university. Several did, in fact, severe ties. Since there was no process for handling the situation, it remained the sole responsibility of the president of the university to decide whether the posters should be removed. Many saw this as a critical decision point in his tenure—at that point he was only in the first three years of his presidency. Faculty felt the issue to be one of academic freedom, while community members saw the issue to be one of abandoning the true Catholic spirit of the institution. However, true to the legacy of Archbishop Ireland, the president, Rev. Dennis Dease, decided that, "the posters are meant to be thought-provoking and represent people whose actions have had a lasting impact on society."[11] He went on to defend the library's right to display all the posters, which included such historical figures as Martin Luther King, Jr., and Mahatma Gandhi.

Despite the controversy, there was much positive that came from the poster debate, even without the benefit of the statement. As a liberal arts, values-centered university, the community realized the following benefits as a result of the controversy:

1. Many students had never heard of Margaret Sanger and thus sought out reading materials about her, to make up their own minds as to the wisdom of having the advocate for Planned Parenthood's poster up on campus.

2. Conversations took place among faculty and students about Sanger's work and the impact on society today, as well as about the potential conflict with church teachings on procreation.

3. This was a "teachable moment" for students to learn more about the Church's teachings on procreation and birth control. Without an "issue," students tend to confine themselves to classroom assignments, but in this case the discussion went beyond the classroom.

4. Student affairs staff was able to join with faculty in discussing issues surfacing as a result of the controversy. The controversy elevated knowledge about abortion, family planning, and contraceptives.

Following this incident, it became even more evident that an intellectual as well as a spiritual community should have a deliberate and welcoming process in place to engage scholarly and practical implications of issues that emerge from time to time. The fact that an issue is controversial should have no bearing on the relevance or ability for the community to discuss. A statement would have provided structure and commonality of purpose for the campus. A statement that was created with widespread input would have moved the sensitive topic through an educational process with more understanding of the role of a university.

Case #2: Common Text, *Heaven's Coast*
(a campus issue following the development of the statement)

The controversial issues statement was a wonderful guide for the campus as we struggled with criticism received from the external community about the common text selected by the English department. The English department each year selects one common text that is taught in all sections of freshman English, allowing for cross section discussions and public lectures and seminars. Other books are studied throughout the semester as well, but can vary depending on the selections of individual faculty members. Since 1986, the department had selected a common text based on literary merit and portrayals of racial, cultural, economic, and ethnic diversity. Past selections have included Toni Morrison's Pulitzer Prize-winning *Beloved*, Carlos Fuentes's *Old Gringo*, and Maxine Hong Kingston's *Woman Warrior*.

In 1997, the department selected *Heaven's Coast* for use in the fall semester of 1998. *Heaven's Coast* marked the first time a common text dealt with issues of sexual orientation, and it also marked the first time the university had been so publicly criticized by members of the external community and questions raised by members of the board of trustees. The book was written by critically acclaimed poet Mark Doty, a faculty member at the University of Houston and recipient of numerous national and international prizes for his writing. In *Heaven's Coast*, he writes about the loss of his partner Wally Roberts to AIDS and of his close friend Lynda Hull in a car accident within two months of each other.

Rather than having the president decide, as had happened with the poster incident, the community was called upon to find ways to address the controversy prior to the fall 1998 semester in which the book was to be used. For one year the community debated whether the text would be appropriate. There were forums and seminars for those who worked more directly with first-year students, including faculty advisors, residence hall staff, and first-year experience faculty and staff. In addition, faculty development's "Diverse Voices in the Classroom" series did an excellent job of hosting discussions on the book, on how to teach a controversial text, and on how to address student reactions. In the end, the choice of *Heaven's Coast* was supported, but the campus conversation continued.

Members of the student affairs staff were active participants in the discussions, educational forums, and seminars. In addition, there were ongoing opportunities to process and discuss with students their thoughts and reactions in the residence halls. All members of the student affairs staff were encouraged to read the book; several "coffee and book review" sessions were conducted. The staff also provided "coping with grief" sessions and grief counseling to persons for whom the controversy triggered personal reactions. As with most invited guest speakers to our campus, we hosted multiple dinners with students and faculty. There were open lecture presentations to the entire community as well as visits to classrooms and various presentations.

Once again, the outcome was a very positive intellectual and spiritual experience for the campus community and resulted in the following:

1. When the students read *Heaven's Coast*, they also received and discussed in many class sections several Catholic Church documents regarding homosexuality. These included the page in the Catholic Catechism that addresses "Chastity and Homosexuality," the Vatican Congregation for the Doctrine of the Faith's 1986 letter on "The Pastoral Care of Homosexual Persons," and portions of two pastoral letters from the U.S. National Conference of Catholic Bishops: the 1997 "Always Our Children: Pastoral Message to Parents of Homosexual Children and Suggestions for Pastoral Ministers" and the 1989 "Called to Compassion and Responsibility: A Response to the HIV/AIDS Crisis."

2. The experience offered an opportunity to engage in open dialogue about issues of coping with grief, homosexuality, and caring for a loved one. This process also provided a forum for the University of St. Thomas to share Catholic values and views on these issues. At the same time, we were able to embrace real concerns facing anyone who is dying, especially the belief that trials and tribulations experienced by the caretakers should not be minimized. The importance of the dignity and worth of each person remain paramount.

3. It was the first time nearly everyone on campus read the same book and discussed it. There were book discussion groups and conversations everywhere. Students wanted to read the book for themselves, rather than simply accepting a critic's response.

4. The experience offered the opportunity to conduct open and heated discussions with respect and civility for all involved, while at the same time never losing sight of the real issues of the sanctity of life and the human person.

5. The experience "alerted" the archbishop and the president of the potential conflict of opinion on what is or can be "academic freedom" and/or what is appropriate to be examined in a liberal arts-based university that is Catholic in tradition and practice. This notification with supporting documentation occurred before the "controversy" erupted, thus making for a much more wholesome understanding of the issues appropriate for debate and dialogue on a Catholic university campus.

The selection of *Heaven's Coast* presented a healthy dialogue for an educational institution that is charged with challenging the mind, cultivating the soul, and energizing the spirit. Not an easy task, and not one that comes without tension, but something that is worth the effort, nevertheless.

Conclusion

The ability to address controversial thoughts and beliefs is a major tenet of a quality institution of higher education. The additional ability of a faith-based institution is to be able to weave through the very essence of every thought, the belief in the human person, and the dignity and respect due all. The conflict, the creation, and the use of the controversial issues statement at the University of St. Thomas is just one way to create a joint understanding as to how we will remain true to our Catholic intellectual tradition and grow as a Catholic university. The statement shows how it is possible to address controversial issues, not banish them. We have no desire to hide from the issues that pose challenge and create tension to our academic community and the community at large.

It is my hope that this chapter has been meaningful to other Catholic institutions planning their own campus approach to addressing controversial issues. This is but one example, but one that I feel continues to keep us true to our heritage, true to our need to approach complex issues of the day, and true to the commitment to educate our students on all topics. If nothing else, this chapter points to the importance of engaging the entire community in the definition of expectations, as university communities address conflict and expectations from multiple sources.

The end result for the University of St. Thomas has been a more inclusive environment for learning. In creating this environment, the hallmarks for Christianity are haled: peace, justice, respect, dignity, and civility.

10

Embracing Both Diversity and Catholic Identity: Spalding University, Louisville, Kentucky

Deborah L. Ford

Introduction

This chapter tells the story of how Spalding University provides a unifying Catholic experience while celebrating diversity. The first part of the chapter will relate how the student affairs staff assesses spiritual needs and strives to meet those needs. Then specific examples that show how Spalding University maintains Catholic identity, celebrates diversity, and meets student spiritual needs will be shared. The final section will present the challenges we face and how we are addressing them.

Spalding University, founded by the Sisters of Charity of Nazareth in 1814, is an independent, liberal arts university located in the heart of Louisville, Kentucky. There are 850 undergraduates in the traditional weekday program, 250 undergraduates in the weekend/evening program, and 500 graduate students in masters and doctoral programs. Currently, there are 150 students from 38 countries including, the United States, Belize, Ireland, Cyprus, Mozambique, Israel, Taiwan, Canada, India, Ghana, Bosnia, Moldova, and Jordan enrolled in degree programs. Since 1994, the university has strived to internationalize the campus by enrolling an increasing number of students from abroad and by offering study abroad programs for American students. These students represent many faiths and denominations, including Apostolic,

Native American, Orthodox, Seventh Day Adventist, Catholic, Baptist, Lutheran, Episcopalian, Jewish, Muslim, and Hindu. The diversity within such a small group of students creates many challenges in delivering services and offering programs. This diversity also creates opportunities for enhanced levels of awareness, understanding, and collaboration in meeting the co-curricular needs, especially spiritual needs, of the student body.

The mission of Spalding University states: "Spalding University is a diverse community of learners dedicated to meeting the needs of the times in the tradition of the Sisters of Charity of Nazareth through quality undergraduate and graduate liberal and professional studies, grounded in spiritual values, with emphasis on service and the promotion of peace and justice." This mission serves as a focus for everyone on the Spalding University campus and is a central part of both the curriculum and co-curriculum.

With the mission in mind, a task force developed a strategic plan to guide Spalding University into the new century. In relation to this chapter, the task force developed a goal to foster an understanding of spiritual values integral to Spalding's vision as a Catholic university. For the purpose of the university, the task force defined *spiritual* as being a fundamental and universal dimension of what it means to be human—to search for a sense of meaning, purpose, and values beyond self. Spiritual values in the educational context includes an open-minded search for truth, the dignity and rights of all persons, the value of community, and a life ethic developed through disciplined study. How does Spalding University embrace its Catholic identity while living out its mission and striving to nourish these spiritual needs in such a diverse student body?

Assessing Spiritual Needs and Meeting Needs

Defining and maintaining Catholic identity is a challenge for Spalding University and other Catholic colleges. Since campus ministry is a part of student affairs, Spalding University must define Catholic identity and nurture it as part of its student affairs programs. Articles from *The Record, The Gospel on Campus*, and *Current Issues in Catholic Higher Education*, author research, and personal experiences serve as the points of reference for the student affairs staff at Spalding University in defining and maintaining Catholic identity.

For example, in a fall issue of the *The Record*, Father Eugene Hemrick noted seven questions that help us at Spalding University assess how well we fulfill our Catholic identity:[1] The chart on page 174 identifies the questions used to assess our effectiveness in fulfilling our mission. To improve the value of these questions we determined what units/functions in student affairs had responsibility for addressing these areas. We believe that all units within student affairs have a role to play in embracing Catholic identity, celebrating diversity, and meeting student spiritual needs.

We use this chart during our annual planning retreats to assess current effectiveness in each area and also use it for future planning. Although the current campus minister has only been a part of the staff for less than a year, she is using these questions as a guide to develop and refine the current spiritual development program.

In addition to the chart noted above, we have used other methods to determine student spiritual needs. In 1996, a doctoral student from the University of Louisville, Leanne Newman, completed a study about the faith development of new students at Spalding University. This was the first study focused on faith development in over ten years with Spalding University students. The staff welcomed the study since most of our time is spent on program development and implementation as opposed to comprehensive studies like this one. Most of the previous research completed by the student affairs staff was in the form of needs assessments. Some of the needs reported by students on surveys and in the focus groups included questions about faith, spiritual and personal development, relationships, faith sharing, support groups, service opportunities, Bible study, and community building.

Many of these issues are not surprising since they often surface for college students as they gain an enriched understanding of their own faith development. James Fowler noted that faith development "is so fundamental that not all of us can live well for very long without it, so universal that when we move beneath the symbols, rituals, and ethical patterns that express it, faith is recognizably the same phenomenon in Christians, Marxists, Hindus, and Dinka, yet it is so infinitely varied that each person's faith is unique."[2] We recognize that Spalding University students bring these and many other needs to campus and expect some of these needs to be met within the context of Catholic identity. The entire student affairs staff agrees with Newman's assessment that the spiritual development of college students is a vast arena

Questions to Assess Catholic Identity	Areas of Focus within Student Affairs
Are students encouraged to think for themselves as having a calling in life, invited to see that God wants them to employ their education on humanity's behalf?	• Career Services • Values Clarification • Leadership Programs • Campus Ministry • New Student Programs • Service Learning
How committed is the college to encouraging students to volunteer and to develop habits of service?	• Service Learning • Reflection
Are students encouraged to reflect on the connection between service and the development of moral character?	• Mentoring • Reflection • Leadership Development • Values Clarification • Residence Life
Are students helped to realize that combining moral character with an astute mind is not only the key to maturity and fulfillment but also the best way to spread goodness into our culture?	• Leadership Development • Connections to Core Curriculum • Residence Life • Campus Ministry
How many spiritual activities are offered on campus?	• Campus Ministry • Student Activities • Leadership Development • Residence Life
Do students have access to the sacrament of reconciliation, the Eucharist, and retreats?	• Campus Ministry • Leadership Development
Are they given spiritual guidance on personal problems and offered opportunities to explore questions they have about their faith?* *See footnote 1.	• Residence Life • Student Counseling Center • Campus Ministry • Pastoral Counseling • Career Services • Leadership Development

of possibilities and potential waiting to be tapped.[3] As a group we are working to tap into this potential.

Newman's research question was, "With such an overt commitment to spiritual values, the question remains as to how the institution is incorporating such a broad statement into the practical daily life of the university. How are students experiencing this commitment to the development of spiritual values and what do they interpret those to be?"[4] Newman's study helped us to examine how students' experiences within the first few weeks on campus shaped their thoughts and feelings with regard to the spiritual aspect of their lives.[5] The entire staff found the results of the study useful in understanding the needs of students and for developing programs and services to meet those needs.

For example, in her study, Newman asked students to define spiritual values. All of the respondents answered this question, and, even though the responses varied, it showed that students understood spiritual values to be a part of their inner selves and values that guide moral decisions. Some of the student responses included, "Spiritual values is recognizing that there is something beyond the human drive."[6] and "Spiritual values are the values and convictions that you hold true to yourself because of your faith and spirituality. It may not be the convictions that other people have, but they are your own because to you something is right and something is wrong because of your faith."[7] Following this study, we reviewed and revised our campus ministry publications to include a mission for campus ministry and definitions for spiritual values in the context of our program offerings. The current mission of the campus ministry program at Spalding University states: "Grounded in the Spirit of Christ and the Catholic tradition of the Sisters of Charity of Nazareth, Campus Ministry at Spalding University promotes a community rooted in spiritual values with an emphasis on holistic personal development, community formation, interfaith sharing, cultural sensitivity, service, and the promotion of peace and justice." As noted in the campus ministry brochure, "each day God offers us a call, a call to faith and services. Campus Ministry seeks to provide opportunities for students, faculty, and staff from all denominations to hear the call and respond through worship, student organizations, retreats, special events, spiritual and vocational resources, and service learning."

Another question sought to understand how students observed spiritual values in action at Spalding. A small group of students did not see anything as having spiritual values at Spalding, while other students tied spiritual values and development to living on campus, the supportive environment, and to the classroom experience. One student stated,

"Overall it's the backbone of everything. It's like they want to provide service and a loving environment and education based in the spiritual foundation. You don't really see it, but you know it is there."[8] Overall, responses to this question were alarming to the student affairs staff, especially the campus minister. The staff analyzed the results and discussed the reasons for the responses. At the time of the survey, the students had been on campus for less than two months and may not have been exposed to the colleague's spiritual development activities. Also, in 1996, we only had one chapel space on campus, which was located in a building used primarily for upper-division courses. The entire staff agreed that we needed to be more intentional about spiritual development and spiritual values. The following fall we adopted "Catch the Spirit" theme for our programming and publications. Our intent for "Catch the Spirit" was both for Spalding's spirit and individual spirituality.

In addition to assessing how students saw spiritual values in action on campus, Newman asked students to comment on any changes in their faith development during the first few weeks of the semester. Some of the students noted a closer relationship to God as a result of being away from home. One student stated, "When I first came here I got homesick but I felt like God was still with me. I have to rely on God more. I know my parents do not know what I am doing, but God does."[9]

Unfortunately, Newman's 1996 study of faith development of new-to-college students has not been replicated to show the significance of change on campus, but the student affairs staff continues to assess needs. The campus minister works with a committee of students, faculty, staff, and administrators to assess student needs through focus groups, surveys, and individual consultation. At the beginning of each academic year, students who live on campus complete surveys to determine interest in activities that support the development of the whole person. The director of residence life shares the survey results with the entire student affairs staff. In addition, students enrolled in the freshman seminar, "Successful Student Strategies," are asked about interests and needs, and this information also is shared with the staff.

This past spring the new campus minister invited a group of students to participate in a focus group so she could introduce herself and get to know students on a more individual basis. Her goal was to increase participation in campus ministry events and to get new ideas for faith and spiritual development. Several of the students who participated were from abroad and expressed interest in gaining a better understanding of their own spirituality. The students also noted interest in ecumenical prayer gatherings as a way of celebrating diversity.

In order to enhance our spiritual development programming and improve our understanding of Catholic identity and student affairs, three student affairs staff members attended the Institute for Student Affairs at Catholic Colleges (ISACC). While attending the institute, we networked with student affairs practitioners from other campuses and learned more about Catholic tradition and how to embrace it on our campus. Overall the institute was rewarding and worthwhile and provided a place for the team to develop a plan to incorporate new ideas into practice. During the institute we created a spiritual development mission and goals that have served as a basis for planning spiritual development programs over the past several years and functioned as an effective way to meet the diverse spiritual needs of the community.

The mission created for spiritual development was, "We will act as a leaven in our diverse community of learners by responding to the needs of the times through the promotion and integration of spiritual values in our programming and personal and professional interactions." The group also developed five goals during the institute. The first goal, to enhance mission effectiveness through the promotion and integration of spiritual values throughout university life with an emphasis on holistic education, is hard to measure and continues to be a focus for the student affairs staff. We developed a leadership program that concentrates on holistic education and includes a component related to spiritual values.

This program, named the Egan Leadership Medallion Program in honor of Spalding University's former president, Dr. Eileen Egan, SCN, provides opportunities for students to increase personal development and career development skills as well as serve others. Members of the program receive skills and opportunities that assist them as they leave Spalding, providing opportunities for skill development through four components: career development, service, problem solving, and personal development. Upon completion of the program, participants are prepared to serve effectively in formal and informal leadership roles in a range of settings; have the skills and experiences necessary to enter graduate school or the job market with a competitive edge; understand the value of community involvement and service; exercise problem-solving skills and make decisions based on moral judgment in the practice of daily life; and understand that leadership is a combination of the ability to communicate with others, the use of critical thinking skills, exerting ethical behavior, and accepting cultural and individual differences between people. Students who successfully complete the Spalding University Leadership Medallion Program are recognized at the annual student appreciation dinner and receive a medallion to be worn during graduation.

In addition to the medallion program, all students are invited to attend programs offered as part of the Egan Leadership Series. The goal of the series is to inspire Spalding University students to explore their individual role as leaders in our community, to raise their awareness of civic involvement and responsibility, and to further enhance their academic experience. Some of the programs offered during the past few years include "Developing Twenty-First Century Leadership Qualities," "Communicating Across Cultures," "Character Wanted," and "Leadership and Character Day."

The second goal, to provide leadership to the campus in the further development and understanding of our Catholic identity, has been accomplished over the past several years. The campus minister serves as the chair of the faculty-appointed campus ministry committee, and serves as a member of the Strategic Planning Task Force on Spiritual Values. We, in student affairs, believe that if student spiritual needs are going to be assessed and addressed, then we must provide continued leadership for the entire campus community.

While attending ISACC we learned that several campuses had created chapel spaces in their residence halls. Thus, another goal was to develop a chapel space in our residence hall. With the residential population growing and the diversity changing, we created a plan to develop a chapel there. We also hoped the chapel space would expose new-to-college students to spiritual development opportunities earlier in the semester. The chapel space was created and is used for Sunday evening liturgy, Bible study, and individual prayer and reflection.

We accomplished the fourth goal, to provide a professional development in-service for the student affairs staff on the integration of *Ex Corde Ecclesiae* and the *Student Learning Imperative*, immediately following the institute. The campus minister and I planned a program for the student affairs team that introduced everyone to the context of *Ex Corde Ecclesiae* and how it was integrated with the newly published *Student Learning Imperative*.

The final goal from our experience at the ISACC institute was to collaborate with the pastoral ministry program to assess current utilization of spiritual symbols and artwork and to develop a plan to enhance such utilization. In some areas of the Spalding campus, it is obvious that you are on a Catholic campus, but this is not consistent in all areas. The campus minister had worked with the pastoral ministry program to identify current utilization of spiritual symbols and artwork, but a plan had not been developed to enhance utilization. This is an important goal to accomplish for the Spalding campus and one that needs urgent attention. With such a diverse community, spiritual symbols and artwork can convey many messages to different audiences at the same time. The student affairs team believes that passive programming, such as symbols, artwork, and publications, can only enhance spiritual development opportunities on campus and show how we celebrate our diversity.

Examples of How Spalding University Embraces Catholic Identity, Celebrates Diversity, and Meets Student Spiritual Needs

Spalding University is similar to many other Catholic colleges in that we offer a wide array of programs and services to embrace Catholic identity and meet student spiritual needs. We believe, though, that some of our programs are unique.

One of the most significant unifying Catholic experiences for all members of the Spalding community is the connection with the founder and founding order of the university. Members of the founding order, the Sisters of Charity of Nazareth, still serve at the institution as trustees, faculty, and administrators. Students gain a stronger sense of the Catholic history of the campus when being taught by one of the sisters. One student noted in Newman's research, "Everybody knows there are a lot of nuns still teaching in the school. So they know that in certain classes with certain teachers, they know they will get more of a religious aspect into the class."[10]

The most symbolic heroine of Spalding University is Mother Catherine Spalding, the founder of the Sisters of Charity of Nazareth and of Spalding University. During campus visits and new student programs, students are told about Mother Catherine and her contributions to the college. For several years, at the new student orientation sessions, students were taken to the founding site of Spalding University in Nazareth, Kentucky. During the visit, the campus minister led students on a tour and discussed the background of Mother Catherine and other prominent sisters in Spalding's history. The spirit of Mother Catherine is still alive on the campus. Her commitment to education and serving the needs of others is at the forefront of the university's mission and, specifically, the goals of the student affairs team. To illustrate the significance of her role, we have a plaque with her picture hanging in the front hall of the university administration building and one in the Dean of Students office.

Spiritual Development in the Residence Hall

Since the residence hall is home to students from thirty-eight countries, the students celebrate holidays, religious and secular, from around the world. Examples include displaying both traditional Christian symbols of a tree and nativity scene during Christmas as well as a menorah to celebrate Hanukah. Toward the end of the year, the Muslim students participate in Ramadan, as the staff and students offer support. In the spring, the Catholic and Greek Orthodox students celebrate Easter, while Jewish students participate in Passover. All of these religious holidays are noted in the student handbook and calendar to ensure that the campus community knows of religious celebrations from around the world.

Campus Ministry

Like many other campuses, Spalding University supports several religious groups and student organizations that enhance spiritual development through cultural understanding. These include the Campus Ministry Committee, Campus Crusade for Christ, Christian Student Fellowship, Fellowship of Christian Athletes, and the International Club. Although these groups are not unique to Spalding, one group, in particular, the International Club, offers distinct programs in celebrating spiritual diversity on the Spalding campus.

The International Club provides an exchange of ideas and cultural exploration opportunities for Spalding's international student population and American-born students. Activities include internationally themed meals and social functions, discussions, and guest speakers on a variety of topics related to cultural and global concerns. At the annual International Day and Banquet, an ecumenical prayer service is held to recognize the many faiths represented on campus. Students offer prayers and songs of peace and thanksgiving in their native languages.

A powerful program planned by the International Club that inspired both students and staff was the Peace Panel. During this program students from Israel, Bosnia, the former Yugoslavia, and Cyprus discussed their experiences of life in a war zone and their perspective of peace. Several students and staff members attended the program to learn more about the home countries of Spalding students and to gain a better awareness of conflicts from around the world. One staff member noted, "This was the best program I have ever attended at Spalding University. It helped me to understand issues from around the world, and to empathize with our students."

Service Learning

Another important part of meeting spiritual needs, celebrating diversity, and maintaining Catholic identity is through our service-learning program. This program enables all students to learn in a different way, a way that embodies Spalding's core curriculum as expressed in the habits of heart and mind. Through intentional service and critical reflection, students develop holistic values and skills, enhance their social awareness, improve school-to-work opportunities, and explore potential careers. Students value their service-learning experiences. Many have noted that it is different from learning in a classroom setting because they have complete ownership of their projects and thus the desire to learn comes from deep within.

Service learning provides more opportunities for students and staff to engage in concrete activities that challenge and/or confirm classroom theory, thereby improving education. In addition, the international service-learning projects provide students with hands-on experiences of life in a new culture. Examples of successful service-learning projects in the curriculum and co-curriculum include:

- *Art:* Students designed and constructed a playground for visually impaired children at a local preschool and are renovating a public park.

- *Social work:* Students developed and produced a resource guidebook and video for people living with AIDS and a guide to recreational activities for children and families.

- *Education:* Students developed and taught lesson plans based on the environment and assisted with the construction of a nature trail at a local school.

- *Occupational therapy:* Students provided direct care, intervention, and consultation to residents in Belize, Central America.

- *Nursing:* Students participated in the Frontier Nursing program, designed and implemented a breast cancer screening, and provided comprehensive care at local agencies.

Spiritual Development during Campus Crisis

On December 8, 1998, the faith of the entire Spalding University community was tested when an outstanding student leader and resident died from a severe seizure. She was a friend to all students, especially international students, and her death affected the entire residence hall community. On the evening of her death, the community gathered to honor her memory and share in the grief process. The students also joined together in the residence hall lounge for Mass for the feast of the Immaculate Conception as a way of working through their grief.

The campus minister offered grief counseling, and worked with students through this difficult time. In addition, the minister planned a celebration of life in honor of the student when the spring semester began and also planned a prayer service on the one-year anniversary of her death. Today, a living and learning scholarship is named in her honor and is awarded to students who contribute to building a stronger residence life community.

In addition to coming together as a community during a time of crisis, tragedies from around the world have affected the Spalding University community. When a devastating hurricane hit Belize and an earthquake struck India, the campus minister planned prayer services to pray for our students and their families and friends and offered support.

Spalding as a Character Building College

Recent national studies suggest that the vast majority of Americans share a common set of core values: honesty, self-control, perseverance, respect, compassion, and service to those less fortunate. Americans also agree that the college years are an ideal time to engage the minds, hearts, and hands of our young people to learn about and practice these virtues.

Since 1995, Spalding University has been twice designated a "character building college" by the John Templeton Foundation. Established in 1987, the foundation works closely with educators, scientists, theologians, medial professionals, and other scholars throughout the world to develop programs that encourage character development in schools. The foundation's guide, *Colleges that Encourage Character Development*, recognizes and profiles exemplary programs and higher education institutions that inspire students to lead ethical and civic-minded lives. Dr. Thomas R. Oates, president of Spalding University, remarked, "We consider character development an integral part of Spalding's mission, and recognize that it is every bit as important to teach students to be responsible members of society as it is to teach them to succeed in the work force." [11]

Challenges Related to Meeting Spiritual Needs and Maintaining Catholic Identity

As we strive to offer programs and services that embrace Catholic identity, celebrate diversity, and meet student spiritual needs, there are many challenges to overcome. One of the biggest challenges faced by the staff is opening students' minds and increasing awareness and sensitivity to other faiths. We are addressing this by offering programs and services. We make sure to include students from different denominations to participate in the planning and the events. One example of how we are increasing awareness was exhibited during the opening community assembly, where a group of students from five countries presented an ecumenical prayer service in their native dress and language. This helped the faculty, staff, and students to get to know a different dimension of our international students.

Another challenge is obtaining adequate information from surveys and assessments to meet the needs of a student population that is less than fifty percent Catholic. We conduct regular surveys, needs assessments, and focus groups to learn about student's spiritual needs. One of the biggest challenges in accomplishing this research and meeting the goals of student affairs and campus ministry is finding enough time and human and fiscal resources. The team is expected to do more with less, which often can lead to enhanced creativity, but can also lead to staff frustration or morale problems. We are cognizant of these challenges and remain focused on the goals we have set and the needs of the students we are trying to meet. One thing that allows us to remain focused as a team is to start our weekly staff meetings with reflections or prayers.

Summary

Spalding University is a diverse community of learners where spiritual values are embraced and diversity is celebrated. As for maintaining our Catholic identity, we strive to meet the following hallmarks of a Catholic education: being a positive role model; being of service to others; possessing strong moral character; serving as an active member of society; spreading the good news; working for humanity; and promoting peace and justice.[12] Spalding University is meeting these hallmarks through its mission, academic programs, and student affairs programs. The university catalog states, "A Spalding University education should, in a special way, prepare the student not only to survive change but also to contribute constructively to its development. Spalding makes a commitment to its students to provide a quality well-rounded education and asks in return for students to share of themselves in the promotion of a just and peaceful world."[13]

11

Connecting Leadership Development and Faith Development: St. Norbert College, De Pere, Wisconsin

Nancy B. Mathias and Julie Donovan Massey

Introduction

This case study describes how one institution learned to integrate, celebrate, and utilize the strengths of both a current student affairs leadership development model and the richness of the Catholic tradition through a single program. As program directors in the departments of campus ministry and leadership and service, we combined our separate-yet-similar service trip programs into one large Turning Responsibility into Powerful Service Program (TRIPS). This new program helped us to better attain our goal of providing opportunities for our students to develop both their leadership abilities and a fuller understanding of their faith. We recognize and appreciate our students' basic desire to serve others—often the initial impulse that brings them to the service trip program. Now we work intentionally to help them explore the possibility and responsibility of working toward social change and to appreciate the rich and sustaining context the Catholic tradition can offer to this work.

Context

St. Norbert College, a private, Catholic, liberal arts college near Green Bay, Wisconsin, was established in 1898. The student body is comprised of just over 2,000 students, 99 percent of whom are traditional aged, 96 percent are Caucasian, 62 percent are Roman Catholic, and about half come from homes less than 100 miles from campus. The mission of St. Norbert College is to "provide a superior education that is personally, intellectually, and spiritually challenging" and to encourage all students to "develop their full potential in understanding and serving their world." When we interpret this mission in light of the Catholic social tradition (CST),[1] we understand service to the world as a mandate for our students to change the world for the better or, in religious language, to do the work of building the kingdom.

Story

For over twenty years, campus ministry has invited students to explore and develop their faith through service trips. The trips were important in that they offered students an intense immersion and service opportunity with communities in need, and provided the time and place for students to grapple with questions of faith and service. Campus ministry found service trips to be particularly in tune with the faith development stage of the young adult. Understanding the young adult's heightened impatience with an imperfect world, skepticism for formal institutions—including religious groups—and desire to make a difference, it was important for campus ministry to embody the message that faith calls us to act in the world.[2] Because the campus ministry staff saw service trips as playing an important role in the faith development of students, their trips included the guiding presence of a priest or campus minister and group prayer and more formal worship experiences. They also incorporated reflection on service and justice in light of faith.

Underlying campus ministry service trips were a number of key values which at times played against one another. Campus ministry service trips were clearly linked to the Catholic social tradition, with its teachings and examples of reaching out to those in need. They were about service as a Christian value. However, campus ministry trips were also influenced by the Norbertine values of hospitality and community. This meant comfortable accommodations, occasional celebrations at "nicer" restaurants (thanks to the gracious support of the Norbertines), and exploration of the local cultural attractions. And while it was understood that the service offered by our students could have a positive impact on the community served, the greater impact that was realistically expected was growth in faith for those who had served. These values, although positive, at times left a confusing impression. Are we going on a trip to work with the poor and needy, or are we going to have a good time?

Meanwhile, in 1989, SNC began its leadership development program. As the leadership field evolved from the "great man" theory and hierarchical models to more collaborative, service-oriented models, a leadership paradigm was found that seemed to best engage our students: the Social Change Model of leadership development (SCM). It is a values-based model concerned with effecting change on behalf of others and society. It describes leadership as a collaborative process rather than a position. It assumes all students (not just those in formal leadership positions) are potential leaders. And it utilizes service as a powerful vehicle for developing students' leadership ability.[3] This model of leadership development became the theoretical impetus for combining the leadership and service programs at the college.

Once the leadership and service programs were combined into one department, exciting possibilities for applying SCM emerged. One example of a program where this combination had the most relevance was the leadership and service trips program. These trips focused on utilizing service as a leadership development tool in a social change context. Leadership and service trips were student led, required collaborative leadership, and focused on the participants' responsibility to address social issues in their community when they returned from the trip.

Thus, we arrived at a place where St. Norbert College was offering two separate, but similar, service trip programs. Students who participated in both the campus ministry and the leadership and service trips were able to compare the trips and began to share emerging concerns. "Why did the cost vary so much for the trips?" "Why do some trips have staff and others just students?" "Why is it so difficult to find general trip information?" More importantly, the students were frustrated by the inconsistencies they saw in the trips' goals. Again, with the heightened idealism that is their gift, students pushed us with some of the difficult questions. "Is it okay to serve the economically disadvantaged all day and then go out to dinner at night?" "How are we responsible for responding to what we encounter on a service trip?" "Aren't trips supposed to be fun?" These concerns became the catalyst for campus ministry and leadership and service to critically reflect on the possibilities and vision of a single trips program; thus the tentative investigation into each other's worlds began.

The first step in developing a unified trips program was to become familiar with each other's theories, departmental philosophies, and service trip traditions. We began by putting SCM in action. An especially talented student intern organized a weekend planning session that included staff and many concerned and committed students. The group outlined the major issues and then developed a mission statement that spoke to the hopes they had for future trips: Turning Responsibility into Powerful Service (TRIPS.)[4] This mission brought to the forefront the common outcome we had both been working for—to help students become value- or faith-based leaders who could make the world a better place.

Over the next two years, we continued our dialogue about the mission and purpose of trips. We identified many other common points: a strong personal and professional commitment to student development, service, and working for justice; a belief that students have a responsibility to understand, serve, and improve their world; and a theoretical and experiential approach to our work. As we looked at the SCM driving the leadership development aspect of the TRIPS program and the CST supporting the faith aspects of the program, we began to see the theoretical overlap in our work.

Social Change Model[5]	Catholic Social Tradition
Individual Values	
Consciousness of self means being aware of the beliefs, values, attitudes, and emotions that motivate one to take action. *Congruence* refers to thinking, feeling, and behaving with consistency toward others. Congruent persons are those whose actions are consistent with their most deeply held beliefs. *Commitment* is the energy that motivates one to serve and that drives the collective effort.	*Gaudium et Spes* (*The Church in the Modern World*) speaks to these values when it promotes *congruence* of belief and action: "Faith needs to prove its fruitfulness by penetrating the believer's entire life, including its worldly dimensions, and by activating him (sic) towards justice and love, especially regarding the needy."[6] Again, in *Justice in the World*, the Church affirms that our relationship with God and our responsibility to human beings are intertwined.[7] The *commitment* to serve and work for justice is rooted in the depths of our faith.

Group Values	
Collaboration is to work with others in a common effort. It is most effective when capitalizing on talents in a diverse group. *Common purpose* means to work with shared aims and values. It is best achieved when all group members share vision and set goals to be achieved. *Controversy with civility* recognizes differences are inevitable and must be aired openly and with respect. At its best, this will lead to new, creative solutions.	In CST, these values emerge in documents such as *Mater et Magistra (Christianity and Social Progress)* with its themes of *interdependence* and concern for the *common good.*[8] *Popularum Progressio (The Development of Peoples)* and *Sollicitudo Rei Socialis (The Social Concerns of the Church)* both discuss the need for international *collaboration* to bring about a global vision of justice.[9]
Societal/Community Values	
Citizenship is being responsibly connected to the community and society. A good citizen works for positive change on behalf of others and the community. *Change* is the ultimate goal of the leadership process—to make a better world for self and others.	*Discipleship* is being called to follow Christ and live one's faith through the work that one does. A good disciple works to build God's kingdom on earth. *Change* is the ultimate goal of discipleship—to create an earthly experience of justice, life, truth, love, freedom, peace, healing, and community.[10]

After long reflection on these similarities, we discovered two important things. Looking through a leadership lens, CST offers a faith perspective that is shockingly relevant to work for justice and positive change in the world. Looking through a ministry lens, the SCM challenges us to recognize change as the path required for those who seek to build the kingdom. In other words, the SCM provides a process to create change, and CST provides a faith imperative to do so. This discovery has allowed us to invite a more diverse group of students to recognize the synergy created by the coming together of people of both faith and action who are committed to change.

Challenges and Opportunities

This newly formed, process-focused TRIPS program provided many challenges and opportunities. As professionals, we had an energizing new way of looking at our work with students, which also happened to be much more time-consuming and demanding. As for students, they now had opportunities to grow in both the faith realm and the leadership realm, which was also more time consuming and demanding. Ultimately, we have decided this extra work is worthwhile as we are beginning to see students with strong values or faith discovering and utilizing their power to create change.

"What does faith have to with this?"

For our students the proper place of faith in this new, combined program was an issue. When campus ministry coordinated their own service trips, the religious grounding of these trips was assumed—by students and staff alike. As an organization interested in providing the benefits of both faith and leadership development to as many students as possible, we struggled with words and activities that both offered a broad welcome and supported the process of *faithing* or meaning-making, as Sharon Daloz Parks describes it.[11]

Acknowledging students' diverse motivations for participating in TRIPS, our mission speaks about the program as "an opportunity for students to put into action their values, convictions, and religious beliefs through service." To speak in terms that could be embraced by all students, we began to describe *faithing* as a process of actively seeking wisdom. We then trained our trip leaders to reflect on their trip experiences with the intention of seeking wisdom. We asked the trip leaders to invite their group members to share/describe their wisdom sources. With a large majority of our students baptized into Christian denominations, a look at wisdom sources could be expected to include Jesus. But it should not be expected to end there. In trying to help our students with the process of faith development we wanted them to identify their varied and genuine sources of wisdom. For today's student that may include anything from Mother Nature to Deepak Chopra to the poet/musician Jewel. The question we seek to push is, Where are you grounded? When you are looking for wisdom or grappling with a problem, where do you turn?

To assist our students in understanding the role that faith can play as a wisdom source for those committed to justice, we deliberately included exposure to role models. Rather than asking our students to read a lengthy papal letter on a service trip, we sought to introduce them to people whose lives were modeled on the principles found in such letters. A spirited African American Catholic community on Chicago's South Side prays together on Sundays and then takes that prayer to the streets when they minister to prostitutes and confront gangs throughout the rest of the week. A woman in the Twin Cities founds a shelter and greets each new guest with the profound act of washing their feet. A group that calls itself Catholic Workers, surprising and new to most of our students, lives out their faith in daily vigils and regular protests. The lesson quietly accumulates: there are men and women of faith who care about the same issues that concern me and who live in a way that really addresses these issues. These role models also demonstrate the importance of a strong faith tradition in sustaining those who work for change over the long haul.[12]

To further the process of seeking wisdom, we encouraged the groups to immerse themselves in the culture of the community in which they are serving, including the local faith community. Students often chose to participate in worship or prayer with the people they met. We asked them to discover how the community's faith traditions respond to inherently theological questions, "If God exists and cares, why is this situation so messed up?" (in theological terms, *theodicy*) and "What am I supposed to do now that I've seen this situation?" (in spiritual terms, *calling*). Individual role models and communities of faith become wisdom sources that serve as touch points for reflection.

"Isn't it a pain to share leadership?"

It is true that it is much easier to plan and lead the trips ourselves. But it is equally true that if our students are to become "change agents" for a better world, we must prepare them with education and practice for this job.

For trip participants, becoming a change agent means attending six to ten trip meetings, choosing a trip leadership role (meals, education, logistics, and so on), and developing a post-trip service/justice/change project. For trip leaders this translates into twenty to thirty hours of training that includes the basics from the BreakAway model,[13] information on facilitating group reflection with attention to seeking wisdom, and lots of team building to create a supportive peer network. This training helps prepare the leaders for the inherent challenges of the program: working through the "storming" stages in group development, encouraging participants to share in responsibilities of community living, supporting them as they share the joys and sorrows of the people they meet on their service trips, and transforming this experience into a lifelong commitment to make a more just world.

For staff, creating change agents means developing a trip leader training program in addition to managing initial trip logistics. It also means providing ongoing trip leader support to address their uncertainty and inexperience, and trying to smooth the way as much as possible without removing the responsibility and ambiguity of the leadership experience. To the extent that we succeed in developing change agents, the staff must now support the new initiatives that emerge when students return from the trips.

During the first year of this new trip model, there was some initial reluctance to take on the extra work. Although we worked hard to include all interested students (and staff), some were not interested in creating a new service trip program. Several experienced trip leaders continued to run trips the way they were used to—without shared leadership or without a faith dimension. But now many of the trip participants are excited and passionate to try out their ideas for making a better world. Examples from this past year include a pilot mentor program for urban youth; a new campus chapter of Amnesty International; and preparation for a campus theme house, "Living for Justice," modeled after a Catholic Worker community encountered on a service trip.

The biggest challenge we continue to face is finding and developing the students who are passionate about justice, grounded in a faith tradition, and able to provide the leadership necessary to create change. We recognize that not all students are interested in or able to commit the time and energy that trips require. We also know that our TRIPS program is challenging and asks for significant maturity and depth from the students who both lead and participate in these trips. Yet students at all developmental stages continue to step up to the challenge. We know that for many we are planting seeds and helping begin the journey to justice; for others who are actively working for justice, we hope to help them as they become more grounded in a wisdom source and connected to others who support their work. The TRIPS program offers all trip participants the rich soil of a collaborative, change-oriented leadership process and the sustaining nourishment that a faith tradition can bring to their work.

Building on Experience

The work we have done on the TRIPS program has offered us several new opportunities to expand our ideas into other areas. We want to continue to provide training that connects leadership skills and faith development as well as improve the quality and quantity of trip leaders and student leaders in general. Thus, we are beginning to focus our energies on two new campus programs.

The first is a leadership certificate program. This program will enhance the student's leadership development by linking training, leadership experiences, and reflection components into a more meaningful, holistic experience. It will offer general leadership training elements and include concepts such as CST, vocation, and spirituality as they relate to leadership. (These latter concepts are being incorporated partly as a result of the collaboration between the leadership and ministry areas.) It requires a leadership experience (trip leader, program intern, resident assistant, and so on) and reflection components (essay, journal, portfolio, and so on). As trip leaders engage in this process, they will not only be better prepared for their positions but will also have a certificate that recognizes their leadership work.

The second program is called the Lilly Leaders, as it is funded by the Lilly Endowment, Inc. It will help students link their gifts and talents to further their own and others' faith development. A select group of students will be chosen and trained to become change agents throughout the campus—as trip leaders, in residence halls, in athletics, and so on—helping their peers connect the interests of their lives with faith/spiritual contexts. This program will attempt to develop students in faith-based leadership. It will thus require the skills and theories of both ministry and leadership. Through the Lilly Leaders, and other programs, we seek to impact the climate of our campus such that all students begin to approach their lives with questions of how they are called to make the world better.

Lessons Learned

In reflecting back on this evolution of connecting leadership development and faith development, we identified many lessons we have learned that may be of interest to other Catholic colleges and universities.

Build on Common Ground

We learned that when collaboratively developing a program, the starting point for common ground is the college's mission statement. As we began our planning, we included a copy of the statement for everyone involved. Then we gathered a group of talented, passionate students and staff to identify the common values and shared outcomes for a unified trips program; these values and outcomes eventually became the new TRIPS program mission and goals statement. Finally, we focused on the links between student development theories and faith traditions. We wanted the students to discover that where the SCM asks value-based leaders to change society for the better, CST asks faith-based leaders to work to bring about the kingdom of justice on earth.

Expand Your Knowledge

Building on common ground assumes a minimal understanding of each collaborator's professional realm. We had to take the time to learn the theoretical bases from which we worked as well as the language unique to each of our fields. We asked lots of questions. In our case, the program director in the leadership area attended the ISACC conference to discover what it meant for student affairs professionals to work at a Catholic college. It brought new insight into how they could bring Catholic traditions into her work in a way that respected the diversity of beliefs (or disbeliefs) held by both colleagues and students. It was a professionally life-changing experience that created fertile ground for a partnership with campus ministry. The program director in campus ministry was drawn to develop her leadership background when she discovered leadership models built around the concept of our shared responsibility to work for a better society.

Build Relationships

Building common ground and expanding knowledge cannot be effective in an environment lacking trust. Both program directors had to overcome a historical distrust between their departments. This distrust came primarily from a lack of awareness of common ground as well as misunderstandings about each other's work. We have learned that there are many potential collaborators who feel they are outsiders in a religious institution, and thus do not feel welcomed or valued in the collaboration process. The best way we have found to chip away at this painful problem is through a practice that is at the heart of the best of ministry and student affairs—building relationships. As our professional relationship has grown, so has our friendship; this has helped to build a bridge between our departments and has opened doors for many new ventures.

Conclusion

By connecting leadership development and faith development, we can help students gain skills and appreciate a faith grounded for social change. College-age students are at an especially poignant moment in their search for meaning. Service trips provide a common ground from which to explore their deep questions, particularly, "How can I make the world a better place?" A Catholic college has a rich tradition of wisdom that can be an empowering resource in this search. The student affairs profession has excellent resources for leadership development. As professionals and people of faith, we have the opportunity and responsibility to offer these resources to help both ourselves and our students live with integrity and make real a vision for a better world.

12

Managing a Crisis at a Catholic University— Lessons Learned and Shared: Seton Hall University, South Orange, New Jersey

*Robert S. Meyer and
Laura A. Wankel*

We must do the things we think we cannot do.
—Eleanor Roosevelt

It was our saddest day. The morning of January 19, 2000, brought tragedy to Seton Hall University. A fire in the freshmen residence, Boland Hall, killed 3 of our first year students, injured 58 others, and left some 650 displaced. It was a dreadful, devastating loss. Forever, we would be changed.

Our saddest day was also our most challenging day as a Catholic institution of higher learning. In addition to the many pressing issues that needed immediate attention, it seemed as if the world was watching. And it very nearly was: the fourteen miles that separate us from New York City, the nation's largest media market, resulted in incredible, continual press coverage. The helicopters hovering overhead, the satellite dishes aimed skyward, and the hourly press conferences were vivid reminders that our response to this crisis would be measured and monitored by countless millions of people. Even so, it was an opportunity for the world to see the unique response of a Catholic university to a terrible tragedy.

While the president's office, as well as the divisions of academic affairs, business and finance, legal counsel, and university affairs all played key, strategic roles in the university response, this short reflection will focus on the work of student affairs professionals. Specifically, it will look at our preparedness before the crisis, as well as immediate and extended responses.

The work and dedication of so many individuals and groups will become evident as these pages unfold. However, we take a moment at the outset to thank the countless Good Samaritans who saw a need and generously responded. Never would we have made it this far without them. Finally, these words are written with two hopes: 1) that the reader will never have to face such a terrible tragedy; and 2) if that should not be the case, that the reader may perhaps learn from our shared experience.

Being Prepared

How can an individual, never mind an institution, be prepared to face and then manage such a tragedy? Nestled in the suburban village of South Orange, Seton Hall's 54 acres is a home for her 2,100 residents; 2,500 undergraduate commuters; 5,000 graduates; as well as over 1,000 faculty and staff. Since 1856 she also has strived to be a home for the mind, the heart, and the spirit. This small community has been preparing servant leaders to serve the global society for almost 150 years. How could she ever have been prepared for such a tragedy?

While it is humanly impossible to ever be fully prepared to face a crisis of this proportion, there are some steps that an institution can take to minimize the impact. Creating a crisis plan is the first step to being prepared to manage a tragedy of this magnitude. Fortunately, Seton Hall had developed a crisis manual long before the fire alarms sounded. The manual identified various types of crisis and clearly defined the lines of communications, follow-up, and support plan necessary to ensure a coordinated institutional response. The crisis manual designated a command center, press center, telephone bank room, as well as the respective professional staff responsible to manage these areas. The existence of a manual is important; however, the implementation of the protocols into routine practice for smaller, less complex incidents is imperative.

Another fundamental element to responsiveness relates to an established communication plan. The plan must include consideration for internal functional needs as well as information management. A plan that efficiently mobilizes key personnel and functions with contact chains that are clear, easy to use, and accurate is essential. Having an established network of telephone numbers, beepers, cell phones, and so on, all enable easy connection to critical "on call" protocols within all departments.

The coordination and management of accurate, timely, and necessary information to all stakeholders is critically important. Segmenting communications specifically tailored to meet the varied needs of each constituency is a major challenge. Rapidly changing circumstances and the need to provide appropriate information strains even the most seasoned personnel and technically prepared environments. While accuracy is primarily important, the diversity of audiences and constituencies may impact depth of information and delivery modes.

Naturally, the public relations staff will be pivotal in the development and dissemination of information to the internal and external communities. An established collaborative relationship that again draws upon practice and trust will facilitate a reduction in chaos.

Creative use of all technological resources must be considered. Mediums such as scheduled e-mails to specific groups, toll-free hotlines, web pages, town hall meetings, radio and television, telephone chains, scheduled briefings of key personnel, and written scripts will all minimize the dissemination of inaccurate information, maximize rumor control, and subsequently protect the institutional image.

The management of the press is also a frustration that requires enormous care, professionalism, and preparation. The public relations staff is best positioned to manage the inevitable invasion of satellite trucks, helicopters, correspondents, reporters, and sensation seekers. The public relations staff can convey the mission of the university and appropriately provide accurate information that responds to the public's need to be informed. Without management of this critical aspect, numerous vulnerabilities may be exploited, which can include significant, irreparable damage to institutional image, reduction in the effectiveness of personnel to attend to critical needs, and most especially, the violation of the dignity and undeniable rights to privacy of the victims, students, and their families. The road to recovery and survival begins to be shaped through these early projections to the world. The Catholic identity of the university must drive and support these decisions and images.

Developing relationships with the key members of the local municipality is another useful tool in crisis management. Hosting officials from the local police department to share common goals, inviting members of the fire department to present on fire safety issues and conduct training sessions, as well as having a university liaison to the village/town officials are other important features of being prepared to manage a tragedy. Seton Hall enjoys these strategic relationships that are mutually beneficial.

Apart from the practical aspects of having a detailed crisis manual and communication plan, and working toward improving collaboration, being prepared entails recognizing both the traditional and "crisis" roles that each of the units and professionals play in responding to a sudden crisis. Our division of student affairs, under the leadership of a vice president, is composed of the departments of athletics and recreational services, the career center, community development, health/counseling, housing and residence life, and public safety and security. While some of these departments, such as health/counseling, housing and residence life, and public safety have obvious responsibilities when a crisis occurs, others, like athletics, community development, and the career center were called to transform their responsibilities to becoming "crisis managers." Members from these staffs became the liaisons to the students most affected by the fire. They quickly developed personal and trusting relationships with students who were at times frightened, confused, and in need of assistance. Exploring these transformed roles is better when planned in advance without the emotional stress endured when actually facing a tragedy.

A final way of being prepared to face a tragic situation is to know the vast student affairs and other resources that are outside of one's own institution. Preparing a list of colleagues, contacts, and other resources is an invaluable tool to have at one's fingertips should a crisis strike. Seton Hall was fortunate to benefit from good, pre-existing relationships with the student affairs professionals from our sister institutions. In addition to providing extra people to deliver a variety of services (clothing and food distribution, counseling, hotline staffing, and so on), the skills needed for certain aspects of the tasks required experience that often results after years of service in student affairs. Having individuals available who possessed experience as chief officers or directors helped to keep agendas and tasks moving on multiple fronts. We could not have managed without them and will be forever grateful.

Immediate Response

Seton Hall University's motto is *Hazard Zet Forward*. These Old English words mean "forward in spite of adversity or difficulty." Perhaps at no other time in our history had those words rung more true. In the early and very cold winter hours of January 19, 2000, soon after the smoke had cleared, our community was called to move forward in spite of adversity, difficulty, and even death.

The Scriptures are filled with sayings, examples, stories, and parables offering guidance and providing principles that are particularly helpful to a community in crisis. The hundreds of immediate responses, large and small, public and private, were guided by the principles that define who we are as a Catholic university. They describe and even capture the essence of our very reason for being in the business of higher education. Those principles most applicable to our crisis situation are *imago dei*, human dignity, freedom and responsibility, and stewardship. The sense of a common bond has never been more evident.

Our shared sense of being overwhelmed and defeated helped to stimulate our community of faith to be more and do more with a capacity that only great faith can muster. While we knew that the residence hall would be repaired and even improved, our community had a long road to rebuilding itself. With students as our number one priority, this rebuilding would take place one "person" at a time.

Calling on the presence of God was both comforting and challenging. Sharing with a family the horrible news that their child had died is the most difficult task any administrator may ever have to perform. Connecting God's spirit and presence between those delivering the message and those receiving the message is a most profound spiritual moment. God was alive and present in those painful moments when we broke the terrible news to Aaron, Frank, and John's families, and we will never forget them.

God's presence and spirit was also alive as members of the university priest community, the priest-president of the university, and the diocesan archbishop went to the various local hospitals to visit the injured students. The healing, sacramental presence of Jesus was already being shared. Remembering God's presence in the angry calls from some parents and students as well as others who had words of criticism, grief, and disappointment was more challenging.

The dignity of the human person is inviolable.[1] This dignity defines the parameters of relationship that humans are to have with one another. These parameters are clearly tested in crisis situations when people are emotional, frustrated, and lethargic. The immediate days after the fire brought unprecedented long and tiring hours of hard work, even for student affairs professionals accustomed to non-conventional service. From regular university updates with students and staff, to meeting with local and state fire officials, to giving direction to the hundreds of volunteers who came and asked, "What can I do to help?" the days were long and oftentimes seemed unending.

In spite of these seemingly endless days, and the incredible number of tasks that never seemed to be completed, we were blessed. We saw the best of humanity and respect in our staff and in the numerous people who came to help us. The presence of police officers from various agencies around the state, the direction and expert guidance from the New Jersey State Emergency Management Team, the generous service of university food services, and the overwhelming response from the sophomore, junior, and senior students were all signs to us in the "crisis control center" that God's generous spirit was alive, well, and working! Their dedication and selfless service to our community demonstrated that they believed that life is sacred and that all of us are indeed God's children. These individuals and groups had lived this principle sometimes twenty hours every day for weeks. For this, we will be forever grateful as God worked through human instruments one person at a time.

In order to attain fulfillment and eternal life, human beings have freedom of choice, which is an "exceptional sign of the image of God in man."[2] Through free choice, each person shapes his or her own character and destiny.[3] Responsibility accompanies freedom. The Bible affirms that each person will be held accountable for his/her choices and actions.[4] From the first morning of the crisis, a control room was established in the main administration building. In this room state and local officials, key university administrators, and police and fire personnel gathered daily to meet, plan, and discuss. These men and women—all supported and surrounded by myriads of laptop computers, beepers, and cell phones—demonstrated the depth of their characters. It was in this room where hard decisions and implementation plans were developed. These incredible people were truly exceptional glimpses of light on a seemingly dark campus.

Stewardship affirms that the ultimate value and sanctity of human life comes from God. To confess that God is the Lord of life and death affirms the fundamental distinction between Creator and created, and it affirms that as creatures, humans owe their existence, value, and ultimate destiny to God. While the earth and all its contents are here for our proper use and enjoyment,[5] no one can ever claim total mastery over one's own or another's life. Human persons have no dominion over this life, but rather hold it in trust for God's purposes. Stewardship takes into account the availability and proper use of the gifts and talents of a person while simultaneously respecting the notion of human dignity.

In crisis situations, understanding and embracing stewardship is key to making proper decisions. It was very important on occasion for staff members to be sent home to rest, be with their own families, to replenish, pray, and refresh. To be good stewards of one's gifts at times means giving two hundred percent and at other times taking time off. The good steward finds the appropriate balance and is able to say and trust in prayer, "God I have given what I have for this day, the rest is up to you."

Extended Response

A crisis of the magnitude that we experienced continues to demand a series of responses from our university. The tragedy has become etched into the history of this institution, and our response to it has in some ways defined us. Each year, as we welcome new students and staff into the community, we are compelled to share with them the knowledge we gained from the terrible tragedy. We continue to respond in the following ways:

- *Counseling*
  University professional counselors continue to be available to assist and support students and staff members who were emotionally affected by the fire. An incredible contingent of professionals supplemented our counseling staff in the days immediately after the incident, and their generous, professional service lifted many a burden. We continue to create environments and support groups for students to come together to process their experiences from this tragedy.

- *Fire Suppression Systems*
  All of our university residence halls have been refitted with sprinkler fire suppression and upgraded detection systems. The local fire department conducts fire drills and supervises evacuation plans. Our resident assistants have also undergone extensive training at a local fire academy. We are reminded that even with the most advanced equipment, safety is a human issue and we are responsible to and for each other.

- *Expert Staff*
  The university has a renewed commitment to the general safety of the university community. Numerous initiatives aimed at improving awareness and refining practice procedure and policy have moved us to a "best practice" model.

- *Public Relations and Media Management*
  The fire has given us incredible opportunities to be a leader and good example in instituting and publicizing new and improved safety practices. The media continues to follow our rebuilding as

well as occasionally runs stories highlighting our student healing and institutional initiatives. We have also been able to demonstrate our Catholic identity in action.

- *Community Standards*
  The university continues to deal seriously with student infractions to the community standards involving fire or safety issues. Students are exposed to safety programming and have grown to understand the seriousness of these initiatives.

- *Honoring*
  We have expressed our thanks in different ways to those who came into our darkness to help us. We have sent letters, run ads in newspapers, and hosted an evening where agencies and individuals were honored and thanked in a public manner. We will be forever grateful.

- *Praying and Remembering*
  We continue to pray for the students who have died and remember those who continue to heal in body, mind, and spirit. Our prayers continue also for the families of all those affected and are in thanksgiving for so many who generously helped us.

Conclusion

In the end, these past months after the tragedy have been quite a challenge. To close, I share this story. I remember being called into the press room for one of the many briefings that would happen in the days immediately after the fire. The public relations spokeswoman for the university thought it might be a good idea that a priest spoke to the press on the current status of the students. Having done a good deal of the background work, I was left with the task of confronting the lights, the cameras, and the reporters—it was the first time I ever had to participate in such an experience.

Public relations explained that the press would be interested in how the students were adjusting to the loss of their friends, the serious injuries of so many others, and of how they would ever get the semester back together. I wondered that myself.

After sharing with the media that I was a priest-resident of Boland Hall, had lived there for eight years, and was also personally affected by the tragedy, it seemed that an interminable number of probing questions came forth. Whatever I was saying, it didn't seem to be what they wanted to hear. I can vividly remember one reporter, almost sarcastically, say, "Yes, Father, all that's fine and good, but how are the students feeling and how, if at all, are they dealing with this terrible tragedy?"

It was at that moment that I recalled a conversation with a Dominican priest from Providence College. He had lived through the fire in that Rhode Island institution years before that had claimed the lives of twelve young women. Fr. Tom came to my office to give me some support and words of encouragement in dealing with the situation as it continued to develop. I will never forget his words, and, presumably, neither will the aggressive reporter to whom I addressed them: "If you dedicate a university to God, and attempt to embody God's principles and teachings in the everyday life of that university and its students, regardless of what happens, God will be there, even in the darkest moments." I trusted in those words and so did our students. The press conference ended.

I still believe those words. As student affairs professionals at Catholic colleges and universities in this country, we find strength and encouragement in those words. Our hard work and efforts will not go unnoticed by the God to whom we dedicate and name our honorable institutions. Tragedies will continue unfortunately to occur on our campuses despite all our best efforts and preparedness. It is in our response, however, that we can expect to be measured and it is in these ways that we can claim our commitment and demonstrate best our Catholic identity.

Hazard Zet Forward!

Endnotes

Introduction

1. Alice Gallin, O.S.U., ed., *American Catholic Higher Education: Essential Documents: 1967-1990* (Notre Dame, IN: University of Notre Dame Press, 1992).
2. Alice Gallin, O.S.U., *Negotiating Identity: Catholic Higher Education since 1960* (Notre Dame, IN: University of Notre Dame Press, 2000).
3. Ernest T. Pascarella and Patrick T. Terenzini, *How College Affects Students* (San Francisco: Jossey-Bass Publishers, 1991).
4. Arthur W. Chickering and Linda Reisser, *Education and Identity*, 2nd ed. (San Francisco: Jossey-Bass Publishers, 1993).
5. William G. Perry, Jr., *Forms of Ethical and Intellectual Development in the College Years: A Scheme* (San Francisco: Jossey-Bass Publishers, 1999).
6. Sandra M. Estanek and Martin F. Larrey, "ISACC: Integrating Student Affairs Practice and Catholic Identity," *Current Issues in Catholic Higher Education* 18 (Spring 1998), 51-63.

Chapter 1

1. John Paul II, "On Catholic Universities," *Ex Corde Ecclesiae* (Washington, D.C.: United States Catholic Conference, 1996).
2. Three texts that illustrate this type of academic discussion are David O'Brien, *From the Heart of the American Church* (Maryknoll, NY: Orbis Books, 1994), Theodore Hesburgh, C.S.C., ed., *The Challenge and Promise of a Catholic University* (Notre Dame, IN: University of Notre Dame Press, 1994), and John Langan, S.J., ed., *Catholic Universities in Church and Society* (Washington, D.C.: Georgetown University Press, 1993).
3. National Conference of Catholic Bishops, *Ex Corde Ecclesiae: An Application to the United States* (Washington, D.C.: United States Catholic Conference, 1999).
4. Ibid, 3.
5. Ibid.

6. American College Personnel Association, *The Student Learning Imperative: Implications for Student Affairs* (Washington, D.C.: American College Personnel Association, 1994), hereafter cited as SLI.

7. SLI, 1.

8. American College Personnel Association and National Association of Student Personnel Administrators, *Principles of Good Practice in Student Affairs* (Washington, D.C.: American College Personnel Association and National Association of Student Personnel Administrators, 1997), in Gregory Blimling and Elizabeth Whitt, *Good Practice in Student Affairs* (San Francisco: Jossey-Bass Publishers, 1999), 205-208, hereafter cited as PGP.

9. John Paul II, "On Catholic Universities," *Ex Corde Ecclesiae*, hereafter cited as ECE.

10. ECE, part I, n. 13

11. SLI, preamble, 1.

12. PGP, n. 2, 206

13. Vatican Council II, "Pastoral Constitution on the Church in the Modern World," *Gaudium et Spes* (Boston: Pauline Books and Media, 1965).

14. Ibid, n. 1, 3.

15. Margaret O'Brien Steinfels, "The Catholic Intellectual Tradition," Association of Catholic Colleges and Universities, *Occasional Papers on Catholic Higher Education 1*, n. 1 (November 1995).

16. Ibid, 7.

17. Pedro Arrupe, S.J., the 28th General of the Society of Jesus in an address to alumni of Jesuit schools in Europe (July 31, 1973), used this phrase in defining the attributes of a graduate of a Jesuit school. It is used widely in the publications of both secondary and higher education institutions of the Jesuits.

18. David O'Brien, *From the Heart of the American Church* (Maryknoll, NY: Orbis Books, 1994), 191.

19. ECE, part I, n. 21.

20. SLI, 2.

21. PGP, n. 7, 207-208.

22. ECE, part I, n. 21.

23. National Conference of Catholic Bishops, *Always Our Children* (Washington, D.C.: United States Catholic Conference, 1997).

24. ECE, part I, n. 22.

25. SLI, 3.

26. PGP, n. 2, 206.

27. ECE, part I, n. 22, 19.

28. Richard McCormick, S.J., "What Is a Great University?" in *The Challenge and Promise of a Catholic University*, ed., Theodore Hesburgh, C.S.C. (Notre Dame, IN: University of Notre Dame Press, 1994), 167.

29. Ibid, 167.

30. ECE, part I, n. 23.

31. SLI, 1.

32. PGP, n. 2, 206.

33. Brian Daley, S.J., "Christ and the Catholic University," *America*, September 11, 1993, 10.

34. Peter-Hans Kolvenbach, S.J., quoted in William Spohn, "The University that Does Justice," *Conversations* 19 (Spring 2001), 11.

35. Daley, 10.

36. ECE, part I, n. 17.

37. SLI, 1.

38. PGP, n. 3, 206.

39. O'Brien Steinfels, 7-8.

40. Michael Buckley, S.J., "The Catholic University and the Promise Inherent in Its Identity," in *Catholic Universities in Church and Society*, ed., John Langan, S.J. (Washington, D.C.: Georgetown University Press, 1993), 85.

41. ECE, part I, n. 21.

42. SLI, 2.

43. PGP, n. 6, 207.

44. Alfred North Whitehead, quoted in Gregory Blimling and Elizabeth Whitt, *Good Practice in Student Affairs* (San Francisco: Jossey-Bass Publishers, 1999), 135.

45. SLI, 3.

46. American Association for Higher Education, American College Personnel Association, and National Association of Student Personnel Administrators, *Powerful Partnerships: A Shared Responsibility for Learning* (Washington, D.C.: American Association for Higher Education, American College Personnel Association, and National Association of Student Personnel Administrators, 1998).

47. Ibid, 11.

48. ECE, part I, n. 33.

49. SLI, 2.

50. PGP, n. 2, 206.

51. Michael Lavelle, S.J., "What Is Meant by a 'Catholic' University?" *America*, February 5, 1994, 4.

52. Daley, 11.

53. ECE, part I, n. 24.

54. SLI, 3.

55. PGP, n. 6, 207.

56. ECE, part I, n. 24.

57. ECE, part I, n. 34.

58. SLI, 3.

59. PGP, n. 1, 206.

60. David O'Brien, "Conversations on Jesuit (And Catholic?) Higher Education: Jesuit Si, Catholic…Not So Sure," *Conversations on Jesuit Higher Education* 6 (Fall 1994), 11.

61. Peter-Hans Kolvenbach, S.J., quoted in William Spohn, "The University that Does Justice," *Conversations on Jesuit Higher Education* 19 (Spring 2001), 12.

62. ECE, part I, n. 38.

63. SLI, 3.

64. PGP, n. 1, 205-206.

65. ECE, part I, n. 45.

66. SLI, 4.

67. PGP, n. 4, 206-207.

68. ECE, introduction, n. 11.

Chapter 2

1. Mary L. Funke, "Preface," *Current Issues in Catholic Higher Education* 10 (Winter 1990): p. 5.

2. Dorothy M. Riley, "ACCU Student Life Questionnaire: A Report," *Current Issues in Catholic Higher Education* 10 (Winter 1990): p. 6–10.

3. Ibid., p. 9.

4. Ibid., p. 7.

5. Ibid., p. 8.

6. Ibid., p. 9.

7. Funke, "Preface," p. 5.

8. Sandra M. Estanek, "A Study of Student Affairs Practice at Catholic Colleges and Universities," *Current Issues in Catholic Higher Education* 16 (Winter 1996): p. 63–72.

9. Ibid., p. 68.

10. Ibid., p. 66.

11. Ibid., p. 72. It is not quite true that a national organization had not existed previously. The Jesuit Association of Student Personnel Administrators was founded in 1954. JASPA has provided student affairs professionals who work at the twenty-eight Jesuit colleges, and the few affiliate colleges, with the forum for training and discussion desired by colleagues at non-Jesuit institutions. Over the years JASPA has resisted the idea of broadening its mission to include all Catholic institutions. Instead, it has been supportive of other efforts.

12. Because of my role in the creation of ISACC and ASACCU, I have had many opportunities since 1994 to participate with colleagues in discussions of student affairs at Catholic colleges. These have included formal presentations at national conferences and individual institutions as well as informal discussions in person and electronically. The characterization I draw of the proposed explanations and solutions is based upon these experiences.

13. *The Cambridge Dictionary of Philosophy*, s.v. "Epistemology," p. 233.

14. National Association of Student Personnel Administrators, *A Perspective on Student Affairs: A Statement Issued on the 50th Anniversary of "The Student Personnel Point of View,"* p. 14.

15. The American College Personnel Association and the National Association of Student Personnel Administrators, *Principles of Good Practice in Student Affairs: Statement and Inventories*, p. 3.

16. The epistemology of the "great books" was first discussed in Sandra M. Estanek, "Student Affairs and Truth: A Reading of the 'Great Books,'" *NASPA Journal* 36 (Summer 1999): pp. 278-287.

17. Florence A. Hamrick and John H. Schuh, "The Great Books of Student Affairs: A Great Conversation?" *NASPA Journal* 30 (Fall 1992): pp. 66–73.

18. *The Cambridge Dictionary of Philosophy*, s.v. "Empiricism," pp. 224-225.

19. Nevitt Sanford, ed., *The American College: A Psychological and Social Interpretation of Higher Learning* (New York: John Wiley & Sons, Inc., 1962), p. 28.

20. Ibid.

21. Jean B. Elshtain, "Critique of Values in the Social Sciences," Presentation to the Association of Catholic Colleges and Universities, Washington, D.C., February 3, 1998, audiocassette.

22. ACPA and NASPA, *Principles of Good Practice*, p. 4.

23. Robert B. Young, *No Neutral Ground: Standing By the Values We Prize in Higher Education* (San Francisco: Jossey-Bass Inc., Publishers, 1997), p. 40.

24. Ibid., p. 53.

25. Ibid., p. 75.

26. Ibid., p. 102.

27. Ibid., p. 111.

28. John Paul II, "On Catholic Universities," *Ex Corde Ecclesiae* (Washington, D.C.: United States Catholic Conference, 1990), p. 5.

29. Ibid., p. 6.

30. Ibid.

31. Richard P. McBrien, *Catholicism: Study Edition* (San Francisco: HarperCollins Publishers, 1995), p. 951.

32. *HarperCollins Encyclopedia of Catholicism*, s.v. "Individualism," p. 662.

33. Ibid., "Common Good," p. 336.

34. Ibid.

35. John Paul II, *Ex Corde Ecclesiae*, p. 31.

36. Ibid., pp. 14, 15–16.

Chapter 3

1. Roman Catholics would not use the ill-sounding term of indoctrination for the impression I am describing. For them it is a plain and simple matter that the pope and the bishops teach them what to believe. The Catholic tradition is taught them much like one's family history is taught youngsters, from those meant to teach to those meant to learn.

2. There is not a distinctive Catholic way of thinking about mathematics or chemistry. But when one mentions the human sciences or social sciences, I would like to think there is a characteristic Catholic way of "contextualizing" a business course or a psychology course, not in the sense that religion enters the subject matter of marketing or of adolescent psychology, respectively, but in the sense that the wider value-horizon of these subjects is quite important. One can teach marketing from a sheer *laissez-faire*, marketplace-is-king attitude or one can offer social justice principles and the wrongs of, say, price gouging.

3. From a phenomenological perspective, I simply intend to describe this Catholic manner of thinking about sacred realities. From a faith perspective, the Catholic Church would assert that the characteristics of this Catholic way of thinking, of theologizing if you will, are gifts of the Holy Spirit, in that Catholicism believes that the Holy Spirit, the Paraclete, maintains the community of faith in religious truth and guides the community into understanding and articulating it age by age.

4. Toward the end of his life, St. Augustine of Hippo wrote a short handbook of Catholic beliefs, *The Enchiridion on Faith, Hope, and Love*. St. Thomas Aquinas wrote a magisterial summary of doctrines, the *Summa Theologiae*. Less theologically formatted than these and more matter-of-fact in their doctrinal presentations are the various catechisms of the Catholic Church, from that of the Council of Trent, to the famous Baltimore Catechism, to the newly released *Catechism of the Catholic Church*. All of these books look at what is taught in the Catholic tradition; I look at the ways of Catholic *thinking* that generate the doctrines.

5. The key references are Acts 2:42 for the first commune, 6:1 for the fight over money, 7:48 for Stephen's anti-Temple position, 8:1 for the selective Sanhedrin persecution of Hellenist Jews, 11:19 for the first preaching to Gentiles, 15:1 for the conservative Jewish undermining of Hellenistic Jewish baptizing practice, and 15:19 for James's (Jesus' blood relative, not James of the Twelve Apostles) decision supporting Paul and Antioch.

6. How one views the "end times" (or Jesus' victory over sin and death) is called *eschatology* by biblical scholars and theologians. To expect Jesus to return very soon, within one's life time in fact, is called *imminent* eschatology. We know this was the eschatology of the earliest disciples, and Paul still is holding to it in the 50s, as we can see from some of his letters. He is convinced he will be alive on earth when Jesus returns in glory, on what he, using Old Testament language, calls "the day of the Lord."

7. Luke is writing Acts in the mid-80s. Peter's initial Jerusalem preaching was in the early 30s. I make no suggestion that the sermons in Acts give us untouched, much less verbatim versions of Peter's words. The sermons carry, no doubt, historical echoes, such as the earliest tendency to describe Jesus as God's Servant, the *ebed Yahweh* of Isaiah 53. A later Lukan theological perspective, which Catholics believe itself to be inspired, permeates Acts; for example, Luke turns the ecstatic utterances in tongues (*glossalalia*) of Pentecost into foreign languages, as if to presage for the reader what the ultimate effects of Spirit-reception will be, namely, the preaching about Jesus going on in many cultures years later. I do not think Peter ever spoke any language other than Aramaic, or possibly some spotty Greek that Galilean Jews picked up in the north of Israel.

8. It is anachronistic to call Stephen and the other six individuals the seven "deacons" of later church ecclesiastical order, even though this story is read at diaconal ordinations to this day. The seven are pastoral ministers who "serve" (*diakonos* in Greek). If one were asked to use a later term to describe Stephen, it would be "bishop" since he had pastoral administrative responsibilities and he evangelized. We have no idea who led in the breaking of the bread, but it was as likely one of the pastoral leaders as anyone else.

9. My composite interpretation of the Acts story is supported by Raymond E. Brown, "Early Church," *New Jerome Biblical Commentary* (Englewood Cliffs: Prentice Hall, 1990), p. 1340 ff.

10. A note on dates in the life of Jesus. The year of his crucifixion cannot be pinned down. It might have been as early as A.D. 29 and as late as A.D. 33. We can date Jesus' birth more closely (about 5 B.C.) since from secular historical records we know that Herod the Great died in 4 B.C. but was alive when Jesus was born. Thus Jesus died in his mid- or late-thirties. About 500 years later a Christian monk proposed a B.C./A.D. calendar situating history up to and after Jesus' birth. Given the spotty archival documents then existing for this monk, the fact that he was only five years or so off in backdating Jesus' birth ought to win our esteem rather the apparent oxymoron that Jesus was born B.C.

11. See Heb. 6:4 about having been first enlightened and then sinning, for example, the question of post-baptismal sins. This letter is clearly not Pauline. Think of it then not as a Christian letter addressed to Jews to accept Jesus but as a letter from Hellenists Jesus-believing Jews to their Hebrew colleagues to stop Jewish practices involving the Temple and its priests, and to recognize that Jesus, the one High Priest, has replaced all Jewish ceremonials. Recall from my first story that the Hellenists' rejection of Temple and Torah unnerved the Hebrews. But here we see the Hellenist insight: Jesus has replaced it all, and this is what the Gospel of John teaches as well.

12. Hrotsvit is interesting as one of the earliest medieval hagiographers. Her retelling of Pelagius's death in Moorish Cordoba is replete with baptismal motifs: the "river of his blood," the "purifying bath" in which his corpse was washed, the "anointing oil" his body received. We are hearing echoes of the baptismal ritual at the time of the Saxon court of Otto the Great. See *Writings of Medieval Women: An Anthology*, ed., Marcelle Thiebaux (New York: Garland, 1994), pp. 188-98.

13. It was to Flemish Dominican Edward Schillebeeckx's credit to have utilized the Dutch word *ontmoeting* to describe what happens in a performed sacrament. The English encounter only partially captures the Dutch. See Edward Schillebeeckx, *Christ the Sacrament of the Encounter with God* (New York: Sheed & Ward, 1963).

14. This may seem a curious expression but it is not. Recall that Mormons see themselves as Christians too, but they believe that just after the apostolic age the Church fell into apostasy, and that it was only in the latter days of Joseph Smith in the early 1800s that the real Church began again with them, the latter-day saints.

15. There were certainly periods of state persecution when Christianity went underground, into the catacombs as it were, for example, during the political turmoil following Emperor Commodus (+191) and during the Decian and Diocletian persecutions of the next century. But the first public defenses of Christianity, by the Apologists, began during the peaceful reigns of Hadrian (+138), followed by his adopted son Antoninus Pius (+161), followed in turn by his adopted son Marcus Aurelius (+180).

16. St. Augustine, *Confessions*, VII.17 [23], trans., Henry Chadwick (Oxford: Oxford University Press, 1991).

17. St. Augustine, *Confessions*, X.27 [38], author's translation.

18. Cardinal Newman's treatment of the Christian movement—he calls it the idea of Christianity, and the word *movement* captures the dynamism of Newman's word—remains a classic. Newman's note of assimilation as a feature of a true development of doctrine is what I call the integrative characteristic of the Catholic tradition. See John Henry Newman, *An Essay on the Development of Christian Doctrine* (London: Longmans, 1878). My use of *unfolding* is suggested by Newman's greatest commentator, Jan Hendrick Walgrave of Louvain. See his *Unfolding Revelation* (Philadelphia: Westminster, 1972).

19. "The new birth [baptism] would not have been appointed only that the first birth was sinful, so sinful that even one who was legitimately born in wedlock says, 'I was shapen in iniquities and in sins did my mother conceive me.'" *Enchiridion*, question XLVI. "Intercourse with one's spouse, sought for its pleasure, is a venial sin" *De bono conjugali*, 6, 6 (PL 40:377-78).

20. In terms of myopia, Arius commands our sympathy. He argued, after all, that the New Testament uses subordinationist language to depict Jesus, for example, "The Father is greater than I." The Council of Nicea in A.D. 325 used a non-biblical word, *homoousion* or consubstantial, to describe the unity of Jesus and the Father, justifying it by claiming that this word captures the upshot of the entire New Testament story about Jesus. What we remember is that an assemblage of bishops, and Emperor Constantine himself, come down on Arius. Thus, his myopia is overcome by a crowd. What if the myopia comes from an illustrious person who is honored by the whole crowd? There was no one for the later Middle Ages more illustrious in theology than St. Augustine.

21. Pope John XXI ordered Archbishop Tempier of Paris to investigate the new Aristotelianism among the theologians at the university. On March 7, 1277, Tempier proscribed over 200 theses and excommunicated all who held them. Some were clearly in Aquinas's writings. Another Pope John, the XXII, rehabilitated Aquinas by canonizing him in 1323.

22. *Enchiridion*, question XXVI.

23. St. Thomas's treatment of original sin is in ST, I-II, q. 81-85. Fine explanatory essays by Thomas C. O'Brien can be found in vol. 26 of the *Summa Theologiae*, ed., Thomas Gilby (New York: McGraw-Hill, 1964).

24. Cardinal Newman is second to none in writing about teaching authority in the Church and also writing about its limitations. For a synopsis of Newman, see Edward Jeremy Miller, *John Henry Newman on the Idea of Church* (Shepherdstown: Patmos Press, 1987), chap. 4. For a theological examination of *magisterium*, see Francis Sullivan, *Magisterium: Teaching Authority in the Catholic Church* (New York: Paulist, 1983).

25. Not every member of the Jerusalem church accepted James's decision at this so-called council of circa A.D. 49. If we grant that the "Hebrews" were to the right of the "Hellenists" (for example, the more conservative versus the more progressive), then among the Hebrews there was a far-right segment that remained convinced one had to be Jewish to be Jesus' disciple, in spite of James's decision. It was these "false brethren," this "circumcision party" in Paul's terms, that harassed his ministry in Galatia and of whom Paul wrote, in a moment of pique, that he wished their circumcision knives would slip from their hands and castrate themselves (Gal. 5:12). I also wish to recognize that Paul's description in Galatians of the Jerusalem meeting differs somewhat from Luke's account in Acts but not over the recognition by Jerusalem of his non-circumcising ministry to Gentiles.

26. The Council of Trent (1545-1563) was a reforming assembly of Catholic church leaders in two senses. The council recognized the legitimacy of some of the Protestant claims of abuses in the Church as well as abuses identified by earlier Catholic reformers, and it sought to correct them. The council also proscribed as heresy many Protestant teachings. The exercise of strong and increasingly centralized teaching authority and pastoral administration reflects the reactions against the abuses and the heresies. Vatican Council II,

four hundred years later, signals a transition from reactive to proactive ministry. About so complex an epoch, I acknowledge I speak in generalizations. There are significant differences between the Catholicism just after Trent and Baroque Catholicism, for instance.

27. There are levels of Roman Catholic *magisterium*, and I am not suggesting the possibility of abuses at every level. There is, for example, the level of solemn extraordinary infallible *magisterium*, such as the dogmatic teaching of an ecumenical council. The Catholic intellectual tradition recognizes this level as a "charismatic moment," that is, as a special assistance of the Holy Spirit maintaining the Church in the truth.

28. In 1877 Newman reedited his 1837 Anglican book, *The Prophetical Office of the Church*. The 1877 edition carried corrective footnotes to the earlier edition and it included the famous preface on the threefold office of Christ. It is now to be found in *The Via Media of the Anglican Church*, vol. 1. (London: Longmans, 1911).

29. Vatican II was a renewal, not a revolution. The possibility for individual private confessions in a confessional box in anonymous fashion on a Saturday afternoon, like years ago, remains. But efforts were made to heighten the experience of community. The "box" is now a prayerfully arranged room; one may confess in full view of the priest or from behind a screen; and the ritual includes a Scripture reading (recall that Scriptures are community documents).

30. Known also by its English title, *The Church in the Modern World*, this pastoral constitution is felt by many scholars of the council to be the council's *raison d'être*. Other essays of our volume draw connections between its message and the work of student affairs on Catholic campuses.

Chapter 4

1. "The *mandatum* is fundamentally an acknowledgment by Church authority that a Catholic professor of a theological discipline is a teacher within the full communion of the Catholic Church" (Guidelines Concerning the Academic *Mandatum*, November 2000).

2. Many would like to think it would be otherwise, however, the reality may also be indicative of the fact that young Catholic students today have been more indoctrinated and are more influenced by the prevailing societal culture than by church teaching, even though many are products of extensive Catholic schooling.

3. The Catholic University of America, for example, has a carefully crafted "Presentations Policy" that may be accessed on the CUA web site www.cua.edu/students/stuhbook.

4. Conscience and its formation will be addressed in greater detail in a later chapter.

5. The "non-Catholic" should not assume that Catholic colleagues and Catholic students are well versed in the fundamentals of Catholic moral teaching. Many may know "what" the Church teaches relative to various moral issues, but far fewer know "why!"

6. The approach is similar to learning about a great artist or sculptor such as Michelangelo by studying his Creation masterpiece in the Sistine Chapel or his magnificent statue of David in Florence, Italy.

7. From the Latin word for teacher, *magister*.

8. "Old" and "New" Testament is used to designate what are more properly the Jewish and Christian Scriptures, respectively.

9. For example, in the Gospel of Mark (7:7ff) Jesus excoriates the Jewish leaders who teach "human precepts as doctrines" and counters their insistence on dietary laws by saying "there is nothing outside a person that by going in can defile, but the things that come out are what defile."

10. The writings of St. Paul can be very explicit in such matters. See note 15 below.

11. "'Homosexual acts are intrinsically disordered.'"*Catechism of the Catholic Church* #2357, 1994; ". . . according to the objective moral order, homosexual relations are acts which lack an essential and indispensable finality [not open to life] . . . Homosexual acts are intrinsically disordered and can in no case be approved of." *Declaration on Certain Questions Concerning Sexual Ethics,* #8, Congregation for the Doctrine of the Faith, 1975. More on this when the distinction is made between "objective evil" and "subjective evil" (sin).

12. Timothy E. O'Connell, *Principles for a Catholic Morality* (San Francisco: Harper and Row, 1990), 134.

13. Robert M. Friday, *Adults Making Responsible Moral Decisions* (Washington, D.C.: National Conference of Catechetical Leadership, 1992), 24.

14. Ibid, 27-29.

15. "Basing itself on Sacred Scripture (Gen. 19:1-29; Rom. 1:24-27;

1 Cor. 6:10; 1 Tim. 1:10), which presents homosexual acts as acts of grave depravity, tradition has always declared that 'homosexual acts are intrinsically disordered.' They are contrary to the natural law. They close the sexual act to the gift of life. They do not proceed from a genuine affective and sexual complementarity. Under no circumstances can they be approved." *Catechism of the Catholic Church* (Collegeville, MN: The Liturgical Press, 1994, #2357), 566.

16. "This inclination, which is objectively disordered, constitutes for most of them [homosexual persons] a trial. They must be accepted with respect, compassion, and sensitivity. Every sign of unjust discrimination in their regard should be avoided." Ibid., #2358, 566.

17. That sexual orientation does appear to so preoccupy persons who are lesbian and gay is reflected in their penchant for including this orientation in almost any statement of personal identity. Sexual orientation is seldom even mentioned by heterosexual persons in self-descriptions. Societal attitudes toward persons who are gay have likely conditioned homosexuals in this preoccupation.

18. The Organization for Lesbian and Gay Student Rights (OLGSR) is an officially registered student organization at Catholic University. Its constitution states that "the purpose of the Organization shall be 1) to oppose discrimination against students, faculty, and staff on the basis of sexual orientation; 2) to provide a forum for discourse, discussion, and the exchange of views; 3) to support the lesbian and gay students of Catholic University through programs to educate the campus community about the injustice of discrimination on the basis of sexual orientation." OLGSR is not to sponsor religious programs nor "sponsor any activity that is contrary to or involves advocacy contrary to Church teachings on human sexuality." The constitution also enjoins the organization not to represent its views as those of the university or in any way to imply that the university views homosexual acts as morally neutral.

19. In the traditional Baltimore Catechism (1949), question 69 asks: "What three things are necessary to make a sin mortal?" Response: "To make a sin mortal these three things are necessary: first, the thought, desire, word, action, or omission must be seriously wrong or considered seriously wrong [that is, "objectively evil"]; second, the sinner [the subject] must be mindful of the serious wrong; third, the sinner [subject] must fully consent to it." In the absence of the subject elements, actions may be labeled wrong or evil, but not sinful.

20. The nature of Christian moral behavior is responding appropriately in and to a love relationship.

21. *Pastoral Constitution on the Church in the Modern World*, #16.

22. Traditionally, Catholic theology has recognized the authority of personal conscience as reflected in this passage from the *Declaration on Religious Freedom*, #3, from the documents of the Second Vatican Council (1965): "On his part, man perceives and acknowledges the imperatives of the divine law through the mediation of conscience. In all of his activity a man is bound to follow his conscience faithfully, in order that he may come to God, for whom he was created. It follows that he is not to be forced to act in a manner contrary to his conscience. Nor, on the other hand, is he to be restrained from acting in accordance with his conscience, especially in matters religious."

Chapter 5

1. By this definition there is no given content as to what the good would look like concretely. This statement does tell us what the Church thinks about the goodness and ability of humanity, a conclusion based on a characteristically Catholic anthropology, which is very optimistic about the human person. Not everyone shares such optimism.

2. This chapter will only skim the ideas found in the vast literature on conscience, giving an incomplete picture of the complexity of the concepts involved. For further detail, the reader might consult Timothy E. O'Connell, *Principles for a Catholic Morality*, rev. ed. (New York: Harper and Row, 1990), pp. 107-108; or Linda Hogan, *Confronting the Truth* (Mahwah, NJ: Paulist Press, 2000), pp. 36-63.

3. Richard M. Gula, S.S., *Reason Informed by Faith: Foundations of Catholic Morality* (Mahwah, NJ: Paulist Press, 1989) p. 131.

4. Ibid., p. 124.

5. A comprehensive and readable treatment of these various aspects of conscience can be found in Robert J. Smith, *Conscience and Catholicism* (Lanham, MD: University Press of America, 1998). For those who wish to pursue the topic further, Smith offers an excellent bibliography.

6. See Charles M. Shelton, "Helping College Students Make Moral Decisions," *Conversations on Jesuit Higher Education* 2 (Fall 1992), p. 12.

7. An understanding of personalism is key to the moral context of Vatican II. Some contextual background is offered in Dolores L. Christie, *Adequately Considered: An American Perspective on the Louis Janssens' Personalist Morals* (Leuven: Peeters Press, 1990), pp. 101-106.

8. *Gaudium et Spes*, n. 16, Walter M. Abbott, S.J., ed., *The Documents of Vatican II* (New York: America Press, 1966).

9. While this is not the place for an extensive treatment of either author, the reader may wish to look further. Walter Conn, in his work *Conscience: Development and Self-Transcendence* (Birmingham: Religious Education Press, 1981), does a good summary of the pertinent material, and features an extensive bibliography, including the pertinent works of Lawrence Kohlberg. The ambitious reader should also look at the work of Carol Gilligan, who has questioned some of the moral theories developed by Kohlberg and others. See Carol Gilligan, *In a Different Voice* (Cambridge, MA: Harvard University Press, 1982).

10. The following treats selected themes from *Gaudium et Spes*. Much of the insight precedes Vatican II, however, and can be found in the work of Louis Janssens. See, for example Christie, *Adequately Considered*, which gives an exposition of a personalist morality that found its way into the council documents.

11. Richard Gula, in his textbook on Catholic morality, details these ideas in a way that may be helpful to someone who has little background in the extended debate that has raged since the council. See *Reason Informed by Faith*, pp. 28-39. See also Hogan, pp. 100-126.

12. Catholic moral thinking has generally used a teleological approach to morality, finding moral rightness in the calculation of consequences, following Thomas Aquinas. If one probes the more rule-centered or deontological approach to morality sometimes seen in Catholicism, the roots of many of the rules are in fact teleological. The idea is that human persons seek the good as the end or conclusion of their moral actions—a teleological approach—and that all good that human beings embrace is ultimately found in God. Other goods are a foretaste of divinity—the final "end" of humanity—and act as pointers or steps along the way to arriving at the ultimate good (God). Rules try to define what leads to God in a kind of

shortcut approach, so every action doesn't have to be thought out individually.

13. The concept of original sin has shifted in modern times as well. Many contemporary thinkers see it not so much as a primordial event that leaves a troubling blot on the soul to be erased in baptism but as the condition of real evil that clouds human judgment about what is good and compromises the ability to do the good when perceived. "Original sin," by that view, is those things that act as impediments to free and knowing human action. An extensive treatment of these ideas can be found in O'Connell, pp. 53-57; 93-97.

14. These ideas predate the council and can be found in a systematic form in the work of Louis Janssens. See Christie, especially pp. 26-58.

15. A person who lived in seventeenth-century America, for example, would be less culpable of keeping slaves than a person in the twentieth century. The human community had not yet completely understood the personhood of all people, not simply white people.

16. A person in a wheelchair would not have the same moral responsibility to jump in to save a drowning friend as a twenty-year-old Olympic swimmer, for example.

17. See discussion in Christie, p. 68. The original material from Janssens's work is in Flemish: "Christendom en geweten," *De gids op maatschappelijk gebied* 49 (1958), pp. 891-894.

18. See Conn, pp. 46-47. Conn treats the insights of Erickson and Piaget at length in his discussion and offers some articles for further reading.

19. Rosemary Haughton, "Children and Sex," *Marriage* 46, no. 3 (March 1964), p. 12.

20. An explanation of this term is necessary. In an earlier *Leave It to Beaver* era, young Catholic girls were encouraged to dress in "modest" clothing, similar to what Jesus' mother, Mary, might have worn. It was a romantic image that drew more snickers than conformity, however, even in those days.

Chapter 7

1. Conrad Kaczkowski, S.M., "Sustaining a Heritage of Meanings and Values" (photocopy, 1991), *www.stmarytx.edu/prayerroom/societyofmary/archives/mheritage.*

2. Ibid.

3. Ibid.

Chapter 8

1. Wingspread Group on Higher Education, *An American Imperative: Higher Expectations for Higher Education* (Racine, WI: Johnson Foundation, 1993).

2. American College Personnel Association (ACPA), The "Student Learning Imperative: Implications for Student Affairs," *Journal of College Student Development* 37, no. 2 (1996): 118-122.

3. See Neil Howe and William Strauss, *Millennials Rising: The Next Generation* (New York: Vintage Books, 2000). See also Barbara Schneider and David Stevenson, *The Ambitious Generation* (New Haven, CT: Yale University Press, 1999).

4. Robert Birnbaum, *How Colleges Work: The Cybernetics of Academic Organization and Leadership* (San Francisco: Jossey-Bass, 1988).

5. Ibid., 11.

6. J. A. Appleyard, S.J., and Howard Gray, S.J., "Tracking the Mission and Identity Question: Three Decades of Inquiry and the Three Models of Interpretation," *Conversations on Jesuit Higher Education* 18 (2000): 4-15.

7. Ibid., 13.

8. National Association of Student Personnel Administrators (NASPA), *Principles of Good Practice in Student Affairs*, NASPA web page, cited June 6, 2001; available from <http://www.naspa.org>.

9. Ibid.

10. Michelle P. Clark, and Terry W. Mason, "Implementation of a Comprehensive System of Program Evaluation: The Iowa State University Experience," *Journal of College Student Development* 42, no. 1 (2001): 34.

11. Dudley B. Woodard Jr., Patrick Love, and Susan R. Komives, *Leadership and Management Issues for a New Century: New Directions for Student Services*, no. 92 (San Francisco: Jossey-Bass, 2000).

12. Theodore K. Miller, ed., *The Book of Professional Standards for*

Higher Education (Washington, D.C.: Council for the Advancement of Standards in Higher Education, 1997).

13. Ibid., 1.

14. Ibid., 10-11.

15. M. Lee Upcraft, and John H. Schuh, *Assessment in Student Affairs: Guide for Practitioners* (San Francisco: Jossey-Bass, 1996).

16. Ibid.

Chapter 9

1. Vatican Council II, *Pastoral Constitution on the Church in the Modern World—Gaudium et Spes* (Boston, MA: St. Paul Books & Media, October 7, 1965), p. 5.

2. Norman W. Larson, *The University of St. Thomas' Statement Regarding the Addressing of Controversial Issues within the Framework of the Idea of the Catholic University* (St. Paul, MN: University of St. Thomas, 1994), p. 2.

3. Ibid., p. 2

4. Ibid., p. 2.

5. Ibid., p. 3.

6. Joseph B. Connors, *Journey toward Fulfillment: A History of the College of St. Thomas* (St. Paul, MN: College of St. Thomas, 1986), p. 39.

7. Ibid., p. 82.

8. Ibid., p. 82,

9. Ibid., p. 82.

10. Ibid., p. 82.

11. Tatsha Robertson, *Minneapolis Star-Tribune*, October 8, 1993.

Chapter 10

1. Eugene Hemrick, "Marks of a Catholic University," *The Record* 118 (February 22, 1996): p. 4.

2. James Fowler, *Stages of Faith* (San Francisco: Harper Collins, 1981), p. xiii.

3. Leanne Newman, "Catch the Spirit at Spalding University: A Study of Faith Development in Freshmen Traditional College Students at

Spalding University" (Unpublished paper, 1996), p. 1.

4. Ibid, p. 8.

5. Ibid, p. 2.

6. Ibid, p. 32.

7. Ibid, p. 33.

8. Ibid, p. 40.

9. Ibid, p. 42.

10. Ibid, p. 39.

11. From an interview with the president of Spalding University, Thomas R. Oates, Ph. D., 1999.

12. Hemrick, p. 4.

13. *Spalding University Catalog of Undergraduate and Graduate Studies* (Louisville: Spalding University, 2001).

Chapter 11

1. Formally, the Catholic social tradition begins with publication of the 1891 papal letter *Rerum Novarum (The Condition of Labor)*. In this letter, Pope Leo XIII calls attention to inhuman working conditions in industrialized nations. Since that time Catholic social teaching has come to include papal encyclicals as well as documents developed and approved by conferences of bishops. The writings have spoken to topics such as labor, poverty, world development, peace, and economic justice. The broader term *Catholic social tradition* can be heard to encompass both these formal church documents and the attempts of groups and communities to embody these teachings.

2. For information on faith development in young adults, see Sharon Parks, *The Critical Years: The Young Adult Search for a Faith to Live By* (San Francisco: Harper & Row, Publishers, 1986) and *Big Questions, Worthy Dreams* (San Francisco: Jossey-Bass, 2000). Young adult faith development is also explored by Evelyn Whitehead Eaton and James D. Whitehead in *Christian Life Patterns: The Psychological and Religious Invitations to Adult Life* (New York: Crossroad, 1993). For a look at the importance experiential faith for young adults, see Robert A. Ludwig, *Reconstructing Catholicism for a New Generation* (New York: Crossroad, 1995).

3. *A Social Change Model of Leadership Development Guidebook: Version III* (Los Angeles: Higher Education Research Institute, 1996), 18.

4. TRIPS Mission and Goals: Turning Responsibility into Powerful Service is the purpose of the St. Norbert College alternative break trips. The TRIPS program is an opportunity for students to put into action their values, convictions, and religious beliefs through service. TRIPS is rooted in the ideal that service can change lives when offered by a community that is willing to reflect and learn together. The goals are to offer trips that will help students *serve*—offer direct service to the members of their group *and* the community they travel to and serve; *learn*—gain a deeper understanding of social issues through ongoing personal and group action and reflection; *live responsibly*—experience shared community responsibility and simple lifestyle; *seek wisdom*—explore the call to service from multiple faith and value perspectives; *understand differences*—value diverse cultures and perspectives through new experiences and viewpoints that may challenge ones faith, understanding, and values; *lead*—strengthen individual and shared leadership through service; and *act*—return to St. Norbert College motivated to continue working in direct service or political action.

5. *A Social Change Model*, 22–23.

6. Michael Walsh and Brian Davies, ed., *Proclaiming Justice and Peace* (Mystic, CT: Twenty-Third Publications, 1991), 171. See also *Gaudium et Spes*, #21.4.

7. Walsh and Davies, 273–274. See also *Justice in the World*, #34.

8. Walsh and Davies, 92–94 and 99. See also *Mater et Magistra*, #59–67 on interdependent social relationships and #96 on the common good.

9. Walsh and Davies, 242 and 415. See also *Popularum Progressio*, #78 and *Sollicitudo Rei Socialis,* #32.

10. Walsh and Davies, 123, 182, 260, 283, 390, 429, and 478. References to a biblical vision of a world that honors justice, life, truth, love, freedom, peace, healing, and community are found in *Mater et Magistra* (#261), *Gaudium et Spes* (#40.2 and #43), *Octagesimo Adveniens* (#37.1), *Justice in the World* (#75 and #76), *Laborem Exercens* (#27.4), *Sollicitudo Rei Socialis* (#48.2), and *Cestesimus Annus* (#62.1).

11. Parks, *The Critical Years* and *Big Questions Worthy Dreams*.

12. Laurent A. Parks Daloz, Cheryl H. Keen, James P. Keen, and Sharon Daloz Parks (Boston: Beacon Press, 1996).

13. *BreakAway: The Chapter Manual 2000–2001* (BreakAway: The Alternative Break Connection, Inc., 2000).

Chapter 12

1. Richard M. Gula, *Reason Informed by Faith: Foundations of Catholic Morality* (New York: Paulist Press, 1989), p. 64.

2. Austin Flannery, O.P., ed., *Vatican Council II: The Conciliar and Post Conciliar Documents*, 2 vols. (Northport, NY: Costillo Publishing Company, 1975), p. 917.

3. Kevin D. O'Rourke and Philip Boyle, *Medical Ethics: Sources of Catholic Teachings*, 2nd ed. (Washington, D.C.: Georgetown University Press, 1993), p. 4.

4. See 2 Corinthians 5:10; Romans 2:23.

5. See Exodus 19:5; Leviticus 25:23; Job 1:21; Luke 16:1-13; 1 Timothy 6:7-9.